TEACHING PALESTINE

Lessons, Stories, Voices

A RETHINKING SCHOOLS PUBLICATION

Teaching Palestine: Lessons, Stories, Voices
Edited by Bill Bigelow, Jesse Hagopian, Suzanna Kassouf,
Adam Sanchez, and Samia Shoman

A Rethinking Schools Publication

Rethinking Schools, Ltd., is a nonprofit publisher and
advocacy organization dedicated to sustaining and
strengthening public education through social justice
teaching and education activism. Our magazine, books,
and other resources promote equity and racial justice in the
classroom.

To request additional copies of this book or a catalog of
other publications, or to subscribe to Rethinking Schools
magazine, contact:
Rethinking Schools
9618 W. Greenfield Ave.
Milwaukee, Wisconsin 53214
800-669-4192
rethinkingschools.org

Cover/Book Design: Nancy Zucker
Cover Illustration: Halima Aziz | @palestinianartist
Proofreading: Lawrence Sanfilippo
Index: Heather Dubnick

ISBN: 978-0-942961-49-2

Library of Congress Control Number: 2024953051

Acknowledgements

We are grateful to the many people who helped make this work come to fruition. Thank you to all of the authors, poets, and artists for your contributions to this book, including the cover artist Halima Aziz. Thank you to our Rethinking Schools family: Wayne Au, Elizabeth Barbian, Linda Christensen, Grace Cornell Gonzales, Cierra Kaler-Jones, Stan Karp, David Levine, Larry Miller, Bob Peterson, Dyan Watson, Ursula Wolfe-Rocca, Moé Yonamine, and Missy Zombor. Thank you to former Rethinking Schools managing editors Jody Sokolower and Ari Bloomekatz — whose work at Rethinking Schools and advocacy for justice for Palestine helped shape our thinking and moved us closer to turning this book into a reality. We also thank indexer Heather Dubnick and our longtime proofreader Lawrence Sanfilippo. A number of scholars, teachers, activists, and colleagues contributed in numerous ways to make this book stronger and more accurate: Kristen Alff, Joel Beinin, Aaron Dixon, Marlene Eid, Mimi Eisen, Steven Goldberg, Mona Khalidi, Jen Marlowe, Deborah Menkart, Stephen Shalom, and Naomi Shihab Nye. Obviously, they are not responsible for any errors. We include several illustrations from the magnificent *Visualizing Palestine: A Chronicle of Colonialism & the Struggle for Liberation*, edited by Aline Batarseh, Jessica Anderson, and Yosra El Gazzar. They granted immediate and warm permission for our use of their materials and our book is stronger for it. To our individual family members, Linda, Anna, Gretchen, Xavier, and Mateo; Sarah, Miles, and Satchel; Michael and Khalil; Madelynn and Yemaya; Feras, Falestine, and Jihad: We love you and are grateful for your love and support. In addition, we acknowledge the loved ones who gave us their opinions in the editorial process or provided other support so that we could be free to work. We could not have done this without you.

Finally, this book could not have been completed without Nancy Zucker, whose tireless design work beautifully brought to life the voices in this book.

Artists of *Teaching Palestine*

Leila Abdelrazaq	Khaled Hourani
Lincoln Agnew	Safia Latif
Rawan Anani	Malak Mattar
Maryam Aswad	Irina Naji
Halima Aziz	Erik Ruin
Mona Chalabi	Robert Shetterly
Sawsan Chalabi	Andy Singer
Molly Crabapple	Nikkolas Smith
Sophia Foster-Dimino	Wael Abu Yabes

CHAPTER 1
Why Teach About Palestine

CHAPTER 2
History of Palestine-Israel

CHAPTER 3
Gaza

CHAPTER 4
Israeli Apartheid and Settler Colonialism

CHAPTER 5
Challenging Zionism and Antisemitism

CHAPTER 6
Solidarity with Palestine

CHAPTER 7
More Teaching Ideas
and Resources

1

Why Teach About Palestine

Palestine in the Classroom

SAWSAN CHALABI

The K–12 curriculum across the United States teaches children what is important, what knowledge matters — and crucially, whose lives matter. But silence is also a part of the curriculum. What is missing from school tells young people what *not* to consider, what *not* to question, and whose lives do *not* count. Palestine has long been one of the great silences in the official curriculum.

Of course, this is most acutely felt by Palestinians themselves. As Nina Shoman-Dajani writes in her article (p. 21): "Of the hundreds of assignments my children have brought home from school over the years, not one of them has referred to Palestine." In describing children's books on Palestine in "Resources for Teaching Palestine" (p. 204), Nadine Foty writes: "As a child, I remember feeling like I didn't belong because I could never walk over to a map in my classrooms and see my father's home, Palestine. When I asked, I was met by responses that Palestine didn't exist." Even in schools that attempt to foster global awareness, Palestinian culture is marginalized, sometimes demonized, as Nassim Elbardouh describes in "I Too Have Hope: Anti-Palestinian Racism in Schools and What We Can Do" (p. 23). She recounts an incident when — on the school's culture day — a principal ordered a 7th-grade Palestinian student to remove his keffiyeh claiming it was a "sign of war."

And there is another kind of silencing. How often have we heard "Israel and Palestine is just too complicated to teach." Of course, everything is complicated. There is no subject in our curriculum that we could not teach in greater depth. But as the articles in this book show, the outline of the conflict in Palestine-Israel is no more complicated than other areas that are classroom staples.

The curricular erasure of Palestine must stop. Not only to welcome Palestinians into our schools and classrooms — although that is essential — but also because widespread U.S. ignorance about Palestine has helped produce the injustice that Palestinians have experienced for decades, and continue to experience today. Indeed, discussing the war on Gaza and the West Bank in 2024, a senior Israeli air force official told *Haaretz* that "without the Americans' supply of weapons to the Israel Defense Forces . . . Israel would have had a hard time sustaining its war." U.S. students need a curriculum that helps them decide whether they want their tax dollars used by Israel to oppress Palestinians.

This book insists that yes, Palestine matters; we need to teach Palestinians' history, stories, struggles, and aspirations and this does not have to come at the expense of silencing or erasing others' stories. Centering Palestinians' stories and voices is not to say that we value Palestinian lives over Israeli lives: As educators, we affirm that every human life is precious. But just as the Black Lives Matter movement draws attention to the devaluing of Black life, we emphasize the dignity and worth of Palestinians, whose humanity is so often disregarded in the mainstream narrative.

Confronting the Backlash

Let's acknowledge at the outset that this endeavor is fraught. Advocates for Israel have long used false accusations of antisemitism to silence supporters of Palestinians and teaching about Palestine. But right-wing politicians and networks have amplified these accusations in the wake of the Israeli assault on Gaza that began in 2023.

Almost half of all children going to public schools in the United States are subjected to either state or school district restrictions on anti-racist teaching. The weaponization of antisemitism — even supported by some "liberal" politicians — means that educators who teach

We need to teach Palestinians' history, stories, struggles, and aspirations.

for social and racial justice in locations previously untouched by the battle over teaching about racism are now targeted.

As we reported in *Rethinking Schools* magazine in the spring of 2024, four teachers in Montgomery County, Maryland, were placed on administrative leave for public expressions of support for Palestinians. A charter school in Los Angeles fired two 1st-grade teachers and placed their principal on leave after one teacher revealed on Instagram they had taught a "lesson on the genocide in Palestine." The Decatur, Georgia, school district suspended their equity coordinator for sharing "Resources for Learning & Actions to Support Gaza." In Philadelphia, several leading educators in the Racial Justice Organizing Committee, where the idea for the national Black Lives Matter Week of Action originated, have been the targets of a campaign to label them antisemitic and remove them from the classroom for speaking out about Israel's atrocities. The campaign has included doxxing, email blasts requesting their termination, and inflammatory mobile billboards sent to teachers' homes and schools.

So in most schools and school districts, "teaching Palestine" takes courage. But it is also a crucial way educators can resist attempts to censor a more socially aware curriculum and silence dissent. This is why the *Rethinking Schools*' spring 2024 "Teach Palestine" issue was our most popular in years, and we had to go back to the printer to keep up with requests. Our subsequent "Teach Palestine" webinar attracted more than 2,000 teachers. Educators across North America want to join a community of conscience to teach a fuller, more truthful history of Palestine and defeat the backlash against social justice teaching.

Our students cannot understand today's Palestine-Israel without knowing key pieces of its history.

It is important that we show up for each other in this work, and not attempt to resist organized repression as unorganized individuals. We need to create and strengthen networks of teachers, parents, and students to defend the teaching of Palestine. We need to push our unions and professional organizations to defend our right to teach about what matters. We need to reach out to community groups that have a stake in a fuller curriculum on Palestine-Israel to hold joint teach-ins, conversations, curriculum fairs, and forums. (See "What We Learned from Our 'Oakland-to-Gaza' K–12 Teach-In," in Chapter 6, "Solidarity with Palestine.") Educators can form *Teaching Palestine* study groups, patterned after other Rethinking Schools study groups around our books *Teaching for Black Lives* and *Teacher Unions and Social Justice*. We hope *Teaching Pal-*

estine: Lessons, Stories, Voices inspires teachers to find, support, and draw courage from each other in this crucial work.

Premises

A glance at our table of contents reveals some of *Teaching Palestine*'s premises. The first is that our students cannot understand today's Palestine-Israel without knowing key pieces of its history. That history did not begin on Oct. 7, 2023, or with the Six-Day War, or even with what Israelis call their war of Independence and Palestinians know as the Nakba, the catastrophe, in 1948. The story of today's Palestine-Israel begins with the 19th-century antisemitic pogroms of Eastern Europe, sparking the Zionist movement, which sought "the creation of a home for the Jewish people in Palestine," as expressed by the World Zionist Congress in 1897 in Basel, Switzerland. The current website of the Israeli Ministry of Foreign Affairs opens its history of Israel with an epigraph by Theodor Herzl, Zionism's founding father: "At Basel I founded the Jewish State."

However, before there was a Jewish state, there was Palestine — ruled by the Ottoman Empire from 1517 to 1917, then by the British Empire under a League of Nations Mandate, until the U.N.-ordered partition of Palestine in 1947. In 1948, Great Britain surrendered its mandate and left. But Palestine was Palestinian, regardless of which imperial power laid claim to it. In our book, we use the term Palestine-Israel, to acknowledge that Palestine preceded Israel, but that the state of Israel exists. The imperial hubris and violence that led to Israel's establishment are often hidden from students, but there is abundant scholarship that reveals the Zionists' partnership with the British, articulated succinctly in the 1917 Balfour Declaration — which simultaneously promised "a national home for the Jewish people" and buried more than 90 percent of Palestinians with the term "non-Jewish communities."

In a sadly prescient letter from Jewish historian Hans Kohn to the Zionist journalist and politician Berthold Feiwel in 1929, Kohn wrote:

> We have been in Palestine for twelve years without having even once made a serious

attempt at seeking through negotiations the consent of the indigenous people . . . I believe that it will be possible for us to hold Palestine and continue to grow for a long time. This will be done first with British aid and then later with the help of our own bayonets . . . by that time we will not be able to do without the bayonets. The means will have determined the goal.

We agree with the thesis of Rashid Khalidi's book *The Hundred Years' War on Palestine* that "the modern history of Palestine can best be understood in these terms: as a colonial war waged against the indigenous population, by a variety of parties, to force them to relinquish their homeland to another people against their will." Of course, there is lots more to be said about these decades of dispossession, but a careful look at the history of Palestine-Israel — some of which is featured in our Chapter 2, "History of Palestine-Israel" — lands on Khalidi's conclusion.

Centering the history of Zionism in the story of Palestine collides with today's attempts to outlaw critical discussion of Zionism in schools — as a number of articles, many from Jewish writers, document in Chapter 5, "Challenging Zionism and Antisemitism." Nowhere in the book do we use "Zionist" as a slur. Zionism animated the quest for an exclusively Jewish state. Without some knowledge of the theory and practice of Zionism, students cannot evaluate any of the competing claims about Israel's genesis. Inherent in academic exploration and learning about multiple perspectives is the right to make up one's own mind about what is factually correct or incorrect, and about what is morally right or wrong. For organizations to insist a priori that anti-Zionism is antisemitism is intellectually dishonest, and disrespects both teachers and students.

That is another premise of our book: that a critical examination of Zionism is central to "teaching Palestine," and is not, on its own, antisemitic. Articles in Chapter 5 insist on this distinction. At the same time, articles in the chapter and elsewhere in the book emphasize the persistence of antisemitism, revealed in common stereotypes and tropes, but also through history

in horrific attacks aimed at Jewish communities, and more recently in white nationalist violence like the 2017 Charlottesville Unite the Right rally, with white men marching with tiki torches and chants of "Jews will not replace us!" and the 2018 murder of 11 people at the Tree of Life Synagogue in Pittsburgh.

As Nina Mehta and Donna Nevel argue in "What Antisemitism Is and What It Is Not" (p. 161), safety for both Jews and Palestinians "never grows from guns, checkpoints, walls, and a police state. True safety is built through forging solidarity with those fighting for a more just world."

Apartheid and Settler Colonialism

Another premise of *Teaching Palestine* is that today's Palestine-Israel is fundamentally unequal. Chapter 4, "Israeli Apartheid and Settler Colonialism," puts this inequality in the spotlight. As Amnesty International describes in a 2022 investigation: "Israel imposes a system of oppression and domination against Palestinians across all areas under its control: in Israel and the OPT [Occupied Palestinian Territories], and against Palestinian refugees, in order to benefit Jewish Israelis. This amounts to apartheid as prohibited in international law."

But these are not simply conclusions teachers should impose on students. Articles in the chapter show how we can engage students in exploring the contours of social inequality through lively activities that respect students as intellectuals. The terms apartheid or settler colonialism are not used as slurs, but as invitations to the questions raised by the movement for justice in Palestine. What is settler colonialism? Does that term help us describe common characteristics of Israel and the United States? Should the term apartheid be applied to Israel? Why or why not? Stories in Chapter 4 — and throughout the book — show how simulation, problem-posing, critical reading, and searching for conceptual patterns can help students discover and describe the nature of Palestine-Israel.

Gaza

We assembled this book through the summer and early fall of 2024, as the genocide in Gaza expanded and intensified. And we use this term genocide precisely in accordance with the U.N. Genocide Convention, which names acts "committed with the intent to destroy, in whole or in part, a national, ethnic, racial or religious group" — and then enumerates what we witness in reports coming out of Gaza every day: "killing members of the group; causing serious bodily or mental harm to members of the group; deliberately inflicting on the group conditions of life calculated to bring about its physical destruction in whole or in part; imposing measures intended to prevent births within the group . . . "

Chapter 3, on Gaza, seeks to present readings, stories, poems, and activities to help young people grasp the enormity of the genocide. In one of the poems, "Aunt May" writes:

My wish is that they drop the bombs on
    us while
we are sleeping and that we all die

together. This is
why we are here together. So that
    nobody is left
alive to mourn those who were killed.

No one should find themselves in circumstances where they wish to die all together. But the chapter seeks to remind students — and all the rest of us — that Gazans are full human beings, and not merely victims of an ongoing genocide. For example, Marta Vidal's evocative "'Birds Know No Borders' — The Love of Bird-Watching in Gaza" describes the work of twin sisters Mandy and Lara Sirdah. Gaza "is one of the world's busiest corridors for bird migration," and Vidal describes how the Sirdah sisters spread the joy of bird-watching throughout Gaza, especially to people with disabilities. Gaza might be an "open-air prison," but it has long been a place where people assert their humanity in loving and imaginative ways.

Is This Book Biased?

In Nassim Elbardouh's article on p. 23, "I Too Have Hope: Anti-Palestinian Racism in Schools and What We Can Do," we include a photo taken inside a school in British Columbia. A question on the wall reads "How does teaching about Palestine benefit all learners?" It's a wonderful question and there are lots of possible answers. One is that when we attempt to look at the world from the standpoint of people who have been invaded, oppressed, exiled, bombed, and discriminated against, we can understand social reality in ways we might otherwise miss. Much about the world comes into focus when looked at from the point of view of people who do not benefit from existing power relations.

Our book's title announces our point of view: The articles, essays, interviews, poetry, and art featured here seek to emphasize Palestinians' perspectives. The educators, writers, and artists bring diverse experiences and viewpoints to this

conversation, but what binds this collection is a commitment to justice for Palestine — and for our students and ourselves. That is not a political program; it is an invitation to imagine what justice looks like, given the long history of colonialism, war, ethnic cleansing, and now, as we argue, genocide. Every classroom should be concerned with this inquiry.

To the question of bias, our answer is: No, we are not biased. What makes a text or curriculum biased is when one's premises are masked, when one claims neutrality but in fact takes sides. Look at Glencoe's *World History* textbook which begins its section on "The Question of Palestine" not with Palestinians, but with Jewish immigrants: "In the years between the two world wars, many Jews had immigrated to Palestine, believing this area to be their promised land." The entire section simply tells Israel's origin story as Israel would tell it — but it feigns objectivity. Holt McDougal's

It is the Israel Defense Forces executing the war against Gazans, but it is the United States of America funding and supplying this war. Since its founding in 1948, Israel has been the world's overall largest recipient of U.S. military aid — $158 billion as of March 2023. As Reuters reported, "Between the beginning of the war in October 2023 and the end of June 2024, the United States "has transferred at least 14,000 of the MK-84 2,000-pound bombs, 6,500 500-pound bombs, 3,000 Hellfire precision-guided air-to-ground missiles, 1,000 bunker-buster bombs, 2,600 air-dropped small-diameter bombs, and other munitions." On Aug. 9, a few days after our five editors met in Portland to shape this book, the United States sent Israel another $3.5 billion to spend on U.S.-made weapons. It bears emphasizing that the provision of U.S. war materiel has long been a bipartisan affair.

This is "our" war, even if we oppose it. And as educators, we have a moral, and an educational, duty to expose our students to the human, cultural, economic, and ecological consequences of the war on Gaza. The charge "Don't stop talking about Gaza" is all over social media. To that we add: Don't stop teaching about Gaza.

Solidarity

Articles in Chapter 6 invite students to consider a variety of ways people have expressed solidarity with Palestine — and can continue to. The chapter has a focus on the special connection that Black activists have felt and enacted with Palestine for decades, beginning most publicly with the Student Nonviolent Coordinating Committee (SNCC) and the Black Panther Party. As writers note in "Teaching Solidarity: The Black Freedom Struggle and Palestine-Israel" (p. 177): "Black Power activists increasingly saw the Palestinians as allies in a common struggle against a global U.S. empire driven by and for racial capitalism." In 1970, here is James Baldwin, author of *The Fire Next Time*:

Modern World History begins its "Conflicts in the Middle East" chapter with "In the years following World War II, the Jewish people won their own state." (Notice the conflation of the Jewish people and Zionists.) The section later laments "The new nation of Israel got a hostile greeting from its neighbors." The first "Critical Thinking" question in the teacher's edition asks "What prevented the establishment of the Arab state in 1948?" The sole possible answer the book offers: "Palestinian Arabs rejected the partition plan."

This is what bias looks like: A story that embeds one group's narrative, yet is presented as a straightforward recapitulation of facts. Bias is also when a text or curriculum implicitly justifies the dehumanization and marginalization of a group of people. From the arrival of the first Zionist settlers in the late 19th century, to the subsequent British invasion and control of Palestine, to the decades-long treatment of Palestine as a geopolitical football, to the violence and forced removal that ultimately established the state of Israel, the bias against Palestinians has been suffocating. In subtle and not-so-subtle ways, teaching materials too often ratify this bias.

Teaching Palestine is partisan in that it centers Palestinian lives, uplifts and celebrates Palestinians' struggle for justice, and denounces racism and inequality. We make our premises explicit. We are not biased. The history, lessons, stories, and poetry in this volume offer a full-throated defense of Palestinian humanity.

"I am against the state of Israel. I don't mean I am against the Jews when I say that. I mean I am against the state of Israel because I think a great injustice has been done to the Arabs." (The title of Palestinian American writer Susan Abulhawa's moving novel, *Against the Loveless World*, is drawn from a James Baldwin quote; Abulhawa notes why Palestinians, in return, feel such connection with Black Americans: "There were others in the world who, like us, were seen as worthless, not expected to aspire or excel, for whom mediocrity was predestined, and who should expect to be told where to go, what to do, whom to marry, and where to live.")

The "Teaching Solidarity" article asks students to imagine themselves as Civil Rights and Black Power activists and to compare what solidarity — with Palestine or with Israel — means to them, and to decide what their position would be on the 1975 U.N. General Assembly Resolution 3379, which declared Zionism a form of racism.

The final article in the chapter, Lara Kiswani's "Educators: Support Boycott, Divestment, and Sanctions," articulates why the call from Palestinian civil society to boycott, divest from, and sanction Israel should matter to teachers here. Given the paucity of ways to influence Israel's stance toward Palestinians, BDS is a nonviolent movement that aims to press Israel toward authentic dialogue with Palestinians. It draws inspiration from the successful anti-apartheid movement of the 1980s that simultaneously raised consciousness about South African racism as it choked off trade, investment, and cultural ties, pressuring the regime to negotiate with leaders of the anti-apartheid movement. North American teachers and students were major players in that movement in solidarity with the anti-racist, democratic struggle in South Africa.

Hope

As we look at the history of Palestine-Israel, from the beginning of the Zionist movement to the Nakba to the events today in Gaza and the West Bank, it seems reasonable to despair. But one of the wonderful things about being an educator is that our work begins with an unshakable belief in the future. To step into a classroom is to express confidence in young people's capacity to learn, to grow, to change, to make a difference — to do good in the world. Education is anchored in hope. A book about teaching Palestine is also a book about teaching hope. Look at the Visualizing Palestine graphic "Palestine Shrinking, Expanding Israel" on pages 48–49. The erosion, the disappearance of Palestine appears inexorable. And yet . . .

Never have there been more people in the world expressing solidarity with Palestine. Never have there been more students demanding justice for Palestinians. Never has there been more consciousness about the ongoing Nakba Palestinians have experienced. There has been a rupture in the silence about Palestine. As Reem Abuelhaj comments in "Talking to Young Children About Gaza" (p. 84), "I never imagined I would walk through my neighborhood in Philadelphia and see people sitting at coffee shops wearing keffiyehs or see so many Palestinian flags in the windows of my neighbors' homes."

We conclude our chapter on Gaza with "Occupied by Hope," an essay by Palestinian American poet and reporter Noor Hindi:

When I ask my father, "Is there hope?," his response is swift.
"Of course there is hope."
"From where?" I ask.
"I haven't let go of my hope."

Here is the truth about being Palestinian: In this lifetime, and the one after, and the one thereafter, we will always choose Palestine. There is little that endures more than our hope.

In the face of the unimaginable, this is what I hold on to.

When we teach about Palestine, this too is what we must hold on to.

■■ ■

—Bill Bigelow, Jesse Hagopian, Suzanna Kassouf, Adam Sanchez, and Samia Shoman

HALIMA AZIZ

Gate A-4

BY NAOMI SHIHAB NYE

Wandering around the Albuquerque Airport Terminal, after learning my flight had been delayed four hours, I heard an announcement: "If anyone in the vicinity of Gate A-4 understands any Arabic, please come to the gate immediately."

Well — one pauses these days. Gate A-4 was my own gate. I went there.

An older woman in full traditional Palestinian embroidered dress, just like my grandma wore, was crumpled to the floor, wailing. "Help," said the flight agent. "Talk to her. What is her problem? We told her the flight was going to be late and she did this."

I stooped to put my arm around the woman and spoke haltingly.
"Shu-dow-a, Shu-bid-uck Habibti? Stani schway, Min fadlick, Shu-bit-se-wee?" The minute she heard any words she knew, however poorly used, she stopped crying. She thought the flight had been cancelled entirely. She needed to be in El Paso for major medical treatment the next day. I said, "No, we're fine, you'll get there, just later, who is picking you up? Let's call him."

We called her son, I spoke with him in English. I told him I would stay with his mother till we got on the plane and ride next to her. She talked to him. Then we called her other sons just for the fun of it. Then we called my dad and he and she spoke for a while in Arabic and found out of course they had 10 shared friends. Then I thought just for the heck of it why not call some Palestinian poets I know and let them chat with her? This all took up two hours.

She was laughing a lot by then. Telling of her life, patting my knee, answering questions. She had pulled a sack of homemade mamool cookies — little powdered sugar crumbly mounds stuffed with dates and nuts — from her bag — and was offering them to all the women at the gate. To my amazement, not a single woman declined one. It was like a sacrament. The traveler from Argentina, the mom from California, the lovely woman from Laredo — we were all covered with the same powdered sugar. And smiling. There is no better cookie.

And then the airline broke out free apple juice from huge coolers and two little girls from our flight ran around serving it and they were covered with powdered sugar, too. And I noticed my new best friend — by now we were holding hands — had a potted plant poking out of her bag, some medicinal thing, with green furry leaves. Such an old country tradition. Always carry a plant. Always stay rooted to somewhere.

And I looked around that gate of late and weary ones and I thought, This is the world I want to live in. The shared world. Not a single person in that gate — once the crying of confusion stopped — seemed apprehensive about any other person. They took the cookies. I wanted to hug all those other women, too. This can still happen anywhere. Not everything is lost.

Naomi Shihab Nye is a poet, songwriter, and novelist. She is the author of numerous books of poetry. This poem is included in Honeybee: Poems & Short Prose.

The Most Important Things
for Students to Learn About Palestine

As executive director of the Middle East Children's Alliance (mecaforpeace.org) in Berkeley, California, Zeiad Abbas works with teachers, teacher educators, and students. Below is an excerpt from his 2013 interview with former Rethinking Schools managing editor Jody Sokolower.

JODY SOKOLOWER: What are the most important things for students to learn about Palestine? What is the framework through which we should be seeing this situation?

ZEIAD ABBAS: There are certain principles: oppression and oppressors, justice and injustice. Students need to use critical thinking to identify who is the oppressor and who is the oppressed. They need to build their stance on justice, and connect the issues together. As Martin Luther King Jr. said, "Injustice anywhere is a threat to justice everywhere." We need to teach children the principles. And Palestine is one of the clearest examples of injustice in the world today.

It is important to look at the whole history. If you start from the Holocaust, you cannot understand. There is a long history, and what happened in Palestine is not the result of the Holocaust. I try to start with how things developed. The first Zionist settlement in Palestine was in 1878; the first Zionist Congress was in 1897. In 1917, in the Balfour Declaration, the British, who were the colonizers then in Palestine, promised it to the Zionists. By the 1920s and '30s, Zionists were organizing Jews all over the world, especially in Europe, to

ERICKA SOKOLOWER-SHAIN

settle in Palestine. Before World War II began, the Zionists had maps of all the Palestinian villages, lists of local leaders, and plans for how to force Palestinians out of Palestine. The plan to colonize Palestine started long before the Holocaust. So it is important to put the history in 1948 and beyond in this larger picture.

Teaching about Palestine should be based in international law and respect for human rights. Under international law, especially U.N. Resolution 194, Palestinians have the "inalienable right" to return to their homeland. There are 11 million Palestinians in the world; 7 million of us are refugees in Gaza and the West

Bank, in neighboring countries in the Middle East, and around the world. Resolution 194 was first passed in 1948; we are still waiting to go home. I have the key to my family house that my mom gave me before she died.

Palestine has been facing an apartheid system, especially in education. Most schools are segregated. Palestinian classrooms have poorer buildings than Israeli classrooms, fewer teachers, larger class sizes, fewer resources. Sometimes teachers can't even get to the school because of the checkpoints. This discrimination is another connection that children in the United States will understand.

JS: There is so much pressure to teach subjects that show up on standardized tests. Why is it important to make time to teach Palestine?

ZA: In the United States, there are special reasons why students need to learn about Palestine. First, it's a basic human rights issue. People in the United States care about human rights and have a right to know what is going on in the world.

Second, the main supporter of the Israeli occupation is the U.S. government. The United States gives money and human resources to support the Israeli military — this is $4 billion a year that could support school budgets, but instead goes to support the occupation of the West Bank and Gaza.

Third, this issue directly involves the people of the United States. Many of the settlers who occupy the West Bank are actually U.S. citizens. They vote in U.S. elections, but also Israeli elections.

Fourth, just to understand world politics, we need to understand the dynamics that involve Palestine. U.S. policy in the Middle East uses Israel to try to control the resources in the region. The United States presents itself as the mediator for peace in the Middle East. In reality, they are supporting the Israeli occupation.

Finally, we cannot have peace in the world without justice in Palestine. It could lead to a third world war; I hate to say it. The new generations in the United States and the world,

they need to know about Palestine. They need to know what's happening in Palestine; they need to know the principles of human rights, the U.N. Declaration of Human Rights, so they can fight for peace. As Americans, this is their responsibility. The world is counting on this new generation to wake up, to confront the injustices their government is doing. Until U.S. public opinion shifts and Americans hold their government accountable for supporting occupation, dispossession, and even genocide, neither the coming generations of Americans nor the world can experience peace. There is no hope for peace without justice for Palestine.

■■ ▪

As a Palestinian American Mother, Here Is the Education I Want for My Children

BY NINA SHOMAN-DAJANI

LA ABDELRAZAQ

Of the hundreds of assignments my children have brought home from school over the years, not one of them has referred to Palestine. As a Palestinian American, and a mother, I want this to change.

My siblings and I often felt like outsiders growing up in California — struggling to find balance between our Palestinian, Arab, Muslim, and American identities. As children of Palestinian immigrants, we knew there was something special about who we were — but this is what caused that outsider feeling at times. My children should not have to struggle with their identity in school as we did.

I am an Arab American Muslim educator, born and raised in the United States. My parents were born and raised in Palestine and moved to the United States in the 1960s for better opportunities following the establishment of Israel and the refugee crisis that followed. My parents instilled a love for Palestine in my heart from a young age and my foreign policy lessons started at about age 3 — as children of parents born in the 1940s during the British Mandate for Palestine, and the subsequent establishment of Israel on Palestinian land, we were surrounded by political discussion at breakfast, lunch, and dinner.

My siblings and I were the only Arabs at our elementary school. We lived dual lives: one filled with tradition and culture — watching Mom make fresh bread over hot stones and learning the Palestinian national anthem in preparation for a community event — and the other filled with attempts to blend in and maintain friends at a school where you had to shop at the Gap to fit in. While I watched classmates ascend from Brownies to Girl Scouts and admired the colorful bows in their hair — I made few friends in elementary school. Once I was invited to a friend's house to play after school and her mother commented to another parent: "Nina is Palestinian . . . isn't that interesting?" I knew even as a child, she was not making a compliment.

It was not until junior high and high school

that I was engaged with peers from other marginalized communities — finally feeling like I was not an outsider. Most of our peers thought my siblings and I were Mexican, and our dark hair and brown eyes allowed us to blend in rather than feel "out" as we did at the predominantly white school that we attended previously.

In college, I made Arab and Muslim friends for the first time, on my large Northern California university campus. I cultivated my love for the Palestinian traditions and culture my parents taught me by getting involved in social and political activities on campus and in the community. As an undergrad when the Second Palestinian Intifada and second war in Iraq started, I joined protests against U.S. involvement in the Middle East. These were not just about opposing war in Iraq — they became a meeting place for like-minded activists to gather and speak out against U.S. hegemony and U.S. policy regarding Palestine.

Hopes for My Three Children

Now, as a mother of three, a daughter and two sons, I reflect on my own life as I attempt to navigate parenthood. Their grandparents on both sides were born and raised in Palestine. In terms of "fitting in," not much has changed since I was their age. My children also attend a predominantly white school as I did. The only time my children hear of Arabs or Muslims on TV is from the news: They hear "terrorist," "threat," or "war" associated with Arab, Muslim, or Palestine. The first and only time that my son came home to tell me that Arabs and Muslims were discussed at school was in the context of learning about the horrific acts of Sept. 11, 2001. He was confused and disheartened, yet adamant that real Muslims would not kill innocent people. I sat my children down and taught them how to discuss Islam when confronted with a situation where their religion or identity is misinterpreted. In the 4th grade, when children are taught that Muslims are terrorists, as in this teacher's lesson, how are they supposed to process who their Muslim classmates are?

Other students ask my children: "Why don't you celebrate Christmas? Do you believe in Jesus? What's Palestine?" These can be difficult questions. The curriculum offers no global perspective;

it is no wonder students turn to my kids with questions. Between my three children and the hundreds of assignments they have completed over the years, no homework assignment or class assignment has referred to Palestine, Arab Americans, or Muslims.

When geography is studied, there is no mention of Palestine. Although some lessons explore "ancient civilizations," the curriculum ignores contributions of Muslim scholars (such as the creation of algebra and discoveries in astronomy). My children have never had an opportunity to write about or present their heritage with their classmates. When I was in 3rd grade, we were invited to dress in cultural clothing and share a traditional dish. My children are now in 2nd, 4th, and 7th grade, and I cannot recall a time when teachers provided such an opportunity. This may seem like a simple example, but the validation such opportunities provide can have a huge impact on how a student views their identity in relation to their classmates, in their community, and within the national conversation.

My children ask me why Palestine is not on the maps at school. I respond, "Palestine exists — it's where your grandparents and great-grandparents were born," and regardless of which map they see, they know where to find Palestine. Now, when we come across a globe in a store, my kids point out Palestine. Of course, we discuss their heritage at home, just as we did when I was growing up, but it would be great to have reinforcement from school, not an erasure of my ancestors' homeland. One of my boys likes to study flags and asked me why the Palestinian flag is not in the almanac he checked out from the library. Why should children have to wait until college to learn the truth? And only then if they seek it out.

I hope that it doesn't take another generation for us to witness a more expansive social studies curriculum that includes Palestine and the history of U.S. involvement in the Middle East — from the perspective of the people who are from the region. Is that too much to ask?

■■ ▪

Nina Shoman-Dajani is a college administrator at a community college in Illinois. She also teaches university courses in Arab American and Middle Eastern studies in Chicago.

I Too Have Hope:

Anti-Palestinian Racism in Schools and What We Can Do

BY NASSIM ELBARDOUH

L ike most people engaging in conversations about Palestine and Israel, I'm afraid of my words being taken out of context, misunderstood, or inadvertently causing harm. I'm especially worried about breaking trust with people and communities about whom I care deeply. As an educator, however, I balance my fears with my responsibility to learn about and teach the issues, especially as they directly impact the learners in my care.

This "fear-responsibility" balancing act isn't new. From lesson plans that encourage students to learn and reflect on their responsibility to engage in truth and reconciliation, to teaching about past discriminatory government policies and actions, to the links between carceral violence and racism, teachers help students to connect what they're learning in school to the complexities of the real world. We need this now more than ever, but it is happening far less when it comes to Palestine and Israel than it should. As an anti-racist educator, I'm called to name this erasure and curricular violence for what it is: anti-Palestinian racism.

I'd like to ground this discussion in two examples of the many harmful incidents that have occurred in Canada, where I teach.

In March 2023, a Palestinian student wore his keffiyeh to his school's culture day. The principal told the student to take it off because, according to the principal, the keffiyeh is a "sign of war."

Telling a student to erase a part of themselves is deeply harmful any day, but the fact that an authority figure asked a Palestinian student to remove his keffiyeh on a *school culture day* speaks volumes to not just the curricular but the cultural-political landscape in North America. What would the principal's reaction have been if they themselves had more accurate, dynamic, and positive representations of Palestinian people and their history to draw on? What if instead of telling the student to remove his keffiyeh, the principal had looked up what keffiyehs actually represent?

When we tell a Palestinian student that they need to take off their keffiyeh because "it is a sign of war," we reinforce dehumanizing stereotypes that there is something inherently violent and divisive about being Palestinian. We show them that despite what our equity statements say about all students belonging, these commitments don't extend to them.

Palestinian students have experienced an increase in this type of behavior since Oct. 7. On Oct. 16, 2023, a Palestinian elementary school student in the Ottawa-Carleton School Board (OCDSB)

When we erase and silence Palestinian culture and people from the curriculum and classroom conversations, we commit curricular violence.

was asked to remove a Palestinian flag from their online profile or risk being removed from class. The principal believed that the Palestinian flag was a "political statement" that would make the other students feel unwelcome. The student protested by saying, "You're not really welcoming me right now."

Would this principal have responded the same to a student displaying the Israeli flag? The Canadian flag? How can we ask Palestinian students to trust and participate in an education system that equates Palestinian identity itself with "a political statement" that has no place in a classroom?

After this story went public, the OCDSB posted an online statement: "While we will not allow imagery that promotes or symbolizes hate, discrimination, or violence, students may express themselves using flags or symbols which represent their identity, background or beliefs."

Of course, a ban on keffiyehs and Palestinian flags is absurd and grossly violates our educational policies, commitments, and responsibilities. And yet, these examples illustrate the pervasiveness of anti-Palestinian racism. Until we reckon with this truth, we will continue to perpetuate profound harm.

These types of inconsistent applications of policy and procedures indicate that the problem isn't the action itself (wearing a keffiyeh or critiquing the actions of the Israeli government), it's the fear of how the action will be perceived. In doing this, we model that we will break where and when people apply pressure. This is destabilizing and scary for young people who require consistency to feel safe enough to ask critical questions and meaningfully engage in the world around them.

The same impacts occur when our values and morals are incongruent with our actions. For instance, we say we value social responsibility and welcome sock drives for Ukrainian refugees but shut down fundraisers for medical aid in Gaza. We say that we support students responding to injustice through student clubs, posters, art installations, fundraisers, and more when it comes to climate justice and women's and queer rights, but when these actions are taken to stand up for Palestinian life, dignity, and freedom, these same students are warned not to "take sides."

Further, when we erase and silence Palestinian culture and people from the curriculum and classroom conversations, we commit curricular violence and contravene our professional responsibilities. If we fail to mention entire portions of history on the principle that these stories are "difficult" or "too complicated," we disconnect students from reality — as well as from how they see history and themselves.

Anti-Palestinian racism can also mean mentioning Palestinians only in the context of violence and terrorism. Lessons begin with the Intifada but fail to mention the Nakba. Teachers cite resources that claim that Israel was a "land without a people for a people without a land" while telling students who question this narrative to stay quiet. When teachers silence Palestinian students and their lived experiences, they abdicate their professional responsibilities and cause emotional and intellectual harm.

Ending curricular violence means coming to terms with the harm that the education system has caused Palestinian students and communities for decades. It means stopping the cycle, working toward repair, and actively preventing ongoing harm. It means recommitting ourselves to humanizing, contextualizing, and honest dialogue about Palestine and Israel. While some media create the delusion of two equal sides in conversations about Palestine and Israel, the reality is more nuanced, and rooted in systems of oppression and occupation. How can we encourage students to listen to learn when the world reinforces an "us vs. them" mentality that leaves little room for dialogue?

When we humanize oppressed groups and center those most marginalized by racism and injustice, we improve safety for everyone. Taking a principled anti-racist approach to current events leads to more safety, not less. And to more hope. Take, for example, the portrait of Palestinian journalist Bisan Owda, painted by grade 10 student, Asha R, at an art school in Vancouver, B.C.

The accompanying artist statement reads:

The central portrait in my piece is of Palestinian and Gazan journalist Bisan

Owda. As a Jew, secular or agnostic as I may be, it is extremely painful to see what is happening in Israel and Palestine in the name of freedom for my people. The Internet's constant overexposure to information and news on this issue, and others, has a tendency to lead people to believe the future is inevitable and bleak; to believe that there is no hope, that there is no point in trying to better the world. I don't think a person in a media-induced despair can ever truly see the beauty in someone like Bisan. The fact that she keeps living and keeps documenting her home as it is destroyed is not a sign of her delusion, or inability to have global awareness. If a woman living through an ethnic cleansing of her people can find something worth fighting for, what's leaving you hopeless?

It's clear that despite what many adults say about the inevitability of violence, many young people see the world, and their future possibilities, differently. They're working hard, and against the odds, to imagine a better world. To do this, they need to be able to tap into their empathy, engage in honest dialogue, and see each other as human beings.

Like Asha, I too have hope. I believe young people want liberation and justice for all and are capable of the difficult conversations required to get there.

■ ▪

Nassim Elbardouh is a teacher and anti-racist educator working in British Columbia. A longer version of this article appeared in the Monitor, *a publication of the Canadian Centre for Policy Alternatives.*

Teachers: Lift Up Palestinian Stories

BY NOURA ERAKAT

SAFIA LATIF

In a recent essay, Palestinian historian Esmat Elhalaby begins by explaining that "genocide begins with the idea of genocide," thus demanding attention to the history of ideas.

According to UNESCO, Israel has damaged or destroyed more than 195 heritage sites, Gaza's main public library and central archives, the Rafah Museum, and more than 100 mosques, including the Great Omari Mosque dating back 1,400 years, as well as the Greek Orthodox Church of St. Porphyrius, the third oldest church in the world. Now, no longer.

Though the International Court of Justice does not recognize cultural genocide, the attack on a people's cultural institutions, its memoirs, books, poems, and poets is a deliberate effort to destroy not only the possibility of their future but a trace of their past.

The campaign against Palestinian existence continues a long tradition. During the 1948 Nakba, David Ben-Gurion, Israel's founding prime minister, ordered the confiscation of Palestinian primary documents — including diaries and photo albums taken from private homes, 642 films, 127 files of photographs, and 6,500 Palestinian books and manuscripts — that today most Palestinians cannot even access so that we can only be written about by others, but cannot adequately write about ourselves.

Edward Said, renowned Palestinian scholar and public intellectual, described this condition as the denial of our permission to narrate. He wrote his essay following the 1982 invasion of Lebanon when the Israeli military stormed the PLO Research Center, looted its library, confiscated its documents, and then bombed the building.

Said details how despite the toll and evidence of Israel's brutalities during the Lebanon invasion, the U.S. media could not properly name Israel's aggression or properly recognize Arab victimhood. He attributed this abysmal failure to a lack of a vocabulary articulating the existence of a Palestinian homeland and its dispossession. A vocabulary that springs from an idea, enabled as much by story and imagination as by the messier grounds of politics.

Hence, today's dominant storytellers in media and government insist that history began on Oct. 7, 2023, in order to erase the Palestinian experience of apartheid and genocide that began before and continue after.

Under international law, three of the specific acts conducted to maintain apartheid are identical to the acts conducted to commit genocide. In the former, they are done with the intent to dominate, in the latter, with the intent to destroy. Martin Luther King Jr. captured this continuum when he said:

> [R]acism is evil because its ultimate logic is genocide . . . if one says that I am not good enough to eat at a lunch counter, or to have a good, decent job, or to go to school with him merely because of my race, he is saying consciously or unconsciously that I do not deserve to exist.

This logic has long sutured Black-Palestinian transnational solidarity. Then as now, this solidarity tells us a story about racism, colonialism, and the legitimacy of violence. When, for example, the coveted right to bear arms in the United States became a national security threat once wielded by the Black Panther Party. When the logic of guilty until proven innocent paved the ground for the assassination of the party's deputy chairman, 21-year-old Fred Hampton.

Then, the dominant storytellers explained that Hampton was killed in a shoot-out. It would be years before the Panthers successfully revealed that the FBI and the Chicago police had planned Hampton's execution in a broader effort to crush Black resistance.

Until we are triumphant, and able to write our own stories, we will be blamed for our own deaths.

As put by Palestinian poet Mahmoud Darwish:

> They put chains on his mouth,
> Bound his hands to the rock of the dead
> And said: You're a Murderer!
>
> They took his food, clothes, and banners,
> And threw him into a condemned cell
> And said: You're a Thief!
>
> They kicked him out of all ports,
> Took his young sweetheart,
> Then said: You're a Refugee!

I will end on a note from another refugee, Hannah Arendt — a political theorist who fled the Nazi regime and who would later be castigated by the Jewish-Zionist establishment for her biting critique of the trials of Adolf Eichmann.

In her musings on so-called human rights, she observed that one of the greatest ironies is that the age that declared life most sacred was the same age that witnessed mass murder on an industrial scale.

She illuminates that the right to life is not rooted in law or states, but only in the actions of people. Rights must be created and the greatest harm that can be inflicted upon anyone of us is not our oppression but the denial of our ability to do something about it.

Teachers bear a great responsibility to this end. How do they teach about an imperfect world? One wherein we have the greatest faith in humanity but are equally cynical of how power, privilege, and interests shape narratives of who deserves to live and who can be left to die. Teachers must both lift up a history of peoples who may not have been invited to pen their own story and must empower the students before them to believe that they can collectively chart new futures.

While the risk of such a basic task is high, I remind you that cowering will not make us safer, but it will most certainly make us less free. I encourage you to create these spaces for your own sake and not just for the Palestinians in Gaza — for they are, in fact, the freest of us all.

May you be protected and strong. May we be triumphant. And may we honor the request of slain poet Refaat Alareer who asked:

> If I must die / let it bring hope / let it be
> a story.

Our task is to ensure that stories of Palestinians are told and that they can be the authors and the narrators who speak for themselves.

■■ ▪

Noura Erakat is a Palestinian American activist, professor, and legal scholar. She is author of Justice for Some: Law and the Question of Palestine.

The Prison Cell

BY MAHMOUD DARWISH

TRANSLATED BY BEN BENNANI

Mahmoud Darwish (1941–2008) has been called Palestine's national poet. In her Rethinking Schools article "Remembering Mahmoud Darwish," Palestinian American poet Naomi Shihab Nye called Darwish the "beacon-voice of Palestinians scattered around the globe." In the article, she tells this story: "My husband, photographer Michael Nye, once photographed in a West Bank Palestinian refugee camp for days, and was followed around by a little girl who wanted him to photograph her. Finally, he did — and she held up a stone with a poem etched into it.

"Through a translator, Michael understood that the poem was 'her poem' — that's what she called it. We urged my dad to translate the verse, which sounded vaguely familiar, but without checking roundly enough, we quoted the translation on the book flap and said she had written the verse. Quickly, angry scholars wrote to me pointing out that the verse was from a famous Darwish poem. I felt terrible.

"I was meeting him for the first and last time the next week. Handing over the copy of the book sheepishly, I said: 'Please forgive our mistake. If this book ever gets reprinted, I promise we will give the proper credit for the verse.' He stared closely at the picture. Tears ran down his cheeks. 'Don't correct it,' he said. 'It is the goal of my life to write poems that are claimed by children.'"

It is possible . . .
It is possible at least sometimes . . .
It is possible especially now
To ride a horse
Inside a prison cell
And run away . . .
It is possible for prison walls
To disappear,
For the cell to become a distant land
Without frontiers:
What did you do with the walls?
I gave them back to the rocks.
And what did you do with the ceiling?
I turned it into a saddle.
And your chain?
I turned it into a pencil.
The prison guard got angry.
He put an end to the dialogue.
He said he didn't care for poetry,
And bolted the door of my cell.
He came back to see me
In the morning.
He shouted at me:
Where did all this water come from?
I brought it from the Nile.
And the trees?
From the orchards of Damascus.
And the music?
From my heartbeat.
The prison guard got mad.
He put an end to my dialogue.
He said he didn't like my poetry,
And bolted the door of my cell.
But he returned in the evening:
Where did this moon come from?
From the nights of Baghdad.
And the wine?
From the vineyards of Algiers.
And this freedom?
From the chain you tied me with last night.
The prison guard grew so sad . . .
He begged me to give him back
His freedom.

"The Prison Cell"

Teaching Idea

BY LINDA CHRISTENSEN

As Mahmoud Darwish portrays in his poem, as long as our minds are free, human-made prisons cannot contain our imaginations. After reading the poem with students, ask: "What imprisons you? Think metaphorically. For example, growing up, poverty imprisoned me. Sometimes, school imprisoned me. Other people's ideas about women's role in society imprisoned me. Create a list of the ways you have been imprisoned."

Share and discuss students' lists. "Now create a second list: things you love. Darwish brings his land to the prison: the Nile River, trees, music.

What do you bring to your prison that helps you escape, that feeds your soul? Notice how specific Darwish is. He names the river, the orchards. He tells us where the wine is from. Get specific. Does your joy come from singing in the Maranatha Church on Sundays? From smelling your grandmother's sweet potato pie?" After students have listed, ask them to share and add to their lists.

Darwish begins with the line "It is possible":

It is possible for [what to disappear? school
    walls? prejudices against women?]
For the cell to become [what is your dream
    place: a library? your neighborhood?]
For example:
It is possible for your contempt for my
    language to disappear.
For the cell to become a room
Where my ancestors' voices can sing again.

Ask students to write a first stanza using Darwish's frame as a model. Ask a few students to share to give others ideas.

Then Darwish moves into conversation with his jailer. Help students notice the question-answer between the poet and the jailer.

Encourage students to begin a dialogue between the oppressor and the liberated as Darwish does.

For example:
What did you do with the rules we created
    for you?
I gave them back to your books that made
    me small.
Where did voices come from?
I freed them from the shame that made their
    voices fade.

Darwish's poem should provide a model, not a prison cell, as students write their own. The intent is to get at the richness that emerges when students begin to name the invisible forces that imprison them.

■ ■

Linda Christensen is a Rethinking Schools editor, and author of Reading, Writing, and Rising Up: Teaching About Social Justice and the Power of the Written Word *and* Teaching for Joy and Justice: Re-Imagining the Language Arts Classroom.

Women playing basketball at the Center for Women's Activities in Kalandia, West Bank, in the 1950s. (UNRWA)

2

History of Palestine-Israel

SAFIA LATIF

But I Heard the Drops

BY SHARIF S. ELMUSA

My father had a reservoir
of tears.
They trickled down
unseen.
But I heard the drops
drip
from his voice
like drops
from a loosened tap.
For 30 years
I heard them.

■ ■ ■

Sharif S. Elmusa is a scholar, poet, and translator. He was the fifth in a family of 12 children, made refugees within a year of his birth in 1947. His father grew figs, grapes, and oranges outside Jaffa until the family moved to the Nuweimeh refugee camp in Jericho.

Teaching the Seeds of Violence in Palestine-Israel

Antisemitism, Zionism, and the British Empire

BY BILL BIGELOW

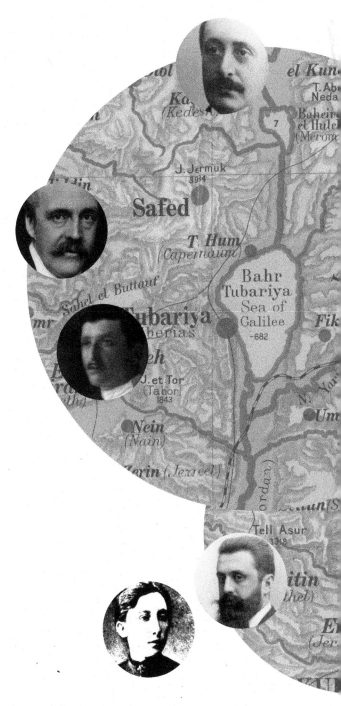

A small group huddled in the back of the classroom. "It all started with antisemitism in the Russian empire, with Jews being forced to leave," said Zack. "Antisemitism led to Zionism — which is just a lot of people searching for safety and a home. The problem is that another huge group of people would be shunted out of the way, pushed to the corner."

Zack, a 9th grader at Grant High School in Portland, Oregon, was trying to name a root cause of today's humanitarian catastrophe in Palestine-Israel. Knowing something about Zionism helped him think about the origins of the conflict there.

Unfortunately, at the very moment students should be learning to think critically about Zionism, prominent voices want to shut down this inquiry. For example, in his influential *Atlantic* magazine article "The Golden Age of American Jews Is Ending," Franklin Foer writes, "There's a reason so many Jews bristle at the thought of anti-Zionism finding a home on the American left: *Zionism* can start to sound like a synonym for *Jew*" [emphasis in the original]. For Foer, criticizing Zionism leads to antisemitism, so we should stop talking about Zionism.

But we cannot understand the long history of oppression — of both Jews and Palestinians — if we abolish "Zionism" from our lexicon, and from our curriculum. Omitting Zionism from our classes makes it impossible to map the route that led to today's horrific violence wracking Palestine-Israel. In fact, the origins of Zionism and the Zionist movement's aim to transform Palestine into a Jewish country should be at the heart of any curricular attempt to probe the cause of today's painful events. (See my article "No, Anti-Zionism Is Not Antisemitism," p. 167.)

When my friend and colleague Suzanna Kassouf invited me to join her in teaching about the "seeds of violence" in Palestine-Israel, I wrote a hybrid mystery-mixer activity that takes students back to when the Ottoman Empire ruled Palestine, and Jews were beginning to flee pogroms — antisemitic violence — in Eastern Europe, and to when the Zionist movement began to partner with the British Empire.

Suzanna teaches five 9th-grade Inquiry classes at Grant High School. Full classes, with about 30 students in each. With gentrification, Grant is whiter and more affluent than when I spent my first year teaching there in the late 1970s. Suzanna taught the "seeds of violence" activities to all five of her classes, and I joined her for three.

We led these lessons during the end of January and early February, as Israel's assault on Gaza was unrelenting. In each class, we began by acknowledging that making sense of the violence depends on when one "starts the clock." On Oct. 7, Hamas fighters attacked Israel and killed about 1,200 people and kidnapped 250 more. That attack triggered Israel's onslaught. But the violence did not begin on Oct. 7. I shared with students a Made in the USA tear gas canister and a handful of so-called rubber bullets — steel ball bearings with a thin plastic coating — that I brought back from Gaza when I'd stayed in the Jabalia refugee camp in late 1989 with Rethinking Schools editors Linda Christensen and Bob Peterson, on an educators delegation. The kids where we stayed in Gaza brought them home after school — they'd been fired into schools by the Israeli military. At the time, during the First Intifada, Gaza was fully occupied by Israel, and military vehicles patrolled the streets during shoot-to-kill dusk-to-dawn curfews, and soldiers regularly shot into schools during the day. But, Suzanna and I emphasized, the violence did not begin in 1989, any more than it began on Oct. 7.

We told students that we were going to do a mystery activity. We would try to solve *What is the source of the violence in Palestine-Israel?* And at the end of the activity, students would determine who or what they thought was at the root of today's violence.

The heart of the lesson is a mixer role play in which students try to "become" one of 17 individuals whose lives touched — or were touched by — events in Palestine, covering the last years of the Ottoman Empire, roughly from 1890 to the British Mandate over Palestine in 1922. There is a lot of history to become familiar with, but students encounter much of this through reading people's stories and meeting one another in character. As we told students: Today's events come into focus when we encounter what unfolded in Palestine at the end of the 19th century and the beginning of the 20th century.

The Mixer

Some of the key individuals students meet in the mixer role play include **Theodor Herzl**, the Viennese "father of Zionism," who believed that the ubiquity of antisemitism made it futile for Jews to pursue assimilation in Europe, and proposed in his 1896 pamphlet *The Jewish State* that Jews seek their own "home"; **Pati Kremer**, an activist with the socialist Jewish Bund in Russia who thought that Zionism's flight-not-fight strategy was wrongheaded, and that what was needed was a class struggle organization to defend Jewish rights throughout Eastern Europe; Britain's foreign secretary **Lord Balfour**, himself an antisemite as well as a Zionist, who sought to block Jewish immigration to Britain but promised in 1917 that the British Empire would support a Jewish homeland in Palestine; **Joseph Baratz**, an idealistic young Zionist who fled murderous pogroms in Russia to live collectively on a kibbutz in Palestine, but who had no room for Palestinians in his vision of an agrarian utopia; and **Yosef Castel**, a Sephardic Jew whose family had lived in Jerusalem for generations and saw the militant ethnic nationalism of the new Zionist arrivals as a threat to his Muslim-Jewish-Christian community.

The Zionists' land purchases in Palestine were problematic, as they bought land from people who held questionable title — hugely wealthy people like the absentee Beirut landowner **Elias Sursuq**, who "owned" and sold vast tracts of Palestinian peasants' land to Zionist settlers. Palestinian peasants, like **Mahmoud Khatib** and **Ahmed Sharabi**, whose families had lived on the land for generations, resisted. And they had support from Palestinian journalists like 'Isa al-'Isa, editor of

Filastin, and **Najib Nassar**, the Christian Palestinian editor of *al-Karmil*, who denounced the Zionist land purchases from absentee landlords, and the Zionist expulsion of Palestinian peasants. And they also had support from Palestinian Ottoman officials like **Shukri al-'Asali**, the district governor for Nazareth, who risked his career and stood up for the peasants against corrupt land sales from rich landowners to Zionist settlers.

Before meeting these and other individuals in the mixer, Suzanna and I sought to familiarize students with key events and issues they would encounter in the mixer with some map work, locating Palestine, the Ottoman Empire, the British Empire, the Russian Empire, and some of the historical context on antisemitism, pogroms, Zionism, World War I, and the Balfour Declaration. (All student materials and detailed teaching instructions can be found at zinnedproject.org/seeds.)

We distributed a different role to each student. In every class, there were more than 17 students, so some students represented the same individual. The roles are fairly detailed, so we urged students not to rush, and to read them several times. Suzanna made recordings of each role so students could listen to them with headphones as they read.

We told students that we wanted them to internalize the information in their roles so that they could "become" this person in the mixer. We asked them to underline or highlight parts they thought were most significant, and to raise questions about anything that seemed unclear. After they finished reading, we asked them to turn over their role sheets and to write on: 1) What are the most important things to know about your character? 2) What fears does your individual have? 3) What hopes do they have?

We distributed name tags so that they could write their mixer name and their location or organization, and then handed out the mixer questions — eight of them — and read these aloud, asking students to star any question they might be able to answer for someone else. These included: "Find someone who supports Zionism. . . . Why do they support Zionism?" "Find someone who opposes or is critical of Zionism. . . . Why are they critical of Zionism or oppose it?" "Find someone who believes that they worked against injustice to

make things more fair. . . . What did they do?"

We reviewed with students the mixer caveats:

- Speak in the "I" voice, as if you are this character. (I know that some teachers are reluctant to ask students to adopt other personas, but the activity works best when students speak in the first person, as their character.)
- Don't adopt an accent or try to "act" the way you think your character would act. (Every role play risks stereotype. We reminded students that individuals in this activity were real people, and to approach them with respect.)
- Use a different individual to answer each question, even if one person's story might apply to multiple questions.
- Take your time. It is not a race.
- Don't group up. Just have one-on-one conversations. And remember, you learn people's stories by talking to them. Don't exchange written roles.
- This is a get up-and-move activity. So if you are able, move throughout the classroom talking with different characters; don't remain seated.
- And this is not *The Twilight Zone*; you can't meet yourself. Some of you have the same character, so if you meet them, just pass on by.

In mixers, I always like to play a role. For one thing, it is more fun, but it also lets me take the temperature of an activity and feel when it is winding down. In Suzanna's classes, I played Elias Sursuq, the Beirut landlord whose family owned enormous parcels of Palestinian land, acquired by taking advantage of Ottoman laws that discriminated against poor and illiterate peasants. Through the years, Sursuq sold much of this land to Zionist settlers, who expelled Palestinian peasants whose families had lived there for generations. In the mixer, Sursuq was not a popular fellow among Palestinians. In a conversation with the student portraying the Palestinian journalist 'Isa al-'Isa I explained that the Ottoman Empire agreed that all my land sales were perfectly legal.

She gave me a look of disgust and said sharply, "It may have been legal, but it was not moral."

In all classes, the mixer was lively, even playful, but without being silly. It may seem paradoxical but the activity shows that although teaching honestly about the world requires us to surface painful history, our curriculum need not be similarly grim.

Debrief

It's always helpful after a frenetic activity like this to allow students to pause and reflect on what they learned. We asked them to write: "Name two people you met who made an impression on you. It could be because you were angered, saddened, or delighted by their story — or because you learned something that was new to you. Who are the people? Explain your thoughts about them. It is fine if one of the people who impressed you was your own character." Suzanna made all the role descriptions available in a Google Doc that students could access online, so if they needed additional details, they were easily located.

I loved reading what students wrote. They were diverse and insightful, and some were poignant. In the mixer, Maria portrayed Palestinian peasant Ahmed Sharabi, evicted from his land when it was purchased by Zionist settlers from the absentee owner. She wrote in part: "Another person who made an impression on me was Theodor Herzl. Our characters had very different views and I thought it was cool to talk. My character was a Palestinian struggling with Jewish settlers, whereas TH was firmly pushing Zionism as a Jew, believing it to be 'justice' for Jewish people. . . . I learned a lot when we were able to compare them side by side as actual humans. It's also sad because you can see that most Jews just wanted safety and to not be mistreated. It's horrible that the plan to make that possible included mistreating other people."

The Jerusalem-based Sephardi Jew Yosef Castel made an impression on a lot of students. James wrote: "Yosef Castel's story makes me feel hopeful because it shows that there can be peace between Palestinians and Jewish people. Their story shows peace with the two sides that could very well be implemented now. It is possible. We just have to

work to make it possible." No doubt, this feels like a distant hope, but learning the story of people like Yosef Castel can help inform that hope.

It is a dense history that students encounter in the mixer. But through conversations with one another, students seemed mostly able to grasp a bigger picture. But full disclosure: As so often happens in school, we suffered from unfortunate timing, ending the activity on the day before a weekend, with three full days sandwiched between the mixer and our mixer discussion. Thus our discussion the following week was not as fresh as had we been able to talk together immediately after the mixer. Suzanna and I were not exactly pulling teeth, but we did need to surface specific individuals in the discussion to remind students of who people were and how they connected to one another. We especially wanted students to recall that there were anti-Zionist Jews — like Pati Kremer and Castel — and antisemitic Zionists, like Lord Balfour. We also wanted to highlight Zionism's fundamental aim of safety for Jews in a separate homeland, which students discovered in Theodor Herzl, Arthur Ruppin, and Joseph Baratz. And we wanted students to recognize that Palestine began as, well, Palestinian, and so surfaced peasants who lost their homes, like Ahmed Sharabi, Mahmoud Khatib, and Razan al-Barawi; as well as Palestinians who stood in solidarity with peasants, like Shukri al-'Asali, Najib Nassar, 'Isa-al-'Isa, Musa Kazim al-Husayni, and Yusuf Diya al-Din Pasha al-Khalidi. And we wanted to remind students that these struggles were not just ethnic, but also grounded in social class — as the wealthy landowner Elias Sursuq was more than happy to sell Palestinian land to the Zionist new arrivals. His abuse of Palestinian peasants did not have religious or ethnic roots; to Sursuq et al., it was just business.

Solving the "Crime"

We returned students to our initial promise that we traveled back more than 100 years to make sense of today. We told students: "When we began the activity, we said that it was kind of like a mystery — that we wanted to figure out how the long-ago history of Palestine could help explain why there is so much violence today. As we said, we can call today's violence the 'crime.' Obviously, this activity goes up only to the early 1920s, right after World War I, and lots happened between then and today. But let's see if we can use that early period to think about responsibility for today's violence. Which 'seeds of violence' were planted back then? What happened in that early history to put Palestine and Israel on a collision course?"

We distributed and read aloud a handout, "Palestine-Israel: Seeds of Violence Possible 'Defendants.'" The possible "defendants" included all of the individuals in the mixer, but also broader defendants like the Ottoman Empire, the British Empire, antisemitism, Zionism, the Balfour Declaration, racism against Palestinians, exploitation by rich landlords — and also invited students to come up with "defendants" not included on the list. The assignment:

1) In your small group, choose three of these individuals, countries, empires, organizations, documents, or ideas that you think were "seeds of violence" planted in the late 19th century or early 20th century. Who or what in Palestine's early history was "guilty" of laying the groundwork, or somehow contributing to today's violence? You can choose from this list or suggest one or more of your own not included here. 2) Give at least three reasons for each of your choices of a possible "defendant." 3) What else would you need to know about the history of Palestine-Israel to be more sure of your answer about the "seeds of violence" there?

We emphasized that we were not looking for "right answers." We also encouraged them to describe how their "indictments" overlapped, and not to feel that they had to list each of these separately.

This small-group work to determine defendants was a delight to witness in the three of Suzanna's five classes I was in. The groups' conversations were animated, imaginative — and smart. Every group had the same "evidence" in front of them, but no two discussions were identical. One thing struck me right away. In most trial role plays

— like "The People vs. Columbus, et al.," for example — students have an easier time blaming individuals than systems or ideologies. But in the papers I read from three 9th-grade classes, 47 students named antisemitism as a key "seed" of today's violence in Palestine-Israel, 29 named Zionism, and 19 accused the British Empire, sometimes all on the same paper. Those were the three leading defendants. But often, groups named three "defendants" culpable in interlocking ways.

Here is from a group in Suzanna's end-of-the-day period 4:

> **Antisemitism**. Without antisemitism there is no Zionism. Without antisemitism Lord Balfour would not have created the Balfour Declaration and the British would not support the Zionists. Without antisemitism there would have been no pogroms, and Jews wouldn't have felt the need to flee Russia. **Zionism**. Without Zionism, the Balfour Declaration wouldn't have been issued. Without Zionism, Palestinian land wouldn't have been bought out and Palestinians wouldn't be forced out of their homes. Without Zionism, there would be less hatred of Palestinians. **Ottoman Empire**. Without the Ottoman Empire, the [1858] Ottoman land code would not have been passed. Without the Ottoman Empire, Zionists would not have been let in. Without the Ottoman Empire, Palestinians could have had independence in their own government. Without the Ottoman Empire, Palestinians could have kept their land.

Whether students landed on the Balfour Declaration, Theodor Herzl, Elias Sursuq, or antisemitism as defendants, students recognized that what began as Palestinians' land ended with appropriation and domination. As one student wrote: "Zionists are invading and the core of Zionism is removing all non-Jews completely. It doesn't try to cooperate at all. Just remove."

Suzanna followed up by asking students to create a poster visualizing who or what was a "seed of violence" in Palestine-Israel. Suzanna's assignment read: "Of the three 'defendants' that your group chose, now choose ONE and create a poster to demonstrate WHY this individual, country, empire, organization, document, or idea is guilty for planting the seeds of the violence we are seeing in Palestine-Israel today. **You MUST draw on evidence from our learning the last three classes.**"

These turned out to be wonderful — visually imaginative with diverse defendants, as in their small-group work: "Antisemitism Planted the Seeds of Violence!" with flames growing up out of seeds; "British Empire Wanted" with plants/crimes emerging from the "soil" of the British flag: "Not mentioning Arabs or Palestinians in the Balfour Declaration," "No political rights," "Evicted Palestinians." One pair of students named the failure to imagine a decent society as the fundamental seed of the violence: "The Belief That No One Can Co-Exist Equally Is Guilty," including an image drawn from the Sephardi Jew Yosef Castel's role, depicting Muslim and Jewish mothers holding each other's babies.

Throughlines

A student who decided on the "indictment" of Palestinian erasure identified a key throughline from past to present: "I think so much of this stems from the racism of not seeing Palestinians as people with rights." In his essential book *The Hundred Years' War on Palestine*, Rashid Khalidi describes correspondence between the Zionist founder Theodor Herzl and Khalidi's great-great-great uncle, the Ottoman/Palestinian scholar and official Yusuf Diya al-Din Pasha al-Khalidi, both of whom are included in the mixer. In his 1899 reply to a long letter from al-Khalidi, Herzl refers to the Indigenous people of Palestine as "the non-Jewish population in Palestine." Herzl's letter anticipates a similar eradication of Palestinians in the 1917 Balfour Declaration, which refers to "Jewish communities" as opposed to unnamed *others*: "existing non-Jewish communities in Palestine" — a denial of Palestinians' humanity repeated five years later in the 1922 Palestine Mandate granted to Great Britain by the League of Nations. Of course, declaring Palestinians nonexistent became part of the Israeli playbook, perhaps most baldly stated by former Prime Minister Golda Meir in 1969:

"There was no such thing as Palestinians."

Then-Zionists', now-Israelis' partnership with empire is another throughline — an early "seed of violence" that has metastasized into what Palestinians experience today in Gaza. As the Zionist leader Ze'ev Jabotinsky wrote in 1923, "Zionist colonization . . . can proceed and develop only under the protection of a power that is independent of the native population [i.e., Palestinians] — behind an iron wall, which the native population cannot breach."

Of course, in 1923, as students see in the mixer, the "power that is independent of the native population" is the British Empire. The abolition of Palestine and the creation of Israel is impossible to imagine without the iron wall of empire. And, speaking of empire, it is worth remembering the essential support for the Balfour Declaration of Woodrow Wilson, another individual in the mixer. As Supreme Court Justice Louis Brandeis wrote, Wilson's support "made possible" the Balfour Declaration. Rashid Khalidi summarizes: "Throughout the intervening century, the great powers have repeatedly tried to act in spite of the Palestinians, ignoring them, talking for them or over their heads, or pretending that they did not exist."

There are lots of moving parts in the "Seeds of Violence" mixer, and inevitably students will remember different facts and draw different conclusions. For me, the important thing is that they grasp that to explain what is going on today, they need to know something of what went on more than 100 years ago. History matters.

Today's violence did not begin on Oct 7. It did not begin in 1967. It did not begin with partition and the Palestinians' Nakba — Israel's "war for independence" — in 1947 and 1948. It did not begin with the Holocaust. No. It began with the Zionist movement's conviction that Palestine should be a Jewish-only country and that Palestinians should disappear.

■■ ▪

Bill Bigelow (bbpdx@aol.com) is curriculum editor of Rethinking Schools.

Visit zinnedproject.org/seeds to access the lesson plan, handouts, and all 17 roles.

Najib Nassar — Palestinian newspaper publisher

I am editor in chief and publisher of the biweekly newspaper *al-Karmil*, which began in Haifa, Palestine, in 1908, in what was then the Ottoman Empire. We didn't have a huge circulation, but nonetheless tens of thousands of Palestinians either read or "heard" my newspaper. As I wrote: "Once I went to one of the Palestinian towns in which there was only one subscriber. Many received me with honor as the owner of *al-Karmil*, which I had not expected and found strange, until I learned that more than 50 persons from that town read the newspaper at the subscriber's [house]." Of course, many Palestinians could not read or write, but they would go to one another's homes and someone would read the paper aloud.

My newspaper led the campaign to prevent the Ottoman government from selling land to the Zionists. The Jewish National Fund had been founded by the Zionist Congress, held in Basel, Switzerland, in 1901, to purchase land in Palestine to support the creation of a Jewish state — the Jewish National Fund saw itself as the "Jewish People's trustee of the land," acquiring and developing more and more land. In 1910, a wealthy absentee Beirut landlord, Elias Sursuq, agreed to sell a huge parcel of land to the Zionists. But this was unfair. Sursuq "owned" this land only because he took advantage of an old Ottoman Empire law to trick the Palestinian peasants out of what rightfully belonged to them. Sursuq only wanted money. The peasants wanted to keep their homes and their land; they resisted, and they were supported by Shukri al-'Asali, the governor of the Nazareth region.

When the Zionists came to our country, they did not care about us Palestinians — they wanted nothing to do with us. They set up their own banking system, their own stores, their own postal system; they even had their own militia. In fact, the Zionists wanted their own Jewish-only country. But no, this was our country. My newspaper wrote many, many articles about what was happening. Some Arab people did not see what the Zionists were doing. So I published a series of articles taken directly from the Zionists' own writing in the Jewish Encyclopedia. I translated this into Arabic. When they write to each other, the Zionists are very open about what they are doing: They want Palestine to be a Jewish-only Zionist country. But Palestinian Arabs have lived here for centuries — Muslims, Christians, and Jews together.

Arthur Ruppin — Zionist Organization Director, Palestine Office, Jaffa, Palestine

I moved from Germany to Palestine in 1907 and became director of the Palestine Office of the Zionist Organization in Jaffa. My job was to organize Jewish immigration to Palestine. I think I knew more about land in Palestine than anyone else. I helped direct what came to be called the Second Aliyah. Aliyah is Hebrew, meaning "rising up." This "rising" was the great migration of Jews to Palestine, 1903 to 1914, when more than 35,000 Jews came to Palestine. Many Jews fled terrible violence throughout Europe, especially in Russia. In Palestine, I wanted to create what the great Zionist thinker Ahad Ha'am described as "a Jewish state and not merely a state of Jews."

To have a Jewish country, everything depended on Zionists acquiring and developing huge amounts of land. As I wrote: "Land is the most necessary thing for our establishing roots in Palestine. Since there are hardly any more arable unsettled lands in Palestine, we are bound in each case of the purchase of land and its settlement to remove the [Palestinian] peasants who cultivated the land so far, both owners of the land and tenants." When I arrived in Palestine, there were some Jewish communities from the First Aliyah migration where all the physical labor was done by Arabs — and Jews were the bosses. That was not the Zionist nation that I wanted to build. I supported what we called "conquest of labor," that all the work in Zionist communities should be done by Jews and only Jews. So whenever my organization bought land, we would evict the previous tenants. Not because we hated the Arab Palestinians, but because we sought to build the Zionist ideal of an all-Jewish nation in Palestine. And for this, Jews and Arab Palestinians had to live separately.

Pati Kremer — Bund (General Union of Jewish Workers of Russia, Lithuania, and Poland)

I have been arrested more times than I can count. Why? Because I am a Jew. Because I am a socialist. Because I am a revolutionary. I was born in Vilna, in the Russian empire. It is true that my father was a wealthy merchant, but soon after I moved to St. Petersburg to study to become a dentist, I became involved in the workers' struggles. I taught workers to read and write, but I also taught about the class struggle — that our enemy is capitalism and the rich capitalist class that has only one thing on their mind: profit. And the more they can squeeze out of workers — with long hours, low pay, unsafe conditions — the bigger the capitalists' profit is. My first arrest came in 1889, when I was just 22.

When I was released, I returned to Vilna and continued my revolutionary work, until I was arrested again in 1897. In that year, we organized the "General Union of Jewish Workers of Russia, Lithuania, and Poland" — but we simply called ourselves the Bund. We were a huge and important organization. We had three main areas of work: 1) To fight for socialism and against the capitalists, including Jewish capitalists, who also exploited workers; 2) To fight for Jewish rights — like the right to have our education in Yiddish — and the right not to be mistreated because we were Jewish; and 3) To oppose Zionism, the movement working to get Jews to leave Europe to form a new country in Palestine. Our motto was "There, where we live, that is our country." The Zionists believed that we could never win our rights here in Russia because of antisemitism — that Jews had to leave and form their own country to be free. But even though members of the Bund were all Jews, we also knew that as workers we were exploited by other Jews. We had no desire to go to Palestine, where Jewish capitalists would continue to exploit us. Interestingly, the first Zionist Congress was also held in 1897, the same year we began the Bund. Working-class Jews had a choice: socialism or Zionism.

Razan al-Barawi — Palestinian peasant, Gaza, Palestine

There is a saying that when elephants fight, it is the grass that is hurt the most. This saying applies to my life. The elephants are the two big empires: the Ottoman Empire and the British Empire. We Palestinians are the grass. Here is my story. As a woman, as a peasant, through the years I farmed part of my family's land and sold our produce. We were not rich and we had to pay taxes to the Ottomans, but we survived. Palestine had been part of the Ottoman Empire since 1517. This was our history. But then a huge war broke out in 1914, and the Ottoman Empire joined the Central Powers — Germany, Austria-Hungary, and Bulgaria — to fight France, Great Britain, and Russia. Even before war was declared, a large number of troops led by Ottoman and German officers began arriving in Gaza in Palestine. They began to position big field artillery. The Ottoman army then started taking our property: food, pack animals, carts, kitchenware, furniture, everything. The Ottomans took over entire buildings to house their soldiers, and they even destroyed some buildings to build up their defenses. Gazans who were more well off sent their families away to other Palestinian towns or villages. But my family was not rich and could not afford to leave.

Up until 1917, there had not been any actual fighting in Gaza. But then we heard that the British were getting closer to Gaza, and so the Ottomans ordered all the civilians to leave. A town crier went through our streets yelling that we must all go away immediately, "even if you have to crawl on your knees!" Soldiers went house to house, with whips, lashing out at anyone who did not leave quickly enough. I was terrified. We could take only what we could carry. How many Gazans were forced to flee? I don't know, but I heard anywhere from 25,000 to 40,000 people. It was awful. In the countryside, we had to beg for mercy. Some of us had to live in caves. We collected twigs to burn for fire, but we really had nothing — only what we took when the Ottomans forced us out of our homes. Many of us went hungry. We wanted to return to Gaza, but soon the British began to bombard Gaza from naval ships, artillery, and even airplanes. As someone who witnessed this described it, the British "treated Gaza to a rain of steel and fire." Much of the city was turned to rubble. So as I say, when the Ottoman and British elephants fight, it is the Palestinian peasants who are trampled.

Independence or Catastrophe?

Teaching 1948 Through Multiple Perspectives

BY SAMIA SHOMAN

The Palmach, part of the Haganah underground Zionist paramilitary organization, arriving in Palestine, July 1947.

Palestinian refugees being trucked out of their village, circa 1948.

Long before I was born in 1975, the course of my life had been drastically altered by history. When David Ben-Gurion declared the creation and independence of the state of Israel on May 14, 1948, my identity as a Palestinian was shaped, along with the history of this region. Throughout my life, I have borne witness to and experienced the ways this day in history changed not only my life, but also the lives of millions of Palestinians and Jews all over the world.

I've made several trips to the region. On many trips, I felt saddened and overwhelmed as I reflected on what the 1948 events had caused: an institutionalized system of oppression and apartheid in what some believe is historic Palestine and others see as Israel. This difference in perspective and personal truth is among the many factors that keep the conflict ongoing.

In my teaching, I use an approach that exposes students to the idea that Palestinians and Israelis have different narratives about the same historical events. The approach encourages critical thinking and allows students the space and opportunity to decide what they think for themselves. At least in my district, it is an approach that has enabled me to build support among a broad range of parents, students, and Middle East scholars — even when I have been challenged by community groups questioning my intentions and curriculum because I am a Palestinian American who teaches the conflict in my contemporary world studies class.

> **I make the point that people come to their own "truths" based on their interpretations and memories of historical events.**

Teaching the conflict takes courage. I write this article in hopes of encouraging teachers who are committed to social justice to take on the challenge. In this context, social justice means exposing students to Palestinian narratives alongside the Zionist narratives that often dominate textbooks. I use the term Zionism and teach it explicitly to my students. Zionism is the support of an exclusively Jewish state in Israel, along with the land that it claims should be part of Greater Israel. An important distinction to make is that not all Jews or Israelis are Zionists, and there are non-Jewish Zionists.

A Framework for Critical Thinking

Before delving into the history of the conflict and the experiences of the people involved, I spend time developing a theoretical framework built on four concepts: Fact, Perspective, Narrative, and Your Truth:

> FACT: Information that can be independently verified; data that is generally accepted as reliable.

> PERSPECTIVE: A particular attitude toward or way of thinking about something; point of view.

> NARRATIVE: The stories we tell and/or believe to explain how a set of facts or events are connected to each other. Our perspective underlies the narratives we tell.

> YOUR TRUTH: In this unit, we use "your truth" as something every person creates for oneself — an interpretation of facts based on one's own perspective.

I teach the students that facts and perspectives inform people's narratives, which lead to individual truths. Facts are pieces of information, data independently verifiable or agreed to by all parties. To take an example from world history, it's a fact that the African continent was almost wholly colonized by European powers during the period from the 1800s through World War I. The dominant European perspective was that their contact with African Indigenous populations brought the blessings of civilization and exposure to God to the "dark continent." Rudyard Kipling's poem "The White Man's Burden" is a narrative based on that perspective. The dominant perspective among African peoples viewed the Europeans as invaders bent on stealing their resources and destroying their cultures. Oral histories passed down about the spiritual and military leadership of Nehanda Nyakasikana in Zimbabwe, for example, are narratives based on that perspective.

I make the point that people come to their own "truths" based on their interpretations and memories of historical events. This helps build a space for students to feel safe reflecting on what they have been taught or exposed to in the past, and to be open to new ideas and information. It gives students a framework from which to understand the conflict, instead of one in which they need to choose sides.

This teaching framework is my attempt to address the histories of the groups involved. There are many people who do not see this conflict as having two equal sides, but exploring it in this way helps students make meaning of the history and current reality.

Before applying the fact, perspective, narrative, and my truth framework to Palestine-Israel, I have students practice with other historical examples, often based on a recently completed unit.

War of Independence or Catastrophe?

I anchor my Palestine-Israel unit in the events of 1948, although the historical background starts long before this, with the First Zionist Congress of 1897 and the Balfour Declaration of 1917. It is important that students understand that Zionist organizations had plans to turn Palestine into a Jewish state long before World War II. (See "Teaching the Seeds of Violence in Palestine-Israel" on p. 33.)

I present the 1948 events as both the Israeli War of Independence and the Palestinian Nakba (Arabic for catastrophe). It is through the events of 1948 that students get their most intimate understanding of how different narratives determine what people see as the truth. For example, my students learn that a Palestinian student in the West Bank or Gaza and an Israeli student in Israel will learn different stories about what happened in 1948. What those students learn shapes their beliefs about the legitimacy of the state of Israel. It is through this lesson that my students begin to grasp the idea of multiple and competing narratives as they read, watch, critique, and analyze text and video footage of things that happened in 1948 from different perspectives. As students work their way through the history, they begin to develop their own truth about what happened.

I ask students to analyze a series of documents about 1948, including primary source accounts, secondary texts, maps, and photos. I set it up as a jigsaw activity: Students work in small groups on one set of documents at a time, then trade them in for another set. The document sets cover the following:

1. Jewish and Palestinian narratives about what happened in 1948 (War of Independence and Al-Nakba)
2. The Deir Yassin Massacre
3. Israeli Declaration of Independence
4. Palestinian Refugees
5. Jewish Immigration to Israel

The first document contains two narratives of 1948, one from an Israeli perspective and one from a Palestinian perspective ("Learning Each Other's Historical Narrative: Palestinian and Israeli" from the Peace Research Institute in the Middle East). The narratives explain that clashes between Palestinians and Jews began quickly after U.N. Resolution 181 to partition Palestine was passed, and continued until an official war broke out on May 15, 1948, after Arab armies entered the newly declared state of Israel.

The Israeli narrative includes the following excerpts:

> The war that began on Nov. 29, 1947, is known as the War of Independence because it resulted in the land of Israel, in spite of the fact that at the beginning local Arabs and then armies from Arab countries tried to prevent it. Local Arab troops and volunteers attacked isolated Jewish communities, Jews in cities with mixed populations, and the roads. They also employed terror tactics — all Jewish people, settlements, and property were considered legitimate targets . . .
>
> During the first stages of the war, Arab residents began leaving their communities in the land of Israel. The first were those who were well-off economically. The result was a significant weakening of the entire Arab community. . . . Most of the Jewish military and civilian leaders in the land welcomed the flight of the Arabs for political reasons (so that the future Jewish state would include as small an Arab minority as possible)

and for military reasons (to distance a hostile population from the field of battle). Haganah [Zionist defense] forces began to deport Arabs. However, not all Arabs were deported and there were no high-level political orders to do so, although military commanders were given freedom to act as they saw fit. Thus the flight was due to deporting and frightening Arabs and because of their own fears without regard to Israeli actions. During the course of the war about 370 Arab villages were destroyed.

The Palestinian narrative includes the following excerpts:

On Nov. 29, 1947, the U.N. General Assembly passed Resolution 181, which called for the partition of Palestine into two states, Arab and Jewish. This was the start of the countdown for the establishment of the state of Israel on May 15, 1948, and the 1948 Catastrophe, which uprooted and dispersed the Palestinian people. The Catastrophe was 1) the defeat of the Arab armies in the 1948 Palestine war; 2) their acceptance of the truce; 3) the displacement of most of the Palestinian people from their cities and villages; and 4) the emergence of the refugee problem and the Palestinian diaspora . . .

The destruction of 418 Palestinian villages inside the green line (pre-1967 Israeli border), concealing the landmarks of Palestinian life, and the massacres against the Palestinian people are the best evidence for the brutality to which the Palestinians were exposed. They were dispersed throughout the world.

Concerning the exodus, the Palestinians did not have the least doubt that it would be for a few days, after which they would return to their houses: "We thought that we would return after one or two weeks. We locked the house and we kept the key, waiting to return."

Some 1,400,000 people inhabited Palestine in 1948. After the Catastrophe, about 750,000 Palestinians wandered with nowhere to go. Families were separated, the elderly died, children carried younger children, nursing children died of thirst. Suddenly Palestinians found themselves exiled from their homes, in an alien world that regarded them as a different kind of frightening human being — refugees! The international community did not focus on learning the reasons for the refugee problem and finding a remedy. Rather than investigating the reasons for the forced migration and displacement, all they did was to provide them with humanitarian assistance.

I have students answer a series of questions, including:

- What are the main differences between the historical narratives recounted by each side? Give two examples.
- List five established facts referred to in both narratives.
- How can the same historical event be known as a War of Independence and a Catastrophe?

"What are some differences between the two narratives?" I asked one group.

"The Israeli narrative says that lots of Palestinians left on their own, but the Palestinian story says they were forced out."

"How would you describe the perspective behind the Israeli narrative?" I asked.

"They believe the land is rightfully theirs for taking."

"They are coming to create Israel because the land was given to them by God."

"They deserve the land because of what survivors of the Holocaust went through."

"What about the perspective behind the Palestinian narrative?" I asked.

"The Jews came in and took their land."

"They were already living there. The Holocaust wasn't the Palestinians' fault, so they shouldn't have their land taken from them."

I moved on to a group that was struggling to understand the two narratives. "Let's start with established facts," I suggested. "What are some facts that both sides agree on?"

"Four hundred and eighteen Palestinian villages got destroyed," read Jorge.

"Do both narratives agree on that?" I asked.

"The Israeli side says 370," Alex pointed out.

"So how could you express that as a fact more likely to be accepted by both sides?" I asked.

"How about: At least 370 Palestinian villages were destroyed," suggested Elizabeth.

The group agreed that would work and moved on to find other facts.

The documents on Palestinian refugees include photographs and this excerpt:

A man from the Nahr Al-Bared refugee camp in Lebanon recalls what happened to his small daughter: I had a daughter — she was 3 years old, and was separated from her mother during the fighting. Some people told me they had seen her going toward the Druze village of Yarka, so I went to look for her. I searched until morning but could not find her. In the morning I went up to Yarka. Some children played in the courtyard. I saw my daughter standing in front of a boy who was eating a piece of bread. She was hungry and asked the boy: "Give me a piece." The boy did not pay any attention to her. I came up behind her, hugged and cradled her in my arms. I couldn't utter a word because of my tears. In just 12 hours our condition changed from honor to humiliation.

Students worked in groups to respond to the questions attached to each document set. As I walked around the room, I heard a range of student comments:

"This whole situation is messed up."

"How come people can't just live peacefully together?"

"It's so sad. What happened to the Palestinians who left their homes?"

"I don't know if this can ever be overcome."

The students had a hard time reconciling the experiences of Jewish people during the Holocaust — and the horror and sadness they had shared as we studied it during our World War II unit — with what they were learning about the Nakba. One of the most common questions students asked throughout the entire unit, often out loud to the entire class, was "How could Jews treat Palestinians without dignity or humanity after what they had experienced?"

When students raised this, I let them engage in discussion with one another and facilitated rather than answered, because I have no answer and do not think there is a single answer. It was an opportunity for students to dig deep on an emotional, academic, and critical thinking level to synthesize historical knowledge with their own perspectives on human behavior.

> "How could Jews treat Palestinians without dignity or humanity after what they had experienced?"

Students were engaged in text analysis and looking at pictures and maps, calling me over for clarification and discussion. They asked me if my family had to flee in 1948 or if I know anyone who did. I explained that my parents were from a village near Jerusalem, were young children in 1948, and were relatively safe; but that my husband's parents were forced to flee to Jordan, where my husband was born.

Students stayed after class, came in at lunch, and hung out after school because they wanted to discuss the situation. My students always have a heightened interest in this unit because it is current, because I have witnessed it firsthand and can share stories, and most of all because it is wrought with emotion, differing realities, and seems never-ending.

To wrap up the document analysis, I asked the students to predict some of the results of 1948 for Palestinians and for Jews in Israel. What might happen next? How might different people have felt? The result was a T-chart. Students wrote:

- Palestinians would be unhappy their homeland was taken away.
- Palestinians would demand changes and want more land, continue to retaliate, and be scared because of the massacres and violence.
- Jews would be happy that their historical homeland became theirs officially.
- Jews would be happy about no more discrimination.
- Jews would justify their actions with their spiritual connections to the land.

After the document analysis, I asked students to apply the framework and their historical understanding to designing a fact, perspective, narrative, and your truth poster for 1948. I had students number off by twos and assigned them to either the War of Independence or the Nakba. As with all student work, there were differing depths of understanding reflected in what students turned in. A high-performing student's work on Israel's independence included the following excerpts:

Fact: The Jewish and Arab people fought a war against each other after tension arose between the two. In 1948, Israel was formed and gained its independence. After the creation of Israel, the Jewish immigration rate increased.

Perspective: The Jewish people believed they had a "natural and historic" right to Palestinian land due to their religious history. Once they gained control of Israel, any Palestinian resistance was seen as a threat that must be dealt with because Arabs were trying to interrupt the land that rightfully belonged to the Jews.

Narrative: Jews were tortured and unaccepted in Europe during the time of the Holocaust. After the Holocaust, Jews were displaced and not united with one another. They saw hope in a land that was full of their history. Families of all ages packed up their belongings and be-

gan the journey to Palestine in hopes of settling into new homes.

My truth: Even though the Jews needed a stable home after the devastation they had been put through in Europe, I believe that they didn't have the right to completely take over land that belonged to another group of people. The Jews should have made a civil compromise with the Arabs before heading to war and pushing them out of their own homes.

In contrast, a hardworking and engaged student with low literacy skills wrote the following about the Nakba:

Fact: Palestinian villages were erased, although the exact number is disputed. After Israel was created, Arab armies invaded. Palestinians ran away from their homes and had to go to refugee camps.

Perspective: The Israeli "independence" is nothing but a catastrophe for us.

Narrative: The Jews made us go to refugee camps and we attacked their villages. Also, more than 300 of our villages were taken over. They came and took our land, killed, and violated rights. We are stuck living in poorly set up camps while they are sleeping in our homes.

My truth: I know that Jews needed a place to stay and the only place they wanted to go was Palestine because it was their birthplace but it was kind of mean of them to go to Palestine and just kick out the Palestinian people because what the Jews went through before was now happening to Palestinians — they had nowhere to go and were living in tents and it was a bad situation for them.

I am fortunate to have six weeks for this unit in a two-year world history cycle, so we continued to study key historical events and issues. I included the First Zionist Congress, the Balfour Declaration, the 1967 and 1973 wars; the First and Second Intifadas and other Palestinian resistance efforts; the Oslo Accords and Camp David negotiations; Israel's security apparatus; the building of the separation wall/security barrier; the effects of the occupation on Palestinians and the effects of the conflict on Israelis; recent events in the Gaza Strip; and current political, economic, and social developments.

The final assessment for the students was participating in a highly structured U.N. conference on solving the conflict based on current facts and the situation on the ground. Never have I seen my students work so hard, become so frustrated by humanity, but be so proud that they were trying to resolve something so difficult and necessary.

To give students a chance to share their personal reactions to our study, after the U.N. conference I asked them to use any medium of their choice (art, poetry, video, collage) to represent what they felt or believed about what they learned during the unit. It could be focused on one particular piece of content, such as the wall/security barrier, or on the entire conflict. The work students turned in was diverse and creative.

Teaching Palestine Is Possible

The impact of 1948 stretches far beyond those directly affected or tied to the region by ancestry and/or religion. The events of that year set off one of the longest conflicts between two peoples in modern world history, making it an educational obligation to those of us teaching contemporary world studies and modern world history. Yet this responsibility has largely been unfulfilled. The typhoon of controversy that swirls around this issue can draw the attention of parents and community members to our curriculum and teaching practices, although what we teach the rest of the year is ignored. The possibility of scrutiny and criticism has dissuaded educators from teaching Palestine-Israel for years or led them to teach a

Palestinian refugees leaving the Galilee, October–November 1948.

watered-down version that does not reflect all experiences and voices.

But teaching Palestine is both possible and ultimately rewarding. I have seen my students flourish as they think, question, and engage. I feel validated that I have helped instill a sense of urgency and humanity in them. That student engagement, strengthening their ability to draw their own conclusions about arguably the most urgent situation in the world, inspires and motivates me to keep teaching about Palestine. I hope that I never lose my courage.

■ ■

For resources from this lesson, go to rethinkingschools.org/articles/independence-or-catastrophe

Samia Shoman taught high school social studies in the San Francisco Bay Area for 16 years and has led teacher professional learning on Teaching Palestine nationwide.

PALESTINE SHRINKI[NG]

1918

1947

UNDER OTTOMAN
RULE, ZIONIST
ORGANISATIONS
INCLUDING
THE JEWISH NATIONAL
FUND BEGIN TO MAKE
**LAND PURCHASES
THROUGHOUT
PALESTINE**
FOR JEWISH
SETTLEMENT.

PRIVATISATION
OF LAND UNDE[R]
THE BRITISH
MANDATE
**ACCELERATES
ITS TRANSFER
AND SALE
TO ZIONIST
ORGANISATIO[NS]**
AND THE
DISPLACEMENT
OF PALESTINIA[N]
INHABITANTS.

SOURCES
Text based on.
BADIL, 2000 **Land Own[ership]**
BADIL, 2012 **Living Lan[d]**
B'Tselem, 2010 **By Hoo[k]**

VISUALIZING**PALESTINE**

WWW.VISUA[LIZINGPALESTINE]
SHARE AND D[ISTRIBUTE]

EXPANDING ISRAEL

FOLLOWING THE **FORCED DISPLACEMENT [NAKBA] OF OVER 750,000 PALESTINIANS** IN 1948, THE NEW STATE OF ISRAEL ENACTS LAWS **TO CONFISCATE THE VAST MAJORITY** OF PALESTINIAN LANDS.

SINCE OCCUPYING THE WEST BANK AND GAZA IN 1967, ISRAEL HAS UNILATERALLY DECLARED **TENS OF THOUSANDS OF HECTARES** OF SO CALLED 'STATE LAND' FOR **ISRAELI SETTLEMENTS.**

20–2000.
The Mewat Pretext In The Naqab.
lement Policy In The West Bank.

Maps adapted from
Malkit Shoshan, 2010. **Atlas of the Conflict: Israel-Palestine**
B'Tselem, 2014. **Map of the West Bank, Settlements and the Separation Barrier.**

Palestinian Land
Zionist Settlements

INE.ORG. MAY 2015.
ELY. CREATIVE COMMONS BY-NC-ND 3.0 LICENSE.

 @visualizingpal
 fb.com/visualizingpalestine

On Teaching the Nakba

BY ABDEL RAZZAQ TAKRITI

We have to apply four principal rules to Nakba education. . . . The first point when we're dealing with Nakba education is to insist that the Nakba happened and to reject denialism in all its forms.

Secondly, we need to insist on the fact that the Nakba is continuing. We have to understand that this is a colonial continuum. This is a structural process. It is not an event. And what we're seeing now in Gaza is very much connected to what happened in 1948.

Thirdly, the Nakba must be stopped. So, it's not enough to commemorate. It's not enough talk about it. We have to stop it right now. And that means the first step to doing that is to stop the genocide in Gaza.

And fourthly, it must be reversed. The Nakba must be reversed. And that means restoring Palestinian political and national rights, not only dealing with this as a humanitarian question, despite the gravity of the humanitarian situation. The humanitarian situation is a byproduct of the denial of the Palestinian political and national rights from the beginning of British colonialism to this very, very day.

▰ ▪

Palestinian historian Abdel Razzaq Takriti is a professor at Rice University. This is excerpted from an interview on Democracy Now! *with Amy Goodman and Juan González, May 15, 2024.*

Palestinians fleeing the village of Qumya in 1948.

Born on Nakba Day

BY MOHAMMED EL-KURD

Mohammed El-Kurd is an internationally touring and award-winning poet, writer, journalist, and organizer from Jerusalem, Occupied Palestine. In 2021, he was named as one of the 100 most influential people in the world by Time *magazine. He is best known for his role as a co-founder of the #SaveSheikhJarrah movement.*

Your unkindness rewrote my autobiography
into punch lines in guts,
blades for tongues,
a mouth pregnant with
thunder.

Your unkindness told me to push
through,

look,
listen.

I was born on the fiftieth anniversary of the Nakba
to a mother who reaped olives
and figs
and other Quranic verses,
watteeni wazzaytoon.
My name: a bomb in a white room, a walking suspicion
in an airport,
choiceless politics.

I was born on the fiftieth anniversary of the Nakba.
Outside the hospital room:
protests, burnt rubber,
Keffiyeh'ed faces, and bare bodies,
stones thrown onto tanks,
tanks imprinted with U.S. flags,
lands
smelling of tear gas, skies tiled with
rubber-coated bullets,
a few bodies shot, dead — died
numbers in a headline.

I
and my sister
were born.

Birth lasts longer than death.
In Palestine death is sudden,
instant,
constant,
happens in between breaths.

I was born among poetry
on the fiftieth anniversary.
The liberation chants outside the hospital room
told my mother
to push.

The United States and Palestine-Israel: Fifty Years of Choices (1956–2006)

BY ADAM SANCHEZ

WIKIMEDIA COMMONS | PUBLIC DOMAIN

President Richard Nixon, Israeli Prime Minister Golda Meir, and Secretary of State Henry Kissinger in the Oval Office, Nov. 1, 1973.

S tudents may be puzzled about the role that the United States has played in Israel's war on Gaza following the Oct. 7, 2023, Hamas attacks. With tens of thousands of civilians killed in Gaza, why has the United States continued to arm Israel?

This lesson looks back at the history of U.S. relations with Palestine-Israel to shed light on the choices the United States faced with respect to Israel, Palestine, and to an extent, the broader Middle East. Using a framework developed by Hyung Nam in his lesson "The U.S. and Iraq: Choices and Predictions," this lesson asks students to focus on critical choice points in U.S. policy toward Palestine-Israel between 1956 and 2006. The goal is to

help students learn what happened over these 50 years, but also see other historical possibilities. In doing so, students gain a deeper understanding of the role the United States has played and continues to play in the conflict.

Beginning in 1956, eight years after the creation of the state of Israel, this lesson is best used after a robust discussion on the events of 1948. (See "Independence or Catastrophe? Teaching Palestine Through Multiple Perspectives," p. 41.) In addition, this lesson ends in 2006 with the rise of Hamas and the siege of Gaza. So, while it provides a framework for understanding contemporary events, the decades after 2006 deserve closer study for students to fully understand today's crisis.

TIME REQUIRED
Two to three class periods

MATERIALS NEEDED
- U.S. Government Response Options — one for each group
- 10 situations and outcomes, cut up — one for each group
- Copies of "Debrief Questions" for every student
- "The United States and Palestine-Israel: Fifty Years of Choices (1956–2006)" Slideshow (bit.ly/USPalChoicesSlideshow)

SUGGESTED PROCEDURE

1. Explain to students that they will examine crucial choice points of U.S. leaders over 50 years of diplomatic relations with Palestine-Israel. For each situation, they will decide how a just U.S. government should have responded and then compare their responses to what actually happened. Tell students: "For this activity, suspend your own beliefs about the U.S. government and imagine that throughout this history we had a government that cared about promoting equality, justice, and ending oppression, and think about how such a government should react in these situations."

2. Put students in groups of three to five and distribute copies of "U.S. Government Response Options." Go through the options, make sure students understand each one, and provide time for questions. For example, you may need to explain economic sanctions: "Sanctions are a way to pressure a government to change its policy or to encourage a people to rise up against the government. Sanctions could be comprehensive, prohibiting any commercial activity with the targeted country, or they could be selective, refusing to sell or buy particular goods. An example of a selective sanction would be refusing to sell weapons, or a particularly destructive type of bomb to a targeted country."

3. Since running the lesson with students, I've developed a slideshow (available at bit.ly/USPalChoicesSlideshow) that displays a map of Palestine-Israel and a table that details the U.S. aid given to Israel and to Palestinians for each time period discussed. Information in the table comes from Congressional Research Service reports as well as the UNRWA commissioner-general annual reports. Until 1975, all the aid given to Palestinians was funneled through UNRWA. Starting in 1975 and expanding significantly after the Oslo Accords, the United States began providing direct Palestinian aid through the U.S. Agency for International Development (USAID).

Because the map changes significantly throughout the history being discussed, looking at the slides can help students better understand the changes taking place. The 1993–1995 map is a particularly useful visual of the areas of control established under the Oslo Accords.

4. Distribute copies of "Situation #1." Ask students to read out loud and discuss the first dilemma in their small groups. Encourage students to individually write down their group's decision for how a just U.S. government would respond to the situation and why. For the first few situations, urge students to share their decisions out loud with the full class. This can help students get an idea of the range of possible responses and rationales; they may discover similarities with other groups in how they chose to respond.

When I taught this lesson at the Academy of Palumbo in Philadelphia, I overheard this conversation between three young women discussing Situation #4, which details the expansion of Israeli settlements in the Occupied Territories following the 1967 Six-Day War and the rise of the Palestine Liberation Organization (PLO):

> Ilana: We should give aid to the civilians being attacked by the PLO in these bombings and hijackings.
> Brianna: OK, but what about the people who are being occupied by the Israeli government? They are being kicked off the land.
> Arya: Right, I think if we're going to provide aid, we should provide aid to the people harmed on both sides.

When this group reported their decision, they found that another group had come to a similar, but different conclusion: suspend aid and publicly criticize Israel's settlement construction in the Occupied Territories.

5. After a few groups share their decision, distribute copies of "Outcome #1" to each group. Give students time to read what really happened and ask for reactions. "Why give Israel more money when it's building these illegal settlements?" Sadie asked after learning the real outcome for Situation #4. "And we're not including the PLO in peace negotiations, so how is there going to be peace without any Palestinian voices at the table?" Leila asked. Ask students to note the actual outcomes on the same paper they write their group's decisions. Tell students that these notes will help them with the debrief questions at the end of the lesson.

6. Distribute "Situation #2." Explain that each situation builds off of the previous outcome — so while students continue to discuss what a just U.S. government might do for Situation #2, they do this not based on what they concluded should have happened in response to Situation #1, but what the actual U.S. government response was historically (detailed in Outcome #1). This becomes important as U.S. aid to Israel and to Palestinians rises over this 50-year period and the possibility of withholding aid becomes an important lever of influence. Follow the same procedure: discussing how students think a just U.S. government should respond, writing their group's conclusions individually, and then sharing with the full class.

7. Continue with the remaining situations. Once everyone understands the assignment, you might no longer have the full class share after every situation as that can make the activity take longer.

8. After students have finished all 10 dilemmas, distribute copies of "Debrief Questions." Give students time to write on the questions before discussing them in class. Or ask students to write on the questions for homework for a discussion the following day.

In her response, Nora wrote, "I disagree with the U.S. response in every situation because it led to more death, brutalization, and destruction." Leila was shocked that the United States continued to "fund Israel with billions of dollars in aid, even after they killed a U.S. citizen! At the very least the U.S. should back their own people over a foreign government." Sadie expressed gratitude for the lesson and stated that it helped her "understand lots of history that I was not clear about."

But not all students responded positively. Ilana wrote in her reflection that she felt the lesson was "one-sided" and did not contain enough details about what "innocent Israelis have gone through." Although I tried to discuss attacks on Israeli civilians when relevant, the lesson aimed to focus on key choice points for the United States in deciding policy toward Palestine-Israel. I acknowledged that in covering 50 years of history much was left out and it would be impossible to choose 10 events over 50 years without using my own judgment about what is important. If I taught this lesson in a longer unit, I would have followed up with an activity where students examine timelines of this period from multiple Zionist and anti-Zionist sources. I'd encourage them to note similarities and differences, debate what they think is most important, and possibly curate their own timeline.

Nevertheless, almost all students seemed to come away with a better understanding of the historical background behind the current conflict and the role the United States has played. Brianna, referring to Hamas' attack on Israel, wrote that the activity "helped me understand the frustration amongst Palestinians that led to Oct. 7." Sadie agreed: "The U.S. helped Israel ruin so many lives and helped kill countless children and civilians. People need to understand this as the buildup to Oct. 7."

■■ ▪

Adam Sanchez (adam@rethinkingschools.org) is the managing editor of Rethinking Schools.

U.S. Government Response Options

Discuss how you think the U.S. government should respond in each case and explain the reasons for your decisions. The range of possible options can include changes or additions to one or more of the following:

• Use military force

• Use economic sanctions (prohibitions on the purchase, sale, or distribution of certain goods to targeted country) to discourage undesirable behavior, and encourage better behavior

• Officially criticize actions

• Ignore the actions

• Support with military aid (money, training, equipment, or personnel)

• Support with economic and humanitarian aid

• Other response (explain)

Palestine-Israel Situations and U.S. Government Responses

SITUATION #1 (1956):
SUEZ CANAL CRISIS

During World War I, Great Britain and France signed a secret treaty that divided the Middle East into spheres of influence and control. The European imperialists were particularly interested in exploiting the region's newly discovered oil as well as utilizing the Suez Canal to access the markets and colonies of Asia. The Arab nationalist movement grew in opposition to European imperialism. After 1948, France became Israel's chief weapons supplier and developed a close diplomatic and military relationship with Israel as a defense against rising Arab nationalism. In 1952, Arab nationalist Gamal Abdel Nasser seized power from the Egyptian monarchy and established the Republic of Egypt. Egypt had been a British protectorate and Nasser forced the last British troops to leave the Suez Canal area in 1954. After Israel attacked Egyptian personnel in Gaza, Nasser tried to purchase arms from Great Britain and the United States. When they refused, he turned to the Soviet Union, the United States' Cold War rival. In response to the Soviet arms deal, the United States canceled promised loans to Egypt that Nasser planned to use to pay for the Aswan Dam. In 1956, Nasser nationalized (took over ownership of) the British- and French-owned Suez Canal Company to raise funds for the dam, which he thought was vital for Egypt's future. Britain, France, and Israel invade Egypt — without first notifying the United States. **How should the U.S. government respond?**

. . . .

OUTCOME #1 (1956):
SUEZ CANAL CRISIS

By the mid-1950s, the Middle East accounted for 40 percent of the world's oil reserves. As oil surpassed coal as the main energy source in industrialized countries, including the United States, the U.S. government became more concerned with Middle Eastern politics. Seeing that Arab nationalists were pushed into the arms of the Soviet Union, the Eisenhower administration publicly condemned the invasion of Egypt. When Israel refused to withdraw troops from Sinai and the Gaza Strip, Eisenhower threatened to apply economic sanctions on Israel. Eisenhower also threatened to sell part of the U.S. government's investment in British bonds and along with many countries, refused to sell oil to Britain and France until they agreed to withdraw. Facing increasing pressure, Israel, France, and Britain withdrew their troops.

. . . .

SITUATION #2 (1960):
NUCLEAR WEAPONS

Despite Israeli assurances that it would "not be the first to introduce nuclear weapons in the Middle East," U.S. intelligence suspects that Israel, with support from France, has secretly begun construction of a heavy-water nuclear reactor that could be used to produce nuclear weapons. If Israel is producing nuclear weapons, it would be an extreme escalation of the arms race in the Middle East between Israel and the surrounding Arab countries. **How should the U.S. government respond?**

OUTCOME #2 (1960):
NUCLEAR WEAPONS

The Kennedy and Johnson administrations pushed for Israel to allow U.S. scientists and intelligence officials to inspect its nuclear facility. Although Israel agreed to the inspections, they placed restrictions on U.S. inspectors that made it difficult to confirm Israeli claims that the nuclear plant was for peaceful purposes only. The United States did not force Israel to accept transparent inspections. According to the Center for Arms Control and Non-Proliferation, Israel likely produced its first nuclear weapon in 1966 or 1967. In *Israel and the Bomb*, Israeli historian Avner Cohen uses interviews with and memoirs by U.S. and Israeli officials to argue that when President Nixon met with Israeli Prime Minister Golda Meir at the White House in 1969, they reached an understanding: Israel would keep its nuclear program secret and not carry out nuclear tests, and the United States would end its inspections, allow Israel's possession of nuclear weapons, and stop pressuring them to sign the 1968 Nuclear Non-Proliferation Treaty. To this day Israel neither confirms nor denies the existence of its nuclear arsenal. Most experts estimate that Israel has about 90 nuclear warheads. Israel is one of four countries that still refuse to sign the Nuclear Non-Proliferation Treaty.

. . . .

SITUATION #3 (1967):
THE SIX-DAY WAR

In the 1950s, Israel began to challenge the 1948 armistice agreement with Syria that established a demilitarized zone between the two countries. In violation of this agreement, Israelis gradually took over parts of this zone, evicting Palestinian villagers and demolishing homes. In retaliation, Palestinians and Syrians fired on Israeli settlements from an area above, called the Golan Heights. In 1966, a new Arab nationalist government took power in Syria and Israeli leaders publicly declared it might go to war with the new regime if it did not end the attacks on Israeli settlements in the Golan Heights. On April 7, the dispute escalated into an air battle. Israel shot down six Syrian fighter jets. Responding to a Syrian request for assistance, in May, Egyptian troops entered the Sinai Peninsula bordering Israel and said they would aid Syria if Israel invaded. Egyptian President Nasser then declared a blockade of the Israeli port of Eilat. Although U.S. intelligence could find no evidence that Egypt was planning attacks on Israel, Israel seeks U.S. approval for a preemptive military strike against Egypt and Syria. Despite widespread fear about Israel's survival in a war with multiple Arab nations, both U.S. and Israeli intelligence estimated that Israel would win a war within a week. **How should the U.S. government respond?**

OUTCOME #3 (1967):
THE SIX-DAY WAR

As Egypt, Syria, and other Arab countries built closer ties to the Soviet Union, the United States increasingly saw Israel as a key ally in the Cold War. By 1965, U.S. annual military aid to Israel had reached $12.9 million. In 1966, the United States had provided $90 million in military aid to Israel. At a meeting on June 1, 1967, U.S. Secretary of Defense Robert McNamara gave Meir Amit, the head of Israel's external intelligence agency, the green light to launch an attack. On June 5, Israeli strikes destroyed the Egyptian and Syrian air forces within a few hours. Jordan joined in the fighting belatedly and was attacked by Israel as well. The war lasted only six days and ended in victory for Israel. As a result, Israel captured the West Bank and East Jerusalem from Jordan, the Gaza Strip and the Sinai Peninsula from Egypt, and the Golan Heights from Syria. During the war, Israel destroyed several Palestinian villages and displaced between 280,000 and 325,000 Palestinians. For the United States, Israel's victory established that country as a key military ally in the Middle East. When Richard Nixon became president in 1969, he declared, "Neither the defense nor the development of other nations can be exclusively or primarily an American undertaking." An Israeli Foreign Office official said something similar earlier in the decade: "The United States has come to the conclusion that it can no longer respond to every incident around the world, that it must rely on a local power — the deterrent of a friendly power — as a first line to stave off America's direct involvement. . . . Israel feels that she fits this definition." William Quandt, a staff member on Nixon's National Security Council, wrote that by 1970 the United States had "a policy based on arming Israel as a strategic asset for American policy in the Middle East."

. . . .

SITUATION #4 (1976):
THE RISE OF THE PALESTINE
LIBERATION ORGANIZATION (PLO)

After the Israeli victory in the June 1967 ("Six-Day") war, Palestinians in the West Bank, East Jerusalem, the Gaza Strip, and the Golan Heights all came under Israeli military occupation. Israel denied Palestinians many basic rights and civil liberties, including freedoms of expression, the press, and political association. Israel criminalized Palestinian nationalism, regularly assassinating Palestinian leaders and making it a crime to display the Palestinian national colors. Between 1967 and 1976, Israel built 44 settlements in the Occupied Territories, often evicting Palestinians who lived there. According to the United Nations, this violated the Fourth Geneva Convention. Several Palestinian resistance organizations united under the Palestine Liberation Organization (PLO). The PLO launched a campaign of armed resistance inside and outside of Israel, some of which could be described as terrorism: PLO-affiliated organizations engaged in high-profile bombings, aircraft hijackings, hostage taking, and killing of Israeli civilians inside and outside of the country. In 1974, the Arab League recognized the PLO as the "sole legitimate representative of the Palestinian people" and granted it full membership. That same year, PLO leader Yasser Arafat called for the PLO's attacks on targets outside of Israel to stop and indicated a new willingness to negotiate with Israel. In 1976, a resolution came before the U.N. Security Council. It was rumored to be backed by the PLO and called for Israel to withdraw from the Occupied Territories, the establishment of an independent Palestinian state, the right of Palestinian refugees to return to their homes, and the right of "all states in the area . . . to live in peace within secure and recognized boundaries." **How should the U.S. government respond?**

OUTCOME #4 (1976):
THE RISE OF THE PALESTINE LIBERATION ORGANIZATION (PLO)

The United States vetoed three 1976 U.N. Security Council resolutions to assert the rights of Palestinians and condemn the Israeli occupation. Throughout the 1970s, despite the building of illegal settlements on Palestinian land, U.S. economic and military aid to Israel continued to rise. Between 1970 and 1979 the United States gave Israel $16.2 billion, 72 percent of which was military aid. After 1976, Israeli settlement construction dramatically expanded. In a secret memorandum of agreement with Israel, the United States promised to "not recognize or negotiate with the Palestine Liberation Organization so long as the Palestine Liberation Organization does not recognize Israel's right to exist and does not accept Security Council Resolution 242." For many years the PLO rejected SC 242 because it recognized only the right of every "state" in the Middle East to "live in security." Accepting SC 242, therefore, meant recognizing Israel without Israel having to recognize Palestinian rights. Israel and the United States also did not accept, as most other countries did, the understanding of SC 242 as requiring Israel to withdraw from all territory occupied in 1967. Nor did they accept, as most other countries did, the establishment of a Palestinian state in the West Bank and Gaza. Despite the United States' secret promise with Israel, senior U.S. intelligence officials established and maintained contact with the PLO. Nevertheless, because Israel opposed Palestinian involvement, the Carter administration did not invite the PLO to participate in the Arab-Israeli peace negotiations held at Camp David in the late 1970s.

. . . .

SITUATION #5 (1982):
GOING TO WAR IN LEBANON

In the 1960s, the Palestine Liberation Organization's primary base of operations was in Jordan, where most Palestinian refugees ended up after 1948. But Jordan's King Hussein saw the power the PLO had built within Jordan as a threat and in 1970 drove the PLO out of the country. The PLO relocated to Lebanon where again it built a sort of state-within-a-state. In July 1981, Israel and the PLO engaged in a two-week exchange of fire across the border. The United States negotiated a ceasefire. Unsatisfied with this outcome, Israeli Defense Minister Ariel Sharon met with U.S. Ambassador Philip Habib to ask for U.S. support for an Israeli invasion of Lebanon to destroy the PLO. According to the recollections of Habib's assistant, Habib described "in graphic detail" to U.S. State Department officials what would happen if they agreed to Israel's request: "We were going to see American-made munitions being dropped from American-made aircrafts over Lebanon, and civilians were going to be killed, there was going to be a hell of a big uproar, and the United States . . . was going to take a full charge of blame." **How should the U.S. government respond to Ariel Sharon's request that the United States support Israel's invasion of Lebanon?**

OUTCOME #5 (1982):
GOING TO WAR IN LEBANON

The United States provided Israel $1.4 billion in military aid in both 1981 and 1982. This paid for the U.S. weapons used in Lebanon by Israel: F-16 fighter-bombers, M-113 armored personnel carriers, 155mm and 175mm artillery shells, air-to-ground missiles, and cluster munitions. When Israeli Defense Minister Ariel Sharon went to Washington to explain plans for the invasion of Lebanon to U.S. Secretary of State Alexander Haig, Haig told Sharon that the United States could not tell Israel "not to defend your interests," and demanded only that there "be a recognizable provocation." When a Palestinian organization not associated with the PLO attempted to assassinate Israel's ambassador in London, Israel invaded Lebanon. After 10 weeks of fighting, more than 19,000 Palestinian and Lebanese — mostly civilians — were killed, and more than 30,000 wounded. More than 650 Israelis — mostly soldiers — were killed and nearly 3,800 wounded.

· ·

SITUATION #6 (1982):
SABRA AND SHATILA

On Sept. 1, 1982, the PLO agreed to leave Lebanon after obtaining assurances from the United States that the remaining Palestinian refugees and civilians would be protected. But two weeks later, despite promises to the United States that it would not do so, the Israeli military entered and occupied West Beirut, Lebanon. On Sept. 15, the Israeli military sealed off the entrance to the Sabra and Shatila refugee camps so no one could leave without Israeli permission. They then allowed the Phalange, a right-wing Lebanese militia that had been armed and trained by Israel, to enter the camps and massacre Palestinian refugees for 43 hours. Estimates have put the death toll between 2,000 and 3,500 civilians and testimonies of survivors describe horrific acts of mutilation and rape. **How should the U.S. government respond?**

· ·

OUTCOME #6 (1982):
SABRA AND SHATILA MASSACRE

U.S. military aid to Israel continued uninterrupted after the Sabra and Shatila Massacre and even increased to more than $1.7 billion annually in 1983 and 1984. On Sept. 17, after the PLO had left Beirut and as the massacres were taking place, President Ronald Reagan instructed Ambassador Morris Draper to hold a meeting with Israeli officials to press Israel to leave Beirut. During the meeting, Israeli Defense Minister Ariel Sharon attempted to justify Israel's continued presence in Lebanon: "There are thousands of terrorists in Beirut. Is it your interest that they will stay there?" After Draper did not challenge this claim that all Palestinian civilians were terrorists, Sharon stated, "So we'll kill them. They will not be left there. You are not going to save them."

SITUATION #7 (1987):
THE FIRST INTIFADA (UPRISING)

In December 1987, an Israeli army vehicle collided with a truck in the Jabalia refugee camp in the Gaza Strip, which killed four Palestinians. This set off a wave of protests across the Occupied Territories known as the First Intifada ("uprising," "shaking off," in Arabic). In January, Israeli Defense Minister Yitzhak Rabin ordered security forces to use "force, might, and beatings" to stop the demonstrations, which were overwhelmingly unarmed. Images of heavily armed Israeli soldiers brutalizing Palestinian teenagers were broadcast around the world; one image of a small Palestinian boy throwing a stone at a massive Israeli tank became a symbol of the uprising. Palestinians engaged in strikes, boycotts, withholding taxes, and other forms of civil disobedience. Protests sometimes turned violent, often started by soldiers using live ammunition, rubber bullets, or tear gas against unarmed or rock-throwing demonstrators. Israel also employed mass arrests without trial and torture to crush the protests and intimidate Palestinians. **How should the U.S. government respond?**

. . . .

OUTCOME #7 (1987):
THE FIRST INTIFADA (UPRISING)

In response to Israeli repression of Palestinian protests, the Reagan administration issued an unusual public condemnation of Israeli security forces for "harsh security measures and excessive use of live ammunition." The First Intifada lasted several years and Reagan's successor, George H. W. Bush took a relatively firmer stance with Israel. He delayed $10 billion in loan guarantees (a form of economic aid) until Israel promised to stop building settlements in the occupied West Bank and participate in a peace conference. Neither president threatened to withhold any of the $1.7 billion in military aid Israel received on average annually from the United States during their presidencies.

. . . .

SITUATION #8 (1992):
MADRID CONFERENCE AND THE OSLO ACCORDS

In 1988, the Palestine Liberation Organization (PLO) adopted the Palestinian Declaration of Independence, which accepted the principles of dividing the land for a two-state solution and a peaceful resolution to the conflict. The PLO simultaneously agreed to Israel's long-held demand that they accept Security Council Resolution 242 as the basis for peace negotiations. (See Outcome #4 for more on SC 242.) Although the Bush administration successfully pressured Israel to send a delegation to the Madrid Peace Conference, Israel continued to oppose any independent Palestinian representation and it attempted to block anyone connected to the PLO in the Jordanian-Palestinian delegation. Nevertheless, this delegation put forward a proposal for a Palestine Interim Self-Governing Authority to create a Palestinian governmental entity, elected by the Palestinian residents of the West Bank, East Jerusalem, and the Gaza Strip, and those displaced from these areas in 1967, as well as those deported since 1967 by Israel. This new authority would have jurisdiction over the Occupied Territories. Israel would freeze settlements and withdraw its troops to the 1967 borders. Israel has so far rejected the proposal. **How should the U.S. government respond?**

OUTCOME #8 (1992):
MADRID CONFERENCE AND THE OSLO ACCORDS

U.S. negotiator Aaron David Miller used the term "Israel's lawyer" to describe how the United States approached the Madrid Conference. The United States refused to pressure Israel to agree to the main Palestinian demands. But they did put pressure on the Palestinian delegation. According to historian Rashid Khalidi, who was at the Madrid Conference, at one point a U.S. diplomat told Palestinian negotiators that if they did not accept a specific offer, the United States could ask its Arab "friends" to put financial pressure on the PLO. Unbeknownst to many of the participants at the Madrid Conference, Israel, frustrated with the lack of progress, simultaneously held separate negotiations with Yasser Arafat, the chairman of the PLO. These negotiations culminated in the Oslo I and II Accords, signed in 1993 and 1995. The PLO agreed to a highly restricted form of self-rule in the Occupied Territories that the Palestinian delegation at the Madrid Conference had rejected. The Oslo Accords carved the West Bank and the Gaza Strip into areas A, B, and C. More than 60 percent of the territory, Area C, was under complete Israeli control. The newly created Palestinian Authority had administrative and security control over 18 percent of the land, Area A. The Oslo Accords were signed in Washington, D.C., on Sept. 13, 1993.

. . . .

SITUATION #9 (2003):
THE SECOND INTIFADA AND THE KILLING OF RACHEL CORRIE

Settlement construction and the demolition of Palestinian homes in the Occupied Territories continued after the Oslo Accords. Israel built a large number of military checkpoints and hundreds of miles of walls and electrified fences carving up the West Bank. Frustrations with continued Israeli aggression and the collapse of the 2000 Camp David peace negotiations led to the Second Intifada as protests erupted across the Occupied Territories. During the first three weeks of the uprising, Israeli forces shot 1 million live bullets at unarmed Palestinian demonstrators. Some Palestinians engaged in suicide bombings and shootings inside Israel's internationally recognized borders. As tensions escalated, Rachel Corrie, a 23-year-old college student from Olympia, Washington, traveled with a group of solidarity activists from the United States to the Gaza Strip. Corrie, a U.S. citizen, was crushed to death by an Israeli bulldozer, while she attempted to nonviolently protect a Palestinian home from being demolished. **How should the U.S. government respond?**

OUTCOME #9 (2003):
THE SECOND INTIFADA AND THE KILLING OF RACHEL CORRIE

U.S. military aid to Israel continued throughout the 1990s, and reached a high of $3.1 billion in 2000. In 2001, Israel elected Ariel Sharon as prime minister. Sharon was the minister of defense during the Sabra and Shatila Massacres and had been found by an Israeli commission of inquiry to be responsible for the slaughter. Sharon rejected a two-state solution. In 1998, as foreign minister, he encouraged Israeli settlers to "run and grab as many [Palestinian] hilltops as they can to enlarge the [Jewish] settlements because everything we take now will stay ours." Despite these comments and Israel's harsh crackdown on Palestinian protests, George W. Bush called Sharon a "man of peace" and endorsed his criticisms of the Palestinian Authority. In 2002, Bush declared "the United States will not support the establishment of a Palestinian state until its leaders engage in a sustained fight against the terrorists and dismantle their infrastructure." Israel called Rachel Corrie's killing a "regrettable accident." The Bush administration accepted this interpretation. The Corrie family launched a civil suit against Israel but an Israeli court dismissed the case. Despite acknowledgement that Israel's investigation into Corrie's death was not thorough and transparent, and despite calls from the Corrie family for the United States to investigate her death, the United States has yet to do so.

. . . .

SITUATION #10 (2006):
THE RISE OF HAMAS

Since its creation out of the Oslo Accords, the Palestinian Authority (PA) had been run by Fatah, the largest group inside the Palestine Liberation Organization (PLO). Frustration with Fatah, the PLO, and the PA increased as it became clear that the PA had no power except that permitted by Israel. Hamas was a group in Gaza that Israel allowed to operate in the 1980s and '90s as an alternative to the PLO — despite its antisemitic program, commitment to armed resistance, and use of suicide bombings to kill Israeli civilians. Hamas grew in popularity during the brutal repression of the Second Intifada. The United States considers Hamas a terrorist organization and supported the Israeli assassination of two of Hamas' key leaders in 2004. But these killings only enhanced Hamas' popularity and power. Hamas ran in the 2006 Palestinian Authority election and won. Hamas claimed it was willing to extend a ceasefire agreement with Israel and attempted to form a coalition government with Fatah. **How should the U.S. government respond?**

OUTCOME #10 (2006):
THE RISE OF HAMAS

The United States and Israel rejected Hamas' participation in the Palestinian Authority and cut off funding to the PA. U.S.-trained, Fatah-controlled security forces in the Gaza Strip tried to unseat Hamas by force. When this failed, Hamas proceeded to set up its own Palestinian Authority in the Gaza Strip. Israel declared that Gaza had become a "hostile territory" and with the support of Egypt, which had become the second largest recipient of U.S. military aid after Israel, imposed a siege on Gaza: Goods entering were reduced to a bare minimum, regular exports were stopped completely, fuel supplies were cut, and leaving and entering Gaza was rarely permitted. In 2018, the U.N. Special Rapporteur for the Occupied Territories described the consequences of the blockade: "With an economy in free fall, 70 percent youth unemployment, widely contaminated drinking water, and a collapsed health care system, Gaza has become 'unlivable.'" Despite Israel's condemnation of Hamas, Israeli Prime Minister Benjamin Netanyahu encouraged the Qatari government to send billions of dollars in aid to the Hamas government, as part of a divide-and-conquer approach toward Palestinians. As Netanyahu told his colleagues in 2019, "Anyone who wants to thwart the establishment of a Palestinian state has to support bolstering Hamas and transferring money to Hamas. . . . This is part of our strategy — to isolate the Palestinians in Gaza from the Palestinians in the West Bank." U.S. military aid to Israel has increased every year since 2006, reaching $3.3 billion annually between 2021 and 2023.

Debrief Questions

Review what your group decided for how the United States should have responded and the actual outcomes of each situation and answer the following questions. Use specific details and facts as evidence.

1. What do you think were the consequences of U.S. policy in Palestine/Israel from 1956 to 2006:
   - on Israeli and Palestinian civilians?
   - on the rest of the world's perception of the United States?

2. Pick two or three of the choices the U.S. government made and discuss why you agree or disagree with those decisions.

3. "Oil is much too important a commodity to be left in the hands of the Arabs."
   —Henry Kissinger, U.S. secretary of state 1973–1977

   "Israel is the largest American aircraft carrier in the world that cannot be sunk, does not carry even one American soldier, and is located in a critical region for American national security."
   —Alexander Haig, U.S. secretary of state 1981–1982

   What do these quotes reveal about the U.S. political and economic objectives in the Middle East? What do these quotes reveal about the way the United States views Israel in relation to those objectives? Did you see evidence for this in the situations and outcomes?

4. How do U.S. government decisions of the past help you understand the crisis in Gaza that began in 2023?

5. What questions do you have that are raised by the information in this lesson?

The United States and Israel

BY STEPHEN R. SHALOM

An Israeli and U.S flag fly in the Negev desert during a joint air defense exercise, 2003.

QUIQUE KIERSZENBAUM | GETTY IMAGES

EDITORS' NOTE: *This is an edited excerpt from an article written for* Against the Current *shortly after the 2009 Israeli assault on Gaza.*

The courageous Israeli journalist Amira Hass, in her 1996 book *Drinking the Sea at Gaza*, tells us that in Israeli slang "go to Gaza" means "go to hell."[1]

She wrote these words long before the recent savage violence, making Gaza a living hell not just in the Israeli imagination, but in reality.

But in creating this nightmare for the people of Gaza, Israel didn't act alone.

It had the support of Egypt, which kept the Rafah crossing between Gaza and Egypt closed. It had the support of the European Union, the second largest arms supplier to Israel.

And most importantly, Israel had the decisive support of the U.S. government: the aircraft, the helicopters, the bunker-buster missiles, the 2,000-pound bombs. And the United States also provided crucial diplomatic backing, making sure that no Security Council resolution could interfere with Israel's agenda.

To understand the role the United States played as Israel's enabler in Gaza, we need to look at what Washington hopes to achieve in the Middle East. The key for the United States is control of oil, what the State Department in 1945 called "a stupendous source of strategic power and one of the greatest material prizes in world history."[2] And this concern to control the region's oil is no less true today than it was in 1945.[3]

Over the years, U.S. control of Middle East oil has faced many challenges. First, there was the competition from other major powers, especially Britain and France. So, following World War II, the United States moved to push these two countries out of Saudi Arabia.

In 1956, Washington opposed the British-French-Israeli aggression against Egypt, keeping its capitalist rivals from reasserting their presence in the region. And in 2003, one cause of the war on Iraq was U.S. competition with France and Russia over Iraqi oil.

But the most important challenge to U.S. control of Middle East oil has been the people of the Middle East. In the early 1950s, a democratically elected Iranian government nationalized the British oil company there, as it was entitled to do under international law. Washington and London responded with a boycott of Iranian oil, which brought Iran's economy to the brink of collapse. Then the U.S. Central Intelligence Agency (CIA) and British intelligence organized a coup, entrenching a quarter-century dictatorship under the Shah and effectively denationalizing the oil company, with U.S. firms getting 40 percent of the formerly 100 percent British-owned company.

The Largest Aircraft Carrier

For U.S. policymakers therefore, the question has always been how can they assure their control of Middle East oil and defend it against all challengers. Middle Eastern public opinion is hostile to the idea of foreign military bases, which its people see — rightly — as an infringement on their independence.

This is where Israel comes in. Israel is, in some respects, the "largest U.S. aircraft carrier in the world," from which U.S.-made planes with U.S.-made weaponry can bombard U.S. enemies from Israeli bases with Israeli pilots.

It is sometimes argued that "if the United States were truly interested in the Middle East's oil it would support the Arabs over Israel." But it's not a question of Israel vs. "the Arabs," but Israel and the pro-American oil oligarchs against any radical and nationalist Arab regimes that might threaten U.S. control of oil.

So in 1959, when Egypt and Iraq were both ruled by nationalist regimes, a memorandum for the National Security Council stated that "if we choose to combat radical Arab nationalism and to hold Persian Gulf oil by force if necessary, a logical corollary would be to support Israel as the only strong pro-West power left in the Near East."[4]

With the so-called Six-Day War in 1967, the U.S.-Israeli alliance began in earnest. Washington officials saw Israel's defeat of Egypt and Syria, both armed by the Soviet Union, as a major contribution to U.S. foreign policy.

When President Richard Nixon took office in 1969, he and his National Security Advisor Henry Kissinger viewed Israel as a Cold War ally that (along with Iran and Saudi Arabia) could tame Soviet-backed regimes of the Middle East. Democratic Sen. Henry "Scoop" Jackson revealed the bipartisan nature of this policy, saying:

> Such stability as now obtains in the Middle East is, in my view, largely the result of the strength and Western orientation of Israel on the Mediterranean and Iran on the Persian Gulf. These two countries, reliable friends of the United States, together with Saudi Arabia, have served to inhibit and contain those irresponsible and radical elements in certain Arab states . . . who, were they free to do so, would pose a grave threat indeed to our principal sources of petroleum in the Persian Gulf.[5]

In 1979, when the pro-American Shah of Iran was overthrown by an anti-American Islamic regime, Israel became even more important to U.S. planners.

Converging Interests

Some people claim that Washington, D.C., is "Israeli-occupied territory" — that the Israel lobby controls U.S. foreign policy, that the Israeli tail wags the U.S. dog and not the other way around.

This view misunderstands the way power works.

Yes, the U.S. and Israeli governments are close allies. They have common interests. They sometimes defer to each other. Allies do that. They cooperate in many areas: They share weapons production; they share intelligence; the United States provides military aid; throughout the Cold War Israel provided Soviet weapons, captured from Arab armies, to countries the United States wanted to support.

This is a close alliance, but that's different from saying that Israel, through the Israel Lobby, controls U.S. policy.

You can't tell "who controls who" if you look only at issues where the interests of the two are the same. But look where their interests diverge — as, for example, over the issue of the Israeli sale of military technology to China. It is easy to see who was boss: The United States imposed sanctions, told Israel to stop its planned arms deal with China, and got Israel to issue a public apology and remove senior defense officials.[6]

Such divergences are rare. Generally, the United States and Israel have the same interests:

- Both the United States and Israel oppose radical Arab regimes.
- Both talk about "democracy," but would rather have a dictator — like Hosni Mubarak in Egypt — than an elected regime where the "wrong people" get elected.
- Both ally themselves with Islamic fundamentalism when it suits their interests: For example, Saudi Arabia is probably the most fundamentalist regime in the world, and one of Washington's closest allies. Israel was happy to support Hamas in Gaza when felt most threatened by the secular Palestine Liberation Organization. And the United States was happy to support Afghan mujahedin against the Soviet Union.

For both the United States and Israel, what's important is not democracy or secularism, but to dominate the region.

What can people do in the United States to make things better? If we educate and mobilize people, maybe we can build enough pressure to put an end to Washington's blank check for Israel. And if we can do that, there's a chance to end the hell on Earth that Israel has created for Palestinians.

[1] Hass, Amira. 1996. *Drinking the Sea at Gaza*. New York: Owl Books.

[2] Chomsky, Noam. 2003. *Hegemony and Survival*. Metropolitan Books.

[3] The United States is not dependent on Middle East oil today (it gets most of its supply from the Western Hemisphere and Africa) just as it was not dependent on Middle East oil in 1945 (when the United States was the world's largest oil producer). Then, as now, the crucial issue was whether Washington could so control global oil supply that it would have leverage over other countries, especially its capitalist competitors.

[4] Chomsky, *Hegemony and Survival*.

[5] Stork, Joe. 1975. *Middle East Oil and the Energy Crisis*. New York: Monthly Review Press.

[6] Marc Perelman, "Israel Miffed Over Lingering China Flap," *Forward*, Oct. 7, 2005, http://www.forward.com/articles/2014/.

■■ ▪

Stephen R. Shalom is Emeritus Professor of Political Science at William Paterson University, where he served for many years as the director of the Gandhian Forum for Peace and Justice and then director of the Middle East Studies program. He is the author of Which Side Are You On? An Introduction to Politics; Imperial Alibis: Rationalizing U.S. Intervention After the Cold War; *and* The United States and the Philippines: A Study of Neocolonialism. *He is on the editorial board of* New Politics *magazine and is a member of Jewish Voice for Peace of Northern New Jersey.*

TIMELINE OF VIOLENCE **SINCE 1988**

26,521
TOTAL PALESTINIANS KILLED

3,027
TOTAL ISRAELIS KILLED

As of November 22, 2023

14,500 Palestinians killed

1,500 Israelis killed

VISUALIZING**PALESTINE**   SOURCES bit.ly/vp-fatalities   NOV2023

Writing My Own Book

BY DANDARA

IRINA NAJI

You took the documents of our houses,
Now you want the ones where our poems are written?
Why are you grabbing our Arab poems?
Why do you want to throw away the national poetry?
What will you leave us with? The romantic poems?
It's not that we are against love
But there are other emotions as well
For example, do you want love?
OK, a couple fell in love
They got married, roses and flowers
They want to live in happiness,
But you took their house, you took their land
So I grab my pen, I write with my pen
No love, no romance, without a homeland

*Dandara, which means "let's make some noise"
or "let's make it happen" in Arabic, is a young
people's hip-hop group at the Madaa Creative
Center in Silwan, just south of Jerusalem's Old
City. As project director Majd Ghaith explains
in* Determined to Stay: Palestinian Youth Fight
for Their Village *(by Jody Sokolower, Interlink
Publishing, 2021): "The Israeli occupation is
forcing Israeli textbooks into our schools. In the
places where there were Palestinian flags, we
see Israeli flags. The history books say that Israel freed the country from the British occupation.
Nothing about the Nakba." In response, Dandara, which creates all their songs collaboratively,
wrote "Writing My Own Book."*

"Why Must You Go Back to Palestine?"

BY FAWAZ TURKI

In 1955, a journalist from England, one of those wretched "area specialists," complete with cameras and images of the Palestinians as the noble savage, came to the [Burj Al-Barajneh refugee] camp to conduct a series of interviews with the men around the cafés. She talks to them, through an UNRWA [United Nations Relief and Works Agency] interpreter, as if they are children — in a slow, deliberate, patronizing manner.

"But why, why must you go back to Palestine?" she asks Abu Samir, thrusting her microphone close to his face. "Why Palestine specifically? There are many Arab countries you can be resettled in."

She was too ignorant of our culture to know how profoundly insulting she was being. No one can make sport of a Palestinian peasant's gods without eliciting a fierce response, yet Abu Samir simply straightens up stiffly in his chair and waits a while before he answers. He has learned over many years how to handle a goat or a mule possessed by a fit of obstinacy. You are gentle with it, suspending your fury a while, till it comes to its senses.

"Sister, let me tell you this," he intones, his eyes almost closed as he puffs on his water pipe. "The land is where our ancestors were born, died, and are now buried. We are from that land. The stuff of our bones and our soul comes from there. We and the soil are one. Every grain of my land carries the memories of all our ancestors within it. And every part of me carries the history of that land within it. The land of others does not know me. I am a stranger to it and it is a stranger to me. *Ardi-aardi*," he concludes. My land is my nobility.

What an English journalist, coming from a culture that wants to "conquer space" and "tame nature," did with that bit of peasant self-definition, no one can say.

■■ ■

Fawaz Turki, a poet and essayist, was born in Haifa, Palestine, in 1940; he fled with his family to Lebanon following the 1948 Nakba, and lived there at Burj Al-Barajneh Refugee Camp.

From Soul in Exile: Lives of a Palestinian Revolutionary, *by Fawaz Turki. Monthly Review Press. 1988; pp. 49–50. Used by permission of Monthly Review Press.*

WAEL ABU YABES

rice haikus

BY SUHEIR HAMMAD

we are women simple
sugar our morning tea
eat rice at all meals

we of simple land
kept the sugar in one sack
rice and another

lived off the brown earth
gave figs to fidayeen*
olives and almonds

when they raided homes
they poured sugar into rice
to ruin them both

with eyelashes and
teeth we tried to sort it out
small grain from small grain

now we eat sweet rice
with our morning tea eat
meals of resistance

fidayeen — popular name for freedom fighters

■■ ■

*Suheir Hammad is a poet, author, and political
activist. She was born in Amman, Jordan. Her
parents were Palestinian refugees who immigrated
to Brooklyn when Suheir was 5 years old.*

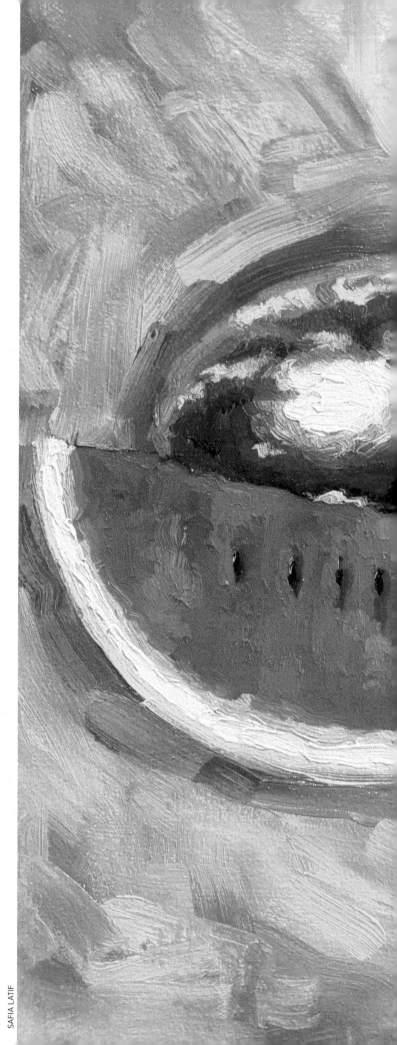

SAFIA LATIF

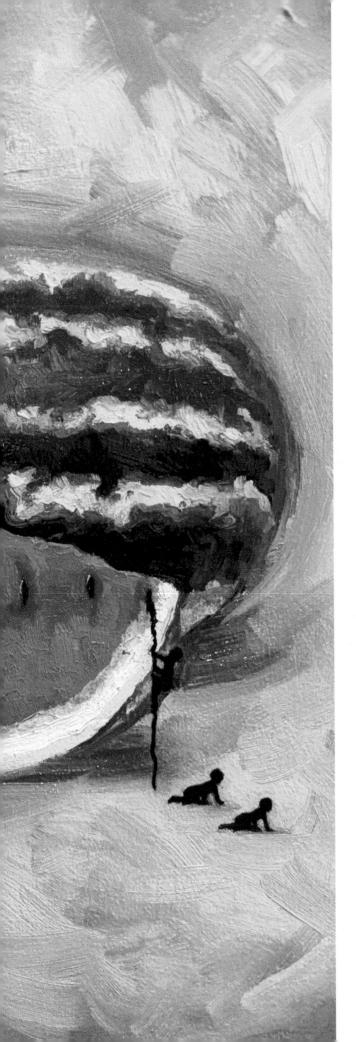

Excerpt from
Hind's Hall 2

BY MACKLEMORE, ANEES, MC ABDUL, AND AMER ZAHR

We don't own the earth
We're killing each other over some lines in the dirt
We bleed the same blood, feel the same hurt
Palestinian life, does it have the same worth? . . .

In our lifetime we will be free
And they can bury us
But they will find out we are seeds.

■■ ■

Macklemore is a Grammy Award-winning artist.

Anees is a Palestinian American rapper/singer.

MC Abdul is a Gaza-born rapper.

Amer Zahr is a Palestinian American comedian, author, singer, and oud player.

3
Gaza

In 2009, as part of an UNRWA-led summer camp, children in Gaza broke a world record by flying 7,000 kites at once. When a Chinese kite flying association broke their record in 2011, the determined kids took it back that summer, flying 12,350 kites on a beach in northern Gaza. The children of Gaza hold that record to this day.

Because of Us

BY EM BERRY

This morning I learned
The English word gauze
(finely woven medical cloth)
Comes from the Arabic word [...] Ghazza
Because Gazans have been skilled weavers for
centuries

I wondered then

how many of our wounds
have been dressed
because of them

and how many of theirs
have been left open
because of us

*Em Berry is an independent writer, poet,
and artist from Aotearoa — New Zealand.
An audio-visual representation of this poem
was published by Al Jazeera and can be
seen at https://youtu.be/TkdMCrNec5I*

"I Think the Word Is Dignity"
— Rachel Corrie's Letters from Gaza

The international media and our government are not going to tell us that we are effective, important, justified in our work, courageous, intelligent, valuable. We have to do that for each other, and one way we can do that is by continuing our work visibly.

...people without privilege will be doing this work no matter what, because they are working for their lives. We can work with them, and they know that we work with them, or we can leave them to do this work themselves and curse us for our complicity in killing them.

Rachel Corrie

On March 16, 2003, an Israeli bulldozer crushed 23-year-old U.S. peace activist Rachel Corrie to death as she tried to prevent the Israeli army from destroying homes in the Gaza Strip. In a series of poignant emails to her family, she explained why she was risking her life.

We share some of those letters here, followed by questions by Bill Bigelow for discussion in high school classrooms or for student written reflections. The Zinn Education Project website features a short video of Rachel Corrie's mother, Cindy Corrie, reading from these letters. The website also includes a link to novelist Alice Walker reading from the letters at a 2006 *Voices of a People's History* event. Or these letters can simply be read aloud in class. See the Rachel Corrie Foundation for Peace & Justice for more resources.

February 7, 2003

Hi friends and family, and others,

I have been in Palestine for two weeks and one hour now, and I still have very few words to describe what I see. It is most difficult for me to think about what's going on here when I sit down to write back to the United States. Something about the virtual portal into luxury. I don't know if many of the children here have ever existed without tank shell holes in their walls and the towers of an occupying army surveying them constantly from the near horizons. I think, although I'm not entirely sure, that even the smallest of these children understand that life is not like this everywhere. An 8-year-old was shot and killed by an Israeli tank two days before I got here, and many of the children murmur his name to me — Ali — or point at the posters of him on the walls. . . . [T]here are 8-year-olds here much more aware of the workings of the global power structure than I was just a few years ago.

Nevertheless, no amount of reading, attendance at conferences, documentary viewing, and word of mouth could have prepared me for the reality of the situation here. You just can't imagine it unless you see it — and even then you are always well aware that your experience of it is not at all the reality: what with the difficulties the Israeli army would face if they shot an unarmed U.S. citizen, and with the fact that I have money to buy water when the army destroys wells, and the fact, of course, that I have the option of leaving. Nobody in my family has been shot, driving in their car, by a rocket launcher from a tower at the end of a major street in my hometown. I have a home. I am allowed to go see the ocean. When I leave for school or work I can be relatively certain that there will not be a heavily armed soldier waiting halfway between Mud Bay and downtown Olympia at a checkpoint with the power to decide whether I can go about my business, and whether I can get home again when I'm done. As an afterthought to all this rambling, I am in Rafah: a city of about 140,000 people, approximately 60 percent of whom are refugees — many of whom are twice or three times refugees. Today, as I walked on top of the rubble where homes once stood, Egyptian soldiers called to me from the other side of the border, "Go! Go!" because a tank was coming. And then waving and "What's your name?" Something disturbing about this friendly curiosity. It reminded me of how much, to some degree, we are all kids curious about other kids. Egyptian kids shouting at strange women wandering into the path of tanks. Palestinian kids shot from the tanks when they peek out from behind walls to see what's going on. International kids standing in front of tanks with banners. Israeli kids in the tanks anonymously — occasionally shouting and also occasionally waving — many forced to be here, many just aggressive — shooting into the houses as we wander away.

. . . There is a great deal of concern here about the "reoccupation of Gaza." Gaza is reoccupied every day to various extents but I think the fear is that the tanks will enter all the streets and remain here instead of entering some of the streets and then withdrawing after some hours or days to observe and shoot from the edges of the communities. If people aren't already thinking about the consequences of this war for the people of the entire region then I hope you will start.

My love to everyone. My love to my mom. My love to smooch. My love to fg and barnhair and sesamees and Lincoln School. My love to Olympia.

Rachel

February 27, 2003
(To her mother)

Love you. Really miss you. I have bad nightmares about tanks and bulldozers outside our house and you and me inside. Sometimes the adrenaline acts as an anesthetic for weeks and then in the evening or at night it just hits me again — a little bit of the reality of the situation. I am really scared for the people here. Yesterday, I watched a father lead his two tiny children, holding his hands, out into the sight of tanks and a sniper tower and bulldozers and Jeeps because he thought his house was going to be exploded. Jenny and I stayed in the house with several women and two small babies. It was our mistake in translation that caused him to think it was his house that was being exploded. In fact, the Israeli army was in the process of detonating an explosive in the ground nearby — one that appears to have been planted by Palestinian resistance.

This is in the area where Sunday about 150 men were rounded up and contained outside the settlement with gunfire over their heads and around them, while tanks and bulldozers destroyed 25 greenhouses — the livelihoods for 300 people. The explosive was right in front of the greenhouses — right in the point of entry for tanks that might come back again. I was terrified to think that this man felt it was less of a risk to walk out in view of the tanks with his kids than to stay in his house. I was really scared that they were all going to be shot and I tried to stand between them and the tank. This happens every day, but just this father walking out with his two little kids just looking very sad, just happened to get my attention more at this particular moment, probably because I felt it was our translation problems that made him leave.

I thought a lot about what you said on the phone about Palestinian violence not helping the situation. Sixty thousand workers from Rafah worked in Israel two years ago. Now only 600 can go to Israel for jobs. Of these 600, many have moved, because the three checkpoints between here and Ashkelon (the closest city in Israel) make what used to be a 40-minute drive, now a 12-hour or impassible journey. In addition, what Rafah identified in 1999 as sources of economic growth are all completely destroyed — the Gaza international airport (runways demolished, totally closed); the border for trade with Egypt (now with a giant Israeli sniper tower in the middle of the crossing); access to the ocean (completely cut off in the last two years by a checkpoint and the Gush Katif settlement). The count of homes destroyed in Rafah since the beginning of this intifada is up around 600, by and large people with no connection to the resistance but who happen to live along the border. I think it is maybe official now that Rafah is the poorest place in the world. There used to be a middle class here — recently. We also get reports that in the past, Gazan flower shipments to Europe were delayed for two weeks at the Erez crossing for security inspections. You can imagine the value of two-week-old cut flowers in the European market, so that market dried up. And then the bulldozers come and take out people's vegetable farms and gardens. What is left for people? Tell me if you can think of anything. I can't.

If any of us had our lives and welfare completely strangled, lived with children in a shrinking place where we knew, because of previous experience, that soldiers and tanks and bulldozers could come for us at any moment and destroy all the greenhouses that we had been cultivating for however long, and did this while some of us were beaten and held captive with 149 other people for several hours — do you think we might try to use somewhat violent means to protect whatever fragments remained? I think about this especially when I see orchards and greenhouses and fruit trees destroyed — just years of care and cultivation. I think about you and how long it takes to make things grow and what a labor of love it is. I really think, in a similar situation, most people would defend themselves as best they could. I think Uncle Craig would. I think probably Grandma would. I think I would.

You asked me about non-violent resistance.

When that explosive detonated yesterday it broke all the windows in the family's house. I was in the process of being served tea and playing with the two small babies. I'm having a hard time right now. Just feel sick to my stomach a lot from being doted on all the time, very sweetly, by people who are facing doom. I know that from the United States, it all sounds like hyperbole. Honestly, a lot of the time the sheer kindness of the people here, coupled with the overwhelming evidence of the willful destruction of their lives, makes it seem unreal to me. I really can't believe that something like this can happen in the world without a bigger outcry about it. It really hurts me, again, like it has hurt me in the past, to witness how awful we can allow the world to be. I felt after talking to you that maybe you didn't completely believe me. I think it's actually good if you don't, because I do believe pretty much above all else in the importance of independent critical thinking. And I also realize that with you I'm much less careful than usual about trying to source every assertion that I make. A lot of the reason for that is I know that you actually do go and do your own research. But it makes me worry about the job I'm doing. All of the situations that I tried to enumerate above — and a lot of other things — constitutes a somewhat gradual — often hidden, but nevertheless massive — removal and destruction of the ability of a particular group of people to survive. This is what I am seeing here. The assassinations, rocket attacks, and shooting of children are atrocities — but in focusing on them I'm terrified of missing their context. The vast majority of people here — even if they had the economic means to escape, even if they actually wanted to give up resisting on their land and just leave (which appears to be maybe the less nefarious of Sharon's possible goals), can't leave. Because they can't even get into Israel to apply for visas, and because their destination countries won't let them in (both our country and Arab countries). So I think when all means of survival is cut off in a pen (Gaza) which people can't get out of, I think that qualifies as genocide. Even if they could get out, I think it would still qualify as genocide. Maybe you could look up the definition of genocide according to international law. I don't remember it right now. I'm going to get better at illustrating this, hopefully. I don't like to use those charged words. I think you know this about me. I really value words. I really try to illustrate and let people draw their own conclusions.

Anyway, I'm rambling. Just want to write to my Mom and tell her that I'm witnessing this chronic, insidious genocide and I'm really scared, and questioning my fundamental belief in the goodness of human nature. This has to stop. I think it is a good idea for us all to drop everything and devote our lives to making this stop. I don't think it's an extremist thing to do anymore. I still really want to dance around to Pat Benatar and have boyfriends and make comics for my co-workers. But I also want this to stop. Disbelief and horror is what I feel. Disappointment. I am disappointed that this is the base reality of our world and that we, in fact, participate in it. This is not at all what I asked for when I came into this world. This is not at all what the people here asked for when they came into this world. This is not the world you and Dad wanted me to come into when you decided to have me. This is not what I meant when I looked at Capital Lake and said: "This is the wide world and I'm coming to it." I did not mean that I was coming into a world where I could live a comfortable life and possibly, with no effort at all, exist in complete unawareness of my participation in genocide. More big explosions somewhere in the distance outside.

When I come back from Palestine, I probably will have nightmares and constantly feel guilty for not being here, but I can channel that into more work. Coming here is one of the better things I've ever done. So when I sound crazy, or if the Israeli military should break with their racist tendency not to injure white people, please pin the reason squarely on the fact that I am in the midst of a genocide which I am also indirectly supporting, and for which my government is largely responsible.

I love you and Dad. Sorry for the diatribe. OK, some strange men next to me just gave me some peas, so I need to eat and thank them.

Rachel

February 28, 2003
(To her mother)

Thanks, Mom, for your response to my email. It really helps me to get word from you, and from other people who care about me.

After I wrote to you I went incommunicado from the affinity group for about 10 hours, which I spent with a family on the front line in Hi Salam — who fixed me dinner — and have cable TV. The two front rooms of their house are unusable because gunshots have been fired through the walls, so the whole family — three kids and two parents — sleep in the parents' bedroom. I sleep on the floor next to the youngest daughter, Iman, and we all shared blankets. I helped the son with his English homework a little, and we all watched *Pet Sematary*, which is a horrifying movie. I think they all thought it was pretty funny how much trouble I had watching it. Friday is the holiday, and when I woke up they were watching *Gummi Bears* dubbed into Arabic. So I ate breakfast with them and sat there for a while and just enjoyed being in this big puddle of blankets with this family watching what for me seemed like Saturday morning cartoons. Then I walked some way to B'razil, which is where Nidal and Mansur and Grandmother and Rafat and all the rest of the big family that has really wholeheartedly adopted me live. (The other day, by the way, Grandmother gave me a pantomimed lecture in Arabic that involved a lot of blowing and pointing to her black shawl. I got Nidal to tell her that my mother would appreciate knowing that someone here was giving me a lecture about smoking turning my lungs black.) I met their sister-in-law, who is visiting from Nuseirat camp, and played with her small baby.

Nidal's English gets better every day. He's the one who calls me "My sister." He started teaching Grandmother how to say "Hello. How are you?" in English. You can always hear the tanks and bulldozers passing by, but all of these people are genuinely cheerful with each other, and with me. When I am with Palestinian friends I tend to be somewhat less horrified than when I am trying to act in a role of human rights observer, documenter, or direct-action resister. They are a good example of how to be in it for the long haul. I know that the situation gets to them — and may ultimately get them — on all kinds of levels, but I am nevertheless amazed at their strength in being able to defend such a large degree of their humanity — laughter, generosity, family time — against the incredible horror occurring in their lives and against the constant presence of death. I felt much better after this morning. I spent a lot of time writing about the disappointment of discovering, somewhat firsthand, the degree of evil of which we are still capable. I should at least mention that I am also discovering a degree of strength and of basic ability for humans to remain human in the direst of circumstances — which I also haven't seen before. I think the word is dignity. I wish you could meet these people. Maybe, hopefully, someday you will.

Rachel

Questions for Reflection and Discussion

1. Rachel Corrie's letters were sent in 2003. The young children she met are today in their 20s or 30s, if they are alive. What are some of the key memories you think these young people might have, based on what is included in Corrie's letters?

2. What questions come up for you in Rachel Corrie's letters? About people in Gaza, about Corrie?

3. Think about the descriptions in Rachel Corrie's letters. What conditions make life so difficult for Palestinians?

4. In one letter, Rachel Corrie says, "I am really scared for the people here." Why is she scared for people?

5. Nowhere in Rachel Corrie's letters does she use the word "courage." Yet at one point in her letters, she describes that "I tried to stand between them [Palestinians] and the tank." What are the experiences in Corrie's life that might lead to this kind of courageous response?

6. Go through Rachel Corrie's letters and underline phrases that you find moving, startling, poignant, poetic. Write a "found poem" from language you find in her letters.

7. Rachel Corrie's mother says that Palestinian violent resistance is making things worse. Rachel asks her mom: "What is left for people? Tell me if you can think of anything. I can't . . ." What do you think about Rachel's statement? What might her mother say?

8. Rachel Corrie writes: "I really can't believe that something like this can happen in the world without a bigger outcry about it. It really hurts me, again, like it has hurt me in the past, to witness how awful we can allow the world to be." Why is it that "we" can allow the world to be so awful?

9. Rachel Corrie writes: "So I think when all means of survival is cut off in a pen (Gaza) which people can't get out of, I think that qualifies as genocide." What do you think of this statement of Corrie's? What does this mean people in Gaza should do? What does it lead Corrie to want to do?

10. What do you think led Rachel Corrie to travel to Gaza to live with the people there in such difficult situations? Try to imagine one experience that Corrie may have had in her hometown of Olympia, Washington, that may have led her to make the decision to travel to Gaza to stand with people there.

11. Based just on what you read in Rachel Corrie's letters, what thoughts do you have about the Palestinians in Gaza whom she spent time with?

12. Rachel Corrie says that Gazans have dignity. "Dignity." What does she mean by that? What leads her to say that? What does the word dignity mean to you?

It's Bisan, from Gaza and I'm Still Alive

Throughout the Israeli assault on Gaza, following Oct. 7, Bisan Owda has posted moving first-person video testimonies that begin with some variation of "I'm still alive." As of the publication of this book, thankfully Owda

is still alive, although her testimonies have also included some of her own health woes. As when Rachel Corrie "reported" from Gaza, Owda is also in her 20s.

After students have read Rachel Corrie's 2003 letters from Gaza, show students videos from Bisan Owda in 2023 and 2024. (These are easily found on the web.) An alternative is to follow a study of the Palestinian 1948 Nakba — catastrophe — with Owda's video "It's Bisan from Gaza, and This Is the Second Nakba," which links what is going on to-

day to 1948. Each "It's Bisan . . ." segment is short, around 10 minutes long. Because Israeli attacks forced Owda to relocate frequently throughout the Gaza Strip, some of her videos are from Rafah, where Rachel Corrie stayed. Ask students:

- How have conditions changed in Gaza since Rachel Corrie was there? What conditions have remained the same?
- Corrie expressed admiration for Gazans. What does Owda admire about Gazans?
- Corrie described Gazans' "dignity." What is Gazans' dignity that you can recognize from Owda's videos — their ability to "remain human" in the midst of such horrific conditions?
- In 2003, Corrie wrote: "I really can't believe that something like this can happen in the world without a bigger outcry about it." Why hasn't there been a "bigger outcry" from people throughout the world to stop the Israeli attacks on Gazans?
- In 2024, Bisan Owda was nominated for an Emmy Award for Outstanding Hard News Feature Story. A pro-Israel organization sought unsuccessfully to have the Emmy nomination withdrawn. Why might an organization not want Bisan Owda's videos widely seen?

Bill Bigelow (bbpdx@aol.com) is curriculum editor of Rethinking Schools.

Talking to Young Children About Gaza

BY REEM ABUELHAJ

Fundamental to our work as educators and caretakers of young children is an obligation to tell them the truth about the world and give them tools to take action. Since Israel launched its assault on Gaza I have watched in grief as Palestinian children have been killed and injured, starved, and denied medical care. It has been challenging to know whether and how to engage with the young children in my life about what is going on. As a Palestinian American elementary school teacher, I found myself unable to look at the 1st and 2nd graders in my classroom without seeing the faces of Gazan children of the same ages. This is a deeply painful time.

Many schools and educational institutions have adopted policies and practices that silence educators from talking about Palestine and Israel under threat of penalty or losing employment. Many adults have chosen not to talk with their children about Israel's genocide in Gaza for fear that it will be too overwhelming or scary.

However, many young children already hear about the genocide in Gaza or even see images of Gaza under siege that pervade social media and the news. Whether from the back seat of the car while a family member listens to the radio, overhearing grown-ups discussing the news in hushed tones from another room, attending a protest with their parents, or even hearing a friend make a reference at school, many young people already sense that something bad is happening to kids in a place called Gaza.

For young children, and all of us, knowing something bad and scary is happening but not having the information to understand it generates fear and a feeling of being out of control. Giving children the information to understand hard and scary events in developmentally appropriate ways, whether in their personal lives or in the global sphere, supports them to feel agency and a sense of emotional safety.

Rather than remain silent when children have questions about Gaza, educators and caregivers of young children can give young people tools to think critically about the world, understand power, and take meaningful action to build a world where everyone has what they need to thrive.

It is not always possible to prepare for a conversation about a tricky topic with a young child. Sometimes a child makes a statement or brings up a question that requires immediate response. Remember, we can always say: I want to think about how to answer that. Can we talk about this again later? The most important thing is to show the child, with our words and our affect, that we are open to answering their questions.

Below are guidelines for conversations between adults and young children about Gaza.

1. Start with what they know. We can always respond to a child's question with another question. For example, if a child asks, "Why are people bombing Gaza?" We might respond, "I'm so glad you asked that question. What have you heard about what's happening in Gaza?"

2. Listen and mirror the language the child is using. Children will use language that they can understand and process. It is the adult's job to listen to the language children use as an indication of their developmental understanding. If a child says, "They are hurting kids in Gaza," we don't need to use the word "kill." If a child says, "They are using

weapons," we don't need to use the word "bombs." If a child says, "People in Gaza don't have enough food," we don't need to use the word "starve."

3. Use concrete, clear, direct language. Think about breaking big concepts down into building blocks that the child can understand. Think about using words they already have references for.

4. Help the child differentiate their experience from the experience of people in Gaza. If the child asks, "Will Israel bomb us here?" We might respond, "No. That isn't going to happen. Here we are safe from bombs. And we can work for a world where everyone is safe from bombs."

5. Check in and affirm feelings (ours and the child's). Conversations about violence and oppression are too often intellectualized by people not directly impacted. It is healthy for adults and children to acknowledge the feelings that arise when talking about this issue. As adults, it's our job to help children notice the feelings that come up and find ways to articulate and work with them. We can also be honest with the child about how we're feeling. It is supportive to talk about how we are feeling with the children in our lives for many reasons, including the fact that children are often aware of our emotions even when we are not naming them. We can name our feelings directly in a way that does not put the child in a position of being our caretaker. For example, if a child asks, "Do you feel sad about Gaza?" We might respond, "Yeah, I do feel sad. I feel that in my heart. Where do you feel it in your body?" After the child responds we might affirm "Yeah, sometimes I feel it there too," and ask, "What are some things we can do when we feel sad?"

6. Make clear moral statements. It is OK, and actually important, to make clear moral statements about social issues. Young children are oriented to justice, and in a world pervasive with oppression it is important for adults to make clear to young children when something is wrong. We can say: "All people deserve to have food, water, and medicine." "It is wrong to stop people from getting food."

7. Give the child a way to take action. One of the most important elements of a conversation with a young child about hard truths is to offer them a sense of agency and opportunities for action. In my classroom, for example, I always pair conversations about climate change, a terrifying and inevitable issue, with lessons about climate justice organizing. Young children need to know there are ways to work against injustice in the world, and that they can participate in taking action. By offering ways of taking action that bring children into the collective (e.g., making protest signs with friends or participating in a letter-writing day), we can use a moment of injustice as an opportunity to build solidarity and community.

* * *

Recently I was having coffee with an acquaintance who said about the genocide in Gaza, "I never imagined this would be happening." I responded that, sadly, as a Palestinian American whose family has been impacted by Israel's escalating military occupation of Palestine, I had known this was possible. However, what I never imagined I would see in my lifetime is the level of resistance and solidarity with the Palestinian people that has erupted in the United States and around the world since Oct. 7, 2023. I never imagined I would walk through my neighborhood in Philadelphia and see people sitting at coffee shops wearing keffiyehs or see so many Palestinian flags in the windows of my neighbors' homes.

In such an unprecedented moment of resistance, we must take seriously the young people who will inherit the struggle for liberation. Giving young children language for understanding the truth about oppression, the tools to fight injustice, and the resources to build communities that can live in collective freedom is world-changing work. Imagine when children across the world today are having these conversations and developing these tools and resources, what more liberatory futures could be possible.

■■ ■

Reem Abuelhaj is an elementary school educator and community organizer in Philadelphia. As an educator, her work focuses on developing and implementing abolitionist practices in the elementary school classroom and supporting young children to learn concrete organizing skills so they can build a more free world.

Sitti's Bird: A Gaza Story — An Introduction to Gaza for Children

BY DONNIE ROTKIN AND JODY SOKOLOWER

Sitti's Bird: A Gaza Story is a beautiful children's book by Malak Mattar, who grew up in Gaza. It's a thoughtful, hopeful introduction to events in Gaza for children. This lesson is aimed at 3rd to 5th graders, but can be adapted for younger or older students.

(In case you can't easily get a copy of *Sitti's Bird*, see the YouTube of a Palestinian girl reading the book. If you have Arabic-speaking students, you may want to use a video that includes the

text read in both English and Arabic. The book starts about nine minutes in. Also see the slide deck to use with the lesson. It includes links to the video of the book. All these materials are at teachpalestine.org.)

Talking about Gaza may be charged for students for a range of reasons, including family connections in Palestine or Israel, demonstrations, and conversations in their homes. Students may have violent images in their minds from the media. Many Palestinian, Arab, and Muslim youth feel targeted by the way the media portrays Palestinians.

Tell students: "We're going to read a book that you may have different ideas and feelings about. Remember our class agreements about listening to each other with open hearts and minds (or however your class agreements are phrased). This might be hard for some of you, but I'm here to help."

Ask students if they have heard that there is a war in Gaza, which is part of Palestine. Ask:

"What questions do you have about that?"

Show students maps of the region and of Palestine-Israel. If you have a standard world map, you can show students how differently Palestine is represented — or omitted — on standard maps.

Tell students: "The book we're going to read is *Sitti's Bird: A Gaza Story*. It's about Malak, who lives in Gaza, which is part of Palestine. Malak wrote the story herself. It's about when she was a few years older than you."

Pre-reading question: "When you feel sad or scared, is there something that makes you feel better? Complete this sentence: When I feel sad, sometimes it makes me feel better to . . ."

"Tell your idea to a reading buddy."

"Who would like to share with the class?"

Tell students: "In the story, Malak is sad and scared, but she finds a way to make herself feel better. Let's find out what happens."

"I'm going to read the story all the way through. You might have questions or ideas during the story. Once we finish, we'll read it again and stop and talk about all your questions and ideas."

Read (or play) the story all the way through. Remind students they will have a chance to ask questions and say what they think and feel in a few minutes.

After you finish the story the first time, ask the class some comprehension questions:

- Why was Malak scared?
- Why couldn't she go to school?
- What did Malak do that made her feel better?
- What happened to Sitti's home?
- Why couldn't Malak go to the international show of her paintings?

Read (or play) the book again, stopping when students have questions or ideas they want to express. Discuss: "Why does Malak ask, 'Sitti, are we in a cage, too?'"

Explain: "As you can see on the map, Gaza is a narrow strip of Palestinian land on the Mediterranean Sea. It is surrounded by fences and walls built by Israel. Israel says it needs the fences and walls to keep it safe. Israel controls all the gates — except one controlled by Egypt. They have ships in the sea that control who can come into or leave Gaza, too. So all the people of Gaza, including Malak and her family, are cut off from the rest of Palestine and the rest of the world. Even before the war happening now, people in Gaza had a lot of trouble getting clean water, books, medical supplies, and food."

"Having all those fences and walls, and not being able to leave — how do you think that makes Sitti feel?"

Talk about the explosions: "The explosions are bombs. Bombs are big, noisy, powerful blasts that blow up buildings and kill people."

"Why can't Malak go to school or leave her house for 50 days?"

"Malak wrote *Sitti's Bird* about her experiences in 2014, when Israel bombed Gaza and then sent in tanks and soldiers for 50 days. Many Palestinian people, including 547 children, were killed. More than 100,000 people lost their homes, like Sitti does. It was a terrible time, but not as bad as the current war."

"Why can't Malak go to the international show of her paintings?"

"Israel controls who can leave Gaza to visit a different country, and who can come to visit Gaza. They wouldn't let Malak leave for her art show. If we wanted to go visit Gaza now to talk to children there, Israel would not let us in."

"Where is Malak now?"

"When Malak got the highest grades of any student in Gaza and the second highest grades in all of Palestine, she was lucky enough to be able to study in Turkey and to travel to other countries. Right now, she is studying art in London, England."

Talk with students about what is happening in Gaza now.

"Right now, there is a terrible war happening in Gaza. Fighters in Gaza, who were angry about how Israel has treated people in Gaza, broke down the wall and killed many Israeli soldiers and Israelis who were at a music festival. They took about 250 Israeli people hostage and took them back to Gaza — they wanted to trade them for Palestinians held in Israeli prisons. This made many people in Israel feel scared and furious. They say they have to make sure that fighters from Gaza can't attack Israel again. With lots of bombs, they have destroyed most of the houses, hospitals, and schools in Gaza. More than 40,000 people have been killed. There is no clean water, and little food. Many people are starving and are very sick. People all over the world are telling Israel to stop the war and open the gates and fences."

"Everyone needs to feel safe. How can people in Israel and people in Gaza be safe?"

"Malak still uses art to share her feelings about Gaza. On her Instagram, we can see pictures of Malak and some of her paintings."

"This is your chance to make a drawing about the book or something it reminds you of. If you want to write about the book instead, that's fine. Or you can do both."

Give students a chance to share and talk about what they drew or wrote.

■ ■

Donnie Rotkin worked as an educator in New York City for more than 35 years. He taught all grade levels, from daycare through 6th grade. After teaching at Central Park East 1, he was a founding member of the Brooklyn New School and Castle Bridge School.

Jody Sokolower is co-coordinator of the Teach Palestine Project at the Middle East Children's Alliance. A former managing editor of Rethinking Schools, she is the author of Determined to Stay: Palestinian Youth Fight for Their Village, *editor of* Teaching About the Wars, *and co-editor of* Rethinking Sexism, Gender, and Sexuality.

A slide deck of this lesson is available at Teach Palestine.

On Politics and Poetry

BY **MARWAN MAKHOUL**

In order for me to write poetry that isn't political,
I must listen to the birds
and in order to hear the birds
the warplanes must be silent.

◼◻

*Marwan Makhoul is a Palestinian poet, born in
1979 in the village of al-Boquai'a, Upper Galilee,
to a Palestinian father and a Lebanese mother.*

MALAK MATTAR | SITTI'S BIRD

"Birds Know No Borders"

The Love of Bird-Watching in Gaza

BY MARTA VIDAL

EDITORS' NOTE: *This article was first published before the Israeli assault on Gaza, beginning after Oct. 7, 2023.*

The skies of Gaza fill with shifting shapes on an early spring morning. At first they are barely visible, only specks soaring above central Gaza's wetlands.

Mandy Sirdah quickly raises her binoculars. "Storks!" she shouts excitedly. Close by, Lara Sirdah, her identical twin sister wearing matching clothes, grabs her long-focus camera and points it to the sky. "So many! So beautiful!" she cries out with joy as she snaps photos of hundreds of white storks flying in circles above her.

Every spring, millions of birds set out from their wintering grounds in Africa and make their way north to Europe and Asia. At the intersection of three continents, the Levant is an important stopover and one of the world's busiest corridors for bird migration.

Many of these birds fly over Gaza, an overcrowded coastal enclave often described as an "open-air prison." The birds soar above more than 2 million people, most of them refugees whose families were forced to leave their villages in 1948 with the establishment of the state of Israel and have been unable to return. Concentrated in refugee camps, Palestinians in Gaza have also been confined by Israeli policies of military closure over many decades and a brutal air, sea, and land blockade imposed since 2007.

"Our movement is very restricted," says Lara, who feels cut off from the rest of the world. "We wish we were birds so we could move freely." Over the past years, bird-watching trips to the Strip's wetlands, groves, and fields have offered the twins a rare opportunity to escape the feeling of confinement. With their heads raised to the sky, they search for birds and dream of flight.

On their early spring exploration of Gaza's wetlands, the Sirdah sisters spotted more than a dozen different species of birds — white-breasted kingfishers flapped their electric-blue wings as black kites soared above yellow wagtails and egrets foraged for food. While Mandy looked through her binoculars and Lara photographed black-headed gulls, swallows swooped down on the twins, flying playfully between them.

The sisters share their photos on social media and help spread awareness about birds and conservation in one of the world's most beleaguered environments. "People are surprised when they see our photos. When they think about Gaza they think it's only blockade, poverty, destruction. But there is also beauty," says Mandy.

Lara and Mandy, who are 47 and live in Gaza City, were never formally trained in wildlife photography or biology. Both work with Atfaluna, an organization supporting deaf people in Gaza. Since they were children they were interested in nature and wildlife, but they started taking bird-watching seriously only in 2015, when they photographed two birds they saw in their garden.

"They looked like the sparrows we usually see in Gaza, but their color was brighter. We published the photo on Facebook, and a bird-watcher in the West Bank told us it was a Spanish sparrow, one of millions of migrating birds that fly over the region," recalls Mandy.

"We started reading more about birds and became very passionate about it. So we started photographing all the birds we saw," she continues. Since then, the twins have spotted 165 species of migrating and resident birds in Gaza.

Despite being hampered by limited resources and restrictions of movement, the Sirdah sisters are committed to spreading knowledge about birds. In collaboration with academic researchers and other bird-watchers they worked on the first checklist of the birds of Gaza, that was published in March 2023.

For the twins, watching birds is a source of solace in the narrow confines of the battered enclave. "The word happiness is not enough to de-scribe what we feel, especially when we see a rare bird for the first time," says Lara. "The birds help us deal with the pressures of our daily lives. They make us forget everything," adds Mandy.

They talk excitedly about the day they managed to spot a European nightjar, a nocturnal species, notoriously hard to find because the dappled plumage blends with their habitat. "I saw the bird resting on an olive branch. It was very well-hidden but we managed to photograph it. It was one of the best days we can remember," Mandy says smiling proudly.

Children who grew up in Gaza witnessing military offensives are more likely to know how to distinguish the sounds of missiles than birdsong. But sometimes there are unexpected connections between birds and bombings. "I used to live in an area that was under bombardment, and a couple of birds came to build their nests in holes made by shrapnel from Israeli F-16 missiles," says Salem Al Qudwa, an architect who focuses on the reconstruction of devastated communities and the possibilities of social transformation.

Across Palestine, birds build nests in shrapnel holes or checkpoints, and perch on the concrete walls, barbed-wire, and fences that segregate and confine Palestinians. "Birds know no borders, they can go wherever they'd like. But we have no freedom," says Abdel Fattah Rabou, a professor of Environmental Studies at the Islamic University of Gaza.

For more than two decades, Rabou has organized trips to the coastal enclave's wetlands to introduce his students to bird-watching and to teach them about Gaza's biodiversity.

He has published several papers on the Strip's fauna and flora, and has spent his career raising awareness about the environment and conservation issues. Recently, he worked with Lara and Mandy on the first checklist of Gaza's bird species.

"In the past, there was a strong culture of hunting here, if people saw a bird, they would shoot it. But in recent years you see more people who are conscious that animals should be protected," says Rabou. While hunting is still popular and a source of income in the deprived enclave, he has noticed changes in attitudes.

"Now there are even people who go to pet

shops and markets to buy birds just to free them from their cages," says Rabou. "Because as a people under occupation, we shouldn't put birds in cages."

Being a bird-watcher in Gaza means facing endless restrictions. Israel controls Gaza's territorial waters, airspace, and the movement of people and goods, except at the border with Egypt. Most Palestinians who grew up in Gaza since the closure imposed in 2007, when Hamas seized control from the Fatah-led Palestinian Authority, have never left the 25- by 7-mile strip.

Egyptian authorities have exacerbated the closures by restricting movement out of Gaza. Israeli authorities justify the closure on "security grounds."

"We found a lot of difficulties getting the equipment," says Lara. Binoculars and zoom lenses are usually not allowed inside Gaza since Israeli authorities consider them "dual-use" items that could be used for military purposes. The twin sisters ordered a long-focus camera for photographing birds, but it was held at the border. It took five months of waiting and a lot of patience handling permissions and questioning to be able to receive their gear.

In an enclave smothered by restrictions where unemployment is about 47 percent and more than half of the population lives in poverty, very few can afford the expensive equipment required for wildlife photography and bird-watching. The twins have to organize and self-fund all their birding trips, as there are no institutions or organizations supporting bird-watchers in Gaza.

The expeditions can also be risky. Several areas in Gaza are military sites closed off to visitors, and border areas are particularly dangerous for someone carrying binoculars and cameras, which Israelis view with suspicion. "It's difficult because there are sensitive areas we're not allowed to enter," adds Lara.

The closure imposed on Gaza also means the twins are unable to attend conferences, exhibitions of their photos, or even ceremonies for awards for their work. "We applied for a lot of permissions but we never managed to leave. We feel we're very restricted," says Lara.

Despite the restrictions, spreading the love of birds and raising more awareness about biodiversity gives the Sirdah twins satisfaction. "We are very happy when people send us photos or recordings of birds they saw or heard and ask us what bird it is. We see more people interested in birds and appreciating wildlife," says Mandy.

To make birding more inclusive, the twin sisters have started making videos in sign language about birds. The response has been encouraging. "We keep being asked when we will post more videos, a lot of people are excited about it," says Mandy.

The twins believe birds can improve the well-being of people with disabilities and be a source of comfort and hope. The deaf can appreciate the beauty of their plumage colors and patterns, and admire their flight. The blind can find joy and tranquility listening to their melodious songs and cheerful twittering.

In Khan Younis, in the south of the Gaza Strip, the Red Crescent Society hosts workshops where people with disabilities make wicker birdhouses for small birds, even when their own homes are threatened with destruction by Israeli bombings.

Zaki Abu Jamus, a craftsman who is visually impaired, says the birdhouses are used locally in gardens and terraces and are also sold abroad. His fingers perform an agile dance as he quickly weaves twigs into a delicate birdhouse. When he is done, he proudly holds up the tiny wicker home. Then smiling, he asks: "Doesn't everyone love birds?"

■■ ▪

Marta Vidal is an independent journalist focusing on social justice and environmental issues across the Mediterranean. Ameera Harouda contributed to this article. This project was supported by the International Women's Media Foundation's Howard G. Buffett Fund for Women Journalists. Used with permission of the author.

Before I Was a Gazan

BY NAOMI SHIHAB NYE

Naomi Shihab Nye is a poet, songwriter, and novelist. She is the author of numerous books of poetry. This poem is included in Everything Comes Next: Collected and New Poems. *Used by permission of the author.*

I was a boy
and my homework was missing,
paper with numbers on it,
stacked and lined,
I was looking for my piece of paper,
proud of this plus that, then multiplied,
not remembering if I had left it
on the table after showing to my uncle
or the shelf after combing my hair
but it was still somewhere
and I was going to find it and turn it in,
make my teacher happy,
make her say my name to the whole class,
before everything got subtracted
in a minute
even my uncle
even my teacher
even the best math student and his baby sister
who couldn't talk yet.
And now I would do anything
for a problem I could solve.

SAFIA LATIF

We Were Children Once

BY AHMED MOOR

Anyone who has been to Gaza knows it's a place of children. They are everywhere. Little girls and boys underfoot, in the streets, arrayed on sandy curbs. They reach into your pockets and make fun of you. Boys on carts pulled by donkeys, peddling goods in tattered clothing and barefoot, baked brown by an unrelenting summer sun. That's the Gaza I remember.

I was born in Rafah in 1984, in the refugee camp there. My family moved when I was young. My father, an orphan who started kindergarten at an UNRWA school at the age of 9 and worked as a child porter for Egyptian soldiers before picking oranges in Israel after 1967, got us out. He finished school and university in Beirut — the only passport available to the Palestinians, then and now — and secured a job with an American NGO. But we went back to Gaza every summer until I was 15, when the Second Intifada started. I haven't been back since.

My earliest memories of Gaza: I remember summer evenings fragrant with jasmine, bright with the Milky Way and the sodium lights of Rafiah Yam, the nearby Jewish settlement, a different kind of bright, searing against the darkness of the Strip. I remember rushing off into the night with other boys, to build plastic bonfires in the dunes and smoke dried molokhia stems, pretending we had cigarettes. And by day, sledding down those same dunes on discarded corn oil containers.

I remember the summer a boy was buried alive when a dune collapsed in his wake. An apocryphal [perhaps made up] story, or a portentous [an ominous] one . . .

I remember trudging through the sandy lanes with my mother to the local telephone operator to call my father, who could rarely join us on those trips home. And I recall, years later, the thrill of watching as the first crew of laborers built a network of telephone exchanges in our corner of Gaza. I remember riding my bike past those high dunes, past Rafiah Yam, and through the checkpoint where Israeli men, armed then, as now, to the teeth, plied small cruelties for fun. I remember "Shlomo's bar" on the beach, which served Palestinian laborers Heineken beer in glass bottles. The prickly pear groves with their fruit — so much like Gaza — sweet, but too often painful.

The dunes are gone now. The sand was used for cinder blocks, the ubiquitous building material in Gaza, where the number of small children has only grown with time. My memories come back to me, relentlessly, with the force of guilt and loss, as I watch the videos of what's being done to those children, more than 10,000 of them now [January 2024]. In one, a cameraman sweeps past a collection of small feet, the only visible parts of small bodies, crushed to death under a collapsed roof in Gaza as they slept. The dunes of my youth turned to cinder blocks, children buried alive under their weight. A timeless story for the children of Gaza, not apocryphal [make believe] at all.

Lately, I catch myself thinking strange thoughts. I imagine a dying sun, 8 billion years from now, swallowing the earth and turning everything to ash. I know I am not alone, and I recognize the dark fantasies of a broken spirit.

And then my children, alive, beautiful, and vivacious — three little girls — wake me from my grim reveries. They pull me back from the precipice. Unknowingly, they hold the genocide at bay. They are too young to know what's being done to their family, so far away from everything in their lives. I write this love letter to Gaza's children, whose lives are brief and whose deaths are meaningless. I write this letter for all the people in Gaza, who were children once, if only briefly, before the awareness of their own worthlessness crept into their lives. I write this letter for myself, and I wonder, when all the children in Gaza are dead, who will pull us back from the precipice?

■ ▪

Ahmed Moor is a Palestinian American writer, born in the Rafah refugee camp in Gaza. He is on the advisory board of the U.S. Campaign for Palestinian Rights. This article, first published in the Nation, *is used by permission.*

The Blockade of Gaza

EDITORS' NOTE: *Israel has restricted the movement of goods and people to and from Gaza since the occupation began in 1967. In 2007, after Hamas won a majority in the Palestinian legislative elections, Israel tightened its blockade. Enacting collective punishment against 2 million Gazans, Israel reduced goods entering Gaza, stopped regular exports, cut fuel supplies, and tightly controlled who could enter or leave. After the Oct. 7, 2023, Hamas attack, Israel expanded the blockade to restrict even essential humanitarian assistance. In September 2024, 15 humanitarian aid organizations declared that Israel was blocking 83 percent of food aid to Gaza and that this reduction meant Gazans were eating an average of one meal every other day. This graphic, created by Mona Chalabi, illustrates some of what was barred from Gaza between 2007 and 2010 based on the findings of Gisha, an Israeli human rights organization. Chalabi won the Pulitzer Prize in 2023 for Illustrated Reporting and Commentary.*

Do You See What I See?

BY LAILA AL-ARIAN

ERIK RUIN FROM 10 PLAGUES OF THE OCCUPATION | JUSTSEEDS

I put down my phone just before closing my eyes to sleep, a final break from the endless stream of horrific news from Gaza. The last posts I see are chilling: Palestinians in Gaza describing the ferocity of Israel's bombing campaign, many of the posts declaring "This is the worst night" yet. Then there are the videos. The screams of terror as 2,000-pound bombs hit homes, the flares of bright orange illuminating Gaza's night skies, and the billowing smoke that follows.

The cycle repeats as night turns into day. I reach for my phone as soon as I wake up and see posts of Gazans taking stock of the events of the previous night: Who was killed, who was rescued from the rubble, who was shot by snipers while fleeing for their safety and waving a white flag.

In the videos, children shake uncontrollably, covered in dust after an air strike, silent and bewildered. The number of children killed and wounded, their limbs amputated, without anesthesia in far too many cases, is so massive that the U.N. has called Gaza "a graveyard for children." Gaza is where Palestinian children go to sleep hungry, where they hold a press conference to beg the world to stop their killing, and where parents write their children's names on their arms and legs in case they need to find them beneath the rubble.

Every time I see a video, photo, or post, I wonder if others are seeing it too — especially Americans, whose tax dollars provide much of the arms for Israel's bombardment. Are they seeing what I'm seeing? I ask over and over again, as each day brings a new brutality that I didn't think was possible.

Israel cut off food, water, fuel, and electricity to Gaza.

It wiped out entire bloodlines.

It stripped men and boys down, photographed, kidnapped, beat, and tortured them.

It executed 11 men in front of their families.

It destroyed cemeteries.

It killed people digging graves for others Israel had previously killed.

It killed a 12-year-old girl who was recovering in a hospital after losing her leg in an earlier air strike that killed her family.

It bombed a hospital live on Al Jazeera. It bombed so many hospitals.

It bombed churches, mosques, schools, universities, U.N. shelters, fishing boats, food storage sites, and bakeries for starving people and convoys of fleeing refugees.

It used white phosphorus, which causes severe burns and even penetrates through bones.

It killed dozens of journalists and even their family members.

It left premature babies to die and then shot the journalist who exposed the story of their decomposing bodies.

I know that if this were happening somewhere else, it would merit wall-to-wall coverage in the United States. Instead, much of what I learn comes from social media and independent or international news outlets.

Israel has barred foreign journalists from entering Gaza unless they are embedded with their military, but even that fact, which would provoke outrage if another country were doing it, has barely made a ripple. Instead, it has fallen on Palestinians to tell their own story — the reporters targeted and killed in record numbers, and the citizen journalists using their phones to capture displacement, starvation, injuries, and death, all evidence of war crimes for which Israel will almost certainly never be held accountable.

It's difficult enough to see the terror unleashed on Gaza's 2.3 million people, nearly half of whom are children. But the complicity and justification from Western countries that have lectured others about human rights for decades makes it unbearable. And then there is the gaslighting, those who deny that any of this is happening at all and claim, for instance, that a dead Palestinian baby is actually a doll.

I am consumed by my feelings — of sadness, grief, and rage — but feel guilty for dwelling on them and even for living life, eating while people are starving, drinking while they are thirsty, sleeping in a warm bed while they are bombed in theirs or sleeping outside in the cold. We Palestinians in the diaspora know that it is fate alone — decisions made by or for our grandparents — that separates us from those in Gaza who are once again enduring Israel's brutality.

In October, I watched a video of two young brothers in the aftermath of an Israeli air strike. The older one, whose face was stained with blood, stood over his younger brother, who was lying down, his head bandaged and face and chest covered in blood. The older boy, no more than 10, was whispering to him to say the declaration of faith that Muslims say when they're dying. This was one of countless videos of Palestinians confronted with the violent deaths of their loved ones, saying goodbye, crying over them in disbelief, and kissing their dead bodies over and over again.

These moments of horrific intimacy are filmed because those who suffer and witness them want to show the world that *this really happened*. But as the death toll reaches higher and higher, I wonder if there is a cost to all the images we're seeing, if they inure people to Palestinian death, if there's no point in intruding on their most vulnerable moments, since those in power have not been moved to stop the carnage.

The day after I saw the video of the two brothers, their images still running through my mind, I asked a member of Congress if he would support the call for a ceasefire. "They've been fighting each other for thousands of years," he responded. It was galling. "That's not true," I responded. "It's been 75 years. My grandparents became refugees after Israel was created." "Thousands of years," he responded, walking away.

This level of ignorance can only come from decades of demonizing Palestinians as "human animals" and "children of darkness" to justify killing them en masse even in the face of the indisputable fact that most of those killed are children, women, and the elderly. *Are they seeing what I'm seeing?*

Most of the videos from Gaza show graphic horror and heartbreaking loss: a child, whose face is covered in blood, writhing and screaming in pain; a father shouting the names of his children as he searches for them under the rubble; a mother screaming in disbelief that her children were killed while they were hungry. But I have found that mundane and familiar footage of everyday life before this onslaught is haunting in its own way. In one video, a young dental school graduate named Abdallah Baghdadi sits in the back of a jeep, wearing a black baseball cap, while on vacation in Turkey, a brief respite from the weight of living under Gaza's blockade. He is smiling, carefree, full of life. Abdallah's grieving friend posted it after he was killed on Oct. 30, to remember him as she knew him.

In the first three weeks of Israel's bombardment of Gaza, I found out that my mother lost 17 members of her extended family in two separate strikes. We had never met them because of Israel's 17-year siege of Gaza, which has cut off the tiny strip from the world and made it nearly impossible for anyone to visit. I've learned that it's possible to mourn people I've never met, like the poet and professor Refaat Alareer, who was killed along with members of his family. Refaat was one of the founders of We Are Not Numbers, a nonprofit that cultivated young writers from Gaza to tell their stories to make sure they don't become statistics. But in the face of so much relentless death, it feels daunting to make sure that each person Israel has killed does not become just a number. How long does it take to recite 40,000 names?

We even worry about the dead in Gaza, as Israel attacks cemeteries throughout the strip. I think about what will become of my late grandfather, who returned to Gaza in 2004 after living abroad as a refugee for much of his life because he wanted to die in his homeland. My grandfather survived Israeli bombardments in 2008, 2012, and 2014. But he can't rest even in death.

What will be left for the people of Gaza when Israel finally ends its campaign of terror? It has destroyed everything that makes a place livable in its determination to end life itself in Gaza, to separate the people from the land. How does life go on when you're surrounded by rubble and mass graves, by children who lost their limbs before they learned to walk, who lost their parents before they learned how to say their names?

Outside of Gaza, to be a Palestinian in this moment is to go through the motions of life while feeling dead inside. It feels like it should be a state of emergency, but all around us life goes on. People do their grocery shopping, gather for the holidays, and blow out their birthday candles, while we are overcome by powerlessness and grief. To be Palestinian right now is to feel betrayed by those who remain silent, whatever their reasons, and to feel gratitude and hope from those who have spoken up.

It's not just Palestinians, though. So many people have told me that this is a life-defining moment for them that has shaped their views in profound ways. *Those people have seen what I've seen.*

Something has broken in all of us, and we will never be the same.

■ ▪

Laila Al-Arian is an investigative journalist and filmmaker, and an executive producer of Fault Lines, *a documentary program on Al Jazeera English.*

Teaching About Gaza

BY SAMIA SHOMAN

The Israeli assault on Gaza that began in 2023 should be taught as part of the longer history of Palestine-Israel. Hamas' Oct. 7 attack should not be the starting point. It's necessary to at least contextualize Hamas' actions in the brutal siege of Gaza that began in 2007. We've provided readings, visuals, films, and poems in this chapter and the Teaching Resources on p. 202 as a starting point.

The multiple narratives framework described in my article "Independence or Catastrophe? Teaching 1948 Through Multiple Perspectives" (p. 41) can also be applied to teaching about Gaza. The premise of this approach is that facts and perspectives inform people's narratives, which lead to individual truths.

At Teach Palestine's website (teachpalestine. org/teaching-gaza-now-2023-2024) teachers can find a lesson applying the multiple narratives approach as well as an international law framework to teach Israel's war on Gaza that began in 2023.

The lesson includes document sets built around two essential questions:

1. To what extent should what is happening in Gaza be considered a global humanitarian crisis? And to what extent do we have a responsibility to do something about it? What is your responsibility?

2. Do current events in Gaza meet the definition of genocide based on the U.N. Convention on the Prevention and Punishment of the Crime of Genocide?

While these document sets were created as events in Gaza were unfolding and will no doubt need to be updated, they can provide a starting point for educators.

■ ■ ■

Samia Shoman taught high school social studies in the San Francisco Bay Area for 16 years and has led teacher professional learning on teaching Palestine nationwide.

What a Gazan Should Do During an Israeli Air Strike

BY MOSAB ABU TOHA

Mosab Abu Toha is a Palestinian poet, short story writer, and essayist from Gaza.

Turn off the lights in every room
sit in the inner hallway of the house
away from the windows
stay away from the stove
stop thinking about making black tea
have a bottle of water nearby
big enough to cool down
children's fear
get a child's kindergarten backpack and stuff
tiny toys and whatever amount of money there is
and the ID cards
and photos of late grandparents, aunts, or uncles
and the grandparents' wedding invitation that's been kept for a long time
and if you are a farmer, you should put some strawberry seeds
in one pocket
and some soil from
the balcony flowerpot in the other
and hold on tight
to whatever number there was
on the cake
from the last birthday.

Israel's War on Gaza Is Also a War on History, Education, and Children

BY JESSE HAGOPIAN

MOHAMMED ABED | GETTY IMAGES

I n one weekend in November of 2023, Israeli airstrikes killed at least 82 Palestinians in Gaza's Jabalia refugee camp, including victims at multiple U.N. schools. As this book went to print, Israel's war on Gaza had killed more than 46,000 Palestinians, including nearly 17,500 children. Gaza's Health Ministry reported in November 2023 that one Palestinian child is killed every 10 minutes. U.N. Secretary-General António Guterres described the carnage as turning Gaza into a "graveyard for children."

Not even the schools have been saved from being turned into cemeteries.

"People in Gaza, sadly, are used to wars, and they're used to sheltering in United Nations Relief and Works Agency (UNRWA) schools, because this is where they feel that there's sanctity, a U.N. and a global understanding that when someone is in the protection of the United Nations, that these buildings will not be targeted," said Tamara Alrifai, spokesperson for UNRWA, the United Nations agency for Palestinian refugees, in an interview on *Democracy Now!* "Sadly, this is not the case."

Since Oct. 7, the 625,000 children enrolled in schools across Gaza have been deprived of education because of Israel's relentless bombardment that had, as of December 2024, destroyed or damaged some 537 schools, comprising more than 95 percent of all schools in Gaza. When Israel blew up Al-Isra University on Jan. 17, it succeeded in destroying every university in Gaza.

In addition to bombing schools, Israel has destroyed or damaged nearly 200 sites of historical importance. This includes leveling Gaza's main public library and two of Gaza's four museums, maintaining Israel's long history of attacking historical knowledge and education. That's because it is difficult to perpetrate ethnic cleansing without also controlling the population's collective memory and erasing the brutality from the historical record.

The destruction of ways of knowing and understanding the world is a practice that sociologist Boaventura de Sousa Santos has called "epistemicide." This includes destroying cultural knowledge, anti-racist ideas, and frameworks for understanding how to challenge oppression and colonization. Israel's actions are part of the violent colonial history of attacking not only the colonized people's bodies, but also bodies of knowledge that can help oppressed populations struggle for freedom.

There are many examples of epistemicide in the United States, from the anti-literacy laws imposed on enslaved African people; to the boarding schools for Native American children designed to strip them of their culture and deny them the truth of how they were dispossessed; to the laws

banning anti-racist education today that impact almost half of all U.S. students. For example, Florida banned the Advanced Placement African American Studies course, and the official state curriculum now declares slavery to have been of "personal benefit" to Black people. Florida teachers can now be charged with a felony, with up to a five-year jail sentence, for being caught with a contraband book about race, gender, or sexuality.

Israel has taken notes on this strategy — while also borrowing from British colonialism — and has long worked to camouflage its settler colonial origin. As Rashid Khalidi explains in his masterful book *The Hundred Years' War on Palestine*, "The British treated the Palestinians with the same contemptuous condescension they lavished on other subject peoples from Hong Kong to Jamaica. . . . As in Egypt and India, they did little to advance education, since colonial conventional wisdom held that too much of it produced 'natives' who did not know their proper place."

The colonial refrain of Israeli settlers that Palestine was a "land without people for a people without land" mirrors the delusion of manifest destiny, where American settlers claimed that God gave them the right to steal land for their own project of colonization. These master narratives, which have informed much of the colonial education in both nations, are the frameworks that allow many people to accept the occupation of Indigenous land and the violence against its inhabitants.

In 2009, Israel's education ministry ordered the removal of the word Nakba from textbooks for Arab schoolchildren. Nakba is Arabic for the catastrophe inflicted on Palestinians in 1947 and 1948 during the establishment of Israel, resulting in the displacement of more than 700,000 Palestinians and the death of some 15,000 Palestinians.

In 2011, Israel passed the "Nakba law," which allows the Israeli government to cut funding to public institutions that teach about the Nakba. "The purpose of the bill is to prevent members of the Arab minority in Israel from exercising their democratic right to commemorate a seminal event in their history," wrote Adalah – the Legal Center for Arab Minority Rights in Israel, as the bill was debated. "This legislation will cause harm to cultural and educational institutions that teach about the Nakba by cutting their funding and will further entrench inequality and discrimination. The bill is both anti-democratic and discriminatory." (See "The Laws of Israel," p. 130.)

On Nov. 9, 2023, Israeli police arrested Meir Baruchin, a Jerusalem history and civics teacher, following his Facebook post opposing the killing of Palestinian civilians. Upon his arrest, authorities confiscated his phone and two laptops, interrogating him on suspicion of treason and intent to disrupt the public order. After spending four days in jail, Baruchin was released, but he was fired from his teaching position and had his teaching certificate revoked.

Israeli police arrested a Jerusalem history and civics teacher following his Facebook post opposing the killing of Palestinian civilians.

"These days Israeli citizens who are showing the slightest sentiment for the people of Gaza, opposing killing of innocent civilians, they are being politically persecuted, they go through public shaming, they lose their jobs, they are being put in jail," Baruchin said in an interview on *Democracy Now!* He added that he believes if he were Palestinian, the consequences would have been more severe.

U.S. educators who believe students should grapple with multiple perspectives on the founding of Israel and the relentless bombardment of Gaza — including with lessons that provide Palestinian perspectives — have faced censure for years. Recently, these attacks have intensified.

Radhika Sainath, a senior staff attorney at Palestine Legal, which defends the free speech rights of advocates for Palestine, revealed the alarming escalation in these attacks: "We've had an exponential surge in requests for legal help. It has been like nothing we've seen before." In the 11 days following Oct. 7, the organization responded to nearly 200 reports of "suppression of Palestinian rights advocacy" in the United States — almost as many incidents as they had addressed in the previous year.

The educational system in Israel and Palestine is shaped by the daily violence of a system of apartheid, followed by the intermittent outbreak of devastating wars. During the 2014 military assault on Gaza, called Operation Protective Edge, Israelis killed 412 students and damaged 14 higher education facilities. Even before the war on Gaza that began in 2023, children in Gaza grappled with profound mental health challenges inflicted by the blockade and attacks on their schools. A Save the Children report published in June 2022 revealed that 80 percent of Gazan children suffer from a state of worry, sadness, and grief, with more than three quarters of children bed-wetting from fear, and a growing number exhibiting reactive mutism.

In Area C of the occupied West Bank, Israel has attacked Palestinian schools and imposed severe restrictions. Area C constitutes 61 percent of the West Bank and has faced continuous limitations on school construction. According to a 2023 report by the Office of the U.N. Special Coordinator for the Middle East Peace Process, the Palestinian population has witnessed a 2.4 percent growth, necessitating the establishment of 600 new schools by 2025.

But Israel significantly hinders construction of new schools. Funding challenges and bureaucratic obstacles have resulted in the construction of only 68 schools since 2020. The U.N. report also explained that since 2010, Israel has conducted 36 demolitions, affecting 20 schools in occupied East Jerusalem and the West Bank.

In September 2017, the United Nations Children's Fund (UNICEF) issued a joint statement with Save the Children decrying Israel's demolition of three elementary schools: "Many children have to study in schools with little protection from the heat or the cold; some face long journeys, delays at military checkpoints, harassment and violence, military activity in or around the school, or have to cross military areas and firing zones."

Israel has created a vicious form of the school-to-prison pipeline. Every year, the military court system prosecutes between 500 and 700 Palestinian children. Since 2000, Israel has detained more than 12,000 youth. And since August 2019, there has been an escalation in Palestinian students subjected to prolonged and arbitrary military detention. Israel routinely detains students for exercising their rights to assembly, association, and expression.

Palestinian students and teachers encounter daily hardships: They're forced to navigate checkpoints and endure delays, detentions, and harassment by Israeli soldiers and settlers. The imposed separation of East Jerusalem from other Occupied Palestinian Territories further hinders Palestinians' access to schools and cultural centers.

Travel bans on students and academics, introduced by Israel since 2000 and exacerbated by the 2007 blockade, have prevented Palestinians in Gaza from pursuing education in the West Bank and from attending universities established for their benefit.

Christopher Rufo, one of the primary instigators of the attack on critical race theory and anti-racist curriculum in the United States, laid out his strategy to help maintain Israeli and U.S. military power: "Conservatives need to create a strong association between Hamas, [Black Lives Matter], [Democratic Socialists of America], and academic 'decolonization' in the public mind. Connect the dots, then attack, delegitimize, and discredit. Make the center-left disavow them. Make them political untouchables."

Despite this strategy, a growing mass movement has coalesced to demand an immediate end to the indiscriminate killing of Palestinians. People across the globe have flooded the streets chanting "Ceasefire Now," and students and educators have played a central role in this struggle. Students for Justice in Palestine has been an important part of the movement. Many teacher union locals have voted for a ceasefire and marched in support of Palestine along with the organization Black Lives Matter at School.

Young Jewish people have also played an important role, including organizing acts of civil disobedience to call for a ceasefire in Gaza. As author Dave Zirin, who is Jewish, wrote, "An entire generation of young Jews, to paraphrase Peter Beinart a decade ago, are feeling forced to choose between their progressive principles and support for Israel's total war — and they are choosing their principles."

These allies are supporting Palestinians across the diaspora who lead the movement for a free Palestine. On Nov. 7, 2023, children held a press conference outside the Al-Shifa Hospital in Gaza City to implore the world to stop Israel's relentless bombing campaign. (See p. 107.)

"Since Oct. 7, we've faced extermination, killing, bombing over our heads — all of this in front of the world," one young spokesperson for the group said in English. "They lied to the world that they kill the fighters, but they kill the people of Gaza, their dreams, and their future. Kids of Gaza run out of their hopes and wants."

Sporting a shirt with a panda bear and gripping a sheet of note paper, he continued: "We came to Al-Shifa Hospital to seek shelter from the bombing, but we suddenly faced death again when they targeted the hospital. The occupation is starving us. We don't find water, food, and we drink from the unusable water. We come now to shout and invite you to protect us."

Standing with his peers, and near a hospital bed with injured children on his right, he concluded: "We want to live, we want peace, we want to judge the killers of children. We want medicine, food, and education. We want to live as the other children live."

Every child deserves medicine, food, and an education that respects their culture and empowers them with the historical lessons they need to challenge war, racism, and oppression today.

■ ■ ▪

Jesse Hagopian is a Rethinking Schools editor, a high school teacher, and on the staff of the Zinn Education Project. He is the co-editor of the Rethinking Schools book Teaching for Black Lives. *He serves on the Black Lives Matter at School steering committee and is a member of Black for Palestine.*

An earlier version of this article appeared in the Progressive.

Droughts and Floods

BY JESSE HAGOPIAN

A bombshell drops
from under the rain clouds:
Twenty Seattle schools will be shuttered.

A funding drought.
Money trees withering.
Barren education,
amidst verdant corporations.

Desolate schoolyards surrounded by
the lush greenbacks of the Amazon jungle.

Parched, blistered lips of children,
while Starbucks' cup runneth over.

Dry riverbeds (where funding once flowed),
amidst a monsoon of Microsoft profits.

Schools on cracked earth, cloven with dry scars
while Boeing makes it rain in Seattle,
until the mansions' gutters
overflow with cash.

Boeing also makes it rain in Gaza
a downpour of GBU-39 bombs
sweeping away every university and hundreds
    of schools.

The Al-Sardi school in Nuseirat was one of them
fourteen children's voices washed away.

One young Palestinian survivor,
    Imad al-Maqadmeh,
asked:
"Why did they bomb us? Why?
I want to know why.
Why? We are all children in the school."

There are those
who dread the torrent of children's questions.
They dam up the resources
that once ran to classrooms;
creating pools of cash for missiles
whose explosions drown out the sound
    of youthful inquiry.

Always enough treasure
to flood the playground with blood.

Never enough
to water the garden of learning and love.

Children's blood is heavier than gold;
it must be conserved,
like the last canteen
when crossing a sun-scorched land.

But if it is to be spilled,
let it irrigate the olive trees
under which students study and dream
let it nurture a global intifada
stretching from the Northwest to Nuseirat.

"We Want to Live as Other Children Live!" Children in Gaza Appeal to the World

On Nov. 7, 2023, children held a press conference outside Al-Shifa Hospital. Days before, an Israeli airstrike, as part of an attack on "schools and health infrastructure," according to the Washington Post, *had killed at least 15 people and injured 60.*

Five months later, Al-Shifa, the largest medical complex and central hospital of the Gaza Strip, lay in ruins. "Heaps of twisted metal, debris, ashes" were all that were left of the hospital and the surrounding neighborhood, NPR reported. Here is the children's plea at the press conference.

Since the 7th of October, we've faced extermination, killing, bombing over our heads — all of this in front of the world. They lied to the world that they kill the fighters, but they kill the people of Gaza, their dreams, and their future. Kids of Gaza run out of their hopes and wants. We came to Al-Shifa to seek shelter from the bombing, but we suddenly faced death again when they targeted the hospital. The occupation is starving us. We don't find water, food, and we drink from the unusable water. We come now to shout and invite you to protect us. We want to live, we want peace, we want to judge the killers of children. We want medicine, food, and education. We want to live as the other children live.

Mediterranean Sea at Gaza City, 2014.

We Had Dreams

Palestinians Living and Dying Under Siege in Gaza

If I die, remember that I, we, were individuals,
humans, we had names, dreams, and
achievements
and our only fault was that we were classified as
inferior.
Belal Aldabbour

What scares me the most is the thought of my
death as a number among the numbers that
increase every minute. I am not a number. It took
me 23 years to become the person you see now. I
have a home and friends, memory, and pain.
Shaharzad

Before we are even
born, we are killed.
Dr. Fadel Naim

I cleaned the house and wiped away the dust and
smell of the shelling next door, hoping that death
would not find any trace of it in our house and
would miss us.
Donia

If we die, write about me and my baby. Tell the
world that I had him after waiting four painful
years and that I didn't even have the chance to
save his face in my memory.
Ruba's Friend

I am not afraid of death. I am afraid of pain and
    my feelings
in the last moments under the rubble. Yesterday,
    when I told
my mom about my fear, she told me to pray to
    God that when
we're bombed, we will die instantly. I do not
know how the
    world goes on, when some of us have given
    up to death, and
our only hope is to die without pain.
@commieruba

I feel helpless. The dead
were given no dignity and
the injured are left in pain.
Adnan El-Bursh

My wish is that they drop the bombs on us while we are sleeping and that we all die together. This is why we are here together. So that nobody is left alive to mourn those who were killed.
Aunt May

I wanna live to see my little kids grow. I wanna watch their graduations not funerals. I wanna hug their souls not bury their bodies. I wanna play scavenger hunt not search for them under the rubble.
Eman Basher

In Gaza every one of us dies
a little death every night
and we are born again every
morning.
Rasha Abushaban

There is no lonelier place in this universe than around the bed of a wounded child who has no more family to look after them.
Ghassan Abu Sittah

Note to self: Only use a Q-Tip after the F-35 has dropped its payload!
J. Shawa

I want to stop. I want to die with my family. I don't want to send photos or anything.
Unnamed Photojournalist

We had our own hopes and dreams. I don't know what's wrong with that.
Ella's Friend

■ ■

We Had Dreams: Palestinians Living and Dying Under Siege in Gaza *is an interactive site that can be found at VisualizingPalestine.org. Visualizing Palestine explains: "With this resource, we uplift the testimonies of Palestinians in Gaza during Israel's genocidal assault in 2023–2024, who have been demonized and dehumanized by the mainstream media and Israeli government officials, as well as North American and European politicians."*

Occupied by Hope

BY NOOR HINDI

HALIMA AZIZ

Recently, I asked my father a simple question: "Is there hope?"

I was standing in my kitchen in Dearborn, Michigan, slicing mangoes. Peering through the doorway, I saw him as I've always seen him: squinting at his phone, his body collapsed on a couch, a tired look on his face.

He had already turned on the news.

I have never been to Palestine. But the chaos of headlines about our homeland is something I am all too familiar with. So is the history that haunts us.

As a child, I was lulled to sleep by the sound of Al Jazeera as I lay on my father's lap. At family gatherings, I listened to our stories: my grandmother surviving the Nakba at 5 years old; my father's upbringing in the Qalandia refugee camp; the trees my great-grandfather planted around his house in Al-Qubab (now al-Ramla), one of 418 Palestinian villages destroyed between 1948 and 1949.

One night last year, I dreamed of Palestine. In the dream, I was kneeling alongside my father, a handful of Palestine's soil in my mouth. I awoke gasping for water, an emptiness in my throat, a hollowness in my body.

I am familiar with emptiness, the cavities of its grief, its hands around my neck. I called my dad later that day.

"We are going to Palestine," I said. "October 2024."

He made one simple demand: He wished to go in August. "For fig season," he said, and I could hear his smile through the phone.

I want to taste Palestine's bitter earth. For

years, I have grieved its soil without ever having touched it. I want to find the exact location of my hurt, the coordinates of my emptiness. I want and I want. Lately, I have been demanding.

At a recent protest in Dearborn, I detached myself from the crowd and stood under a tree. I was trying to catch my breath. I played hide-and-seek with my body, begging my feet to find the ground they were standing on, to find comfort in a country I am not built for.

I watched a father chase after his son. The boy was barefoot. Hysterical with laughter. He picked up a single red leaf. He flung it in the air. He was a mess of joy, of life.

I don't know what future we are leaving him.

For months, Gazans have made the violence they are facing at the hands of Israel indisputable. Before mourning, before reckoning with all they have lost, before even allowing Allah himself to bear witness to such tragedy, they point their cameras.

I refuse to re-create most of these images here. To describe what is indescribable. But here is what I can say.

In October, doctors in Gaza held a press conference at Al-Ahli Baptist Hospital. A sea of dead Gazan children, their tiny bodies wrapped in white cloth, surrounded them. And yet, Israel continues to kill thousands more. The world watches.

In November, Gazan children held their own press conference in front of Al-Shifa Hospital. They spoke in English. They begged us to protect them. And yet, Israel continues to kill thousands more. The world watches. (See p. 107.)

On Instagram, Gazans like Motaz Azaiza and Bisan Owda, armed only with their phones and their voices, are broadcasting their own genocide — the constant bombardment, the mass displacement, the poisoning of the water, the starvation of the people, the endless grief. And yet, Israel continues to kill thousands more. The world watches.

What more needs to be seen?

Palestinians do not get to mourn our dead. We must argue our humanity, must make our trauma irrefutable, must prove over and over again that we do not deserve our fate. It has been 75 years and counting.

This is the genesis of my frustration, the pri-vate anguish lurking in the background of my everyday movements: We have nothing but the stories we use as shields. And this is not enough.

There is little that is more dislocating than witnessing the genocide of your own people: on Twitter, on Instagram, in waiting rooms at doctors' offices, on the radio, and during all the mundane tasks of survival. There is little that is more demoralizing than watching the world deny a violence that is so simply seen, heard, and broadcast by the people experiencing it themselves.

I have become impatient with the headlines. With "solutions." With the empire's demand that we treat this crisis as "complex" — a demand that only seems to arise when the people dying are Palestinian. With the insistence that every conversation start with Oct. 7, when we know that was far from the beginning of this crisis.

I refuse. I want my country back. This is not complicated.

I am writing for a future I no longer know is possible. I am making art for a future I no longer know is possible. I am dreaming of a Palestine I may never encounter.

Yet still, I am dreaming.

When I ask my father, "Is there hope?" his response is swift.

"Of course there is hope."

"From where?" I ask.

"I haven't let go of my hope."

Here is the truth about being Palestinian: In this lifetime, and the one after, and the one thereafter, we will always choose Palestine. There is little that endures more than our hope.

In the face of the unimaginable, this is what I hold on to.

◾ ▫

Noor Hindi is a Palestinian American poet and reporter. Her debut collection of poems, Dear God. Dear Bones. Dear Yellow, *was an honorable mention for the Arab American Book Award.*

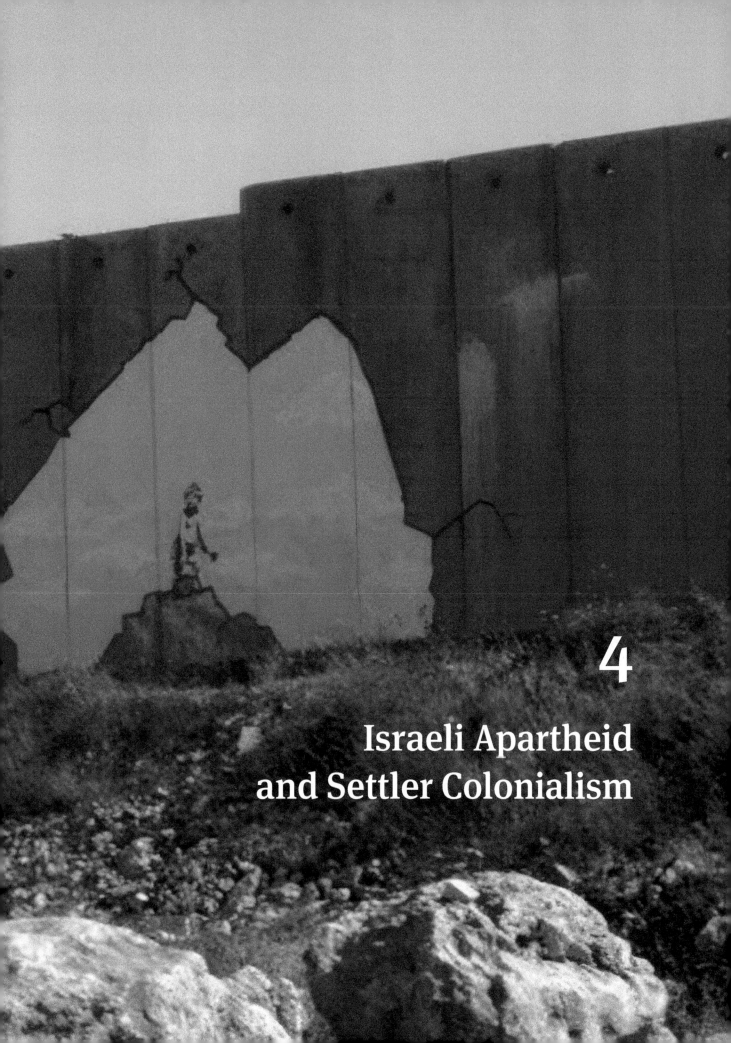

4

Israeli Apartheid
and Settler Colonialism

IRINA NAJI

"We Teach Life, Sir."

BY RAFEEF ZIADAH

Today, my body was a TV'd massacre.

Today, my body was a TV'd massacre that had to fit into sound bites and word limits.

Today, my body was a TV'd massacre that had to fit into sound bites and word limits filled enough with statistics to counter measured response.

And I perfected my English and I learned my U.N. resolutions.

But still, he asked me, Ms. Ziadah, don't you think that everything would be resolved if you would just stop teaching so much hatred to your children?

Pause.

I look inside of me for strength to be patient but patience is not at the tip of my tongue as the bombs drop over Gaza.

Patience has just escaped me.

Pause. Smile.

We teach life, Sir.

Rafeef, remember to smile.

Pause.

We teach life, Sir.

We Palestinians teach life after they have occupied the last sky.

We teach life after they have built their settlements and apartheid walls, after the last skies.

We teach life, Sir.

But today, my body was a TV'd massacre made to fit into sound bites and word limits.

And just give us a story, a human story.

You see, this is not political.

We just want to tell people about you and your people so give us a human story.

Don't mention that word "apartheid" and "occupation."

This is not political.

You have to help me as a journalist to help you tell your story which is not a political story.

Today, my body was a TV'd massacre.

How about you give us a story of a woman in Gaza who needs medication?

How about you?

Do you have enough bone-broken limbs to cover the sun?

Hand me over your dead and give the list of their names in one thousand two hundred word limits.

Today, my body was a TV'd massacre that had to fit into sound bites and word limits and move
those that are desensitized to terrorist blood.

But they felt sorry.

They felt sorry for the cattle over Gaza.

So, I give them U.N. resolutions and statistics and we condemn and we deplore and we reject.

And these are two equal sides: occupier and occupied.

And a hundred dead, two hundred dead, and a thousand dead.

And between that, war crimes and massacre, I vent out words and smile "not exotic," "not terrorist."

And I recount, I recount a hundred dead, a thousand dead.

Is anyone out there?

Will anyone listen?

I wish I could wail over their bodies.

I wish I could just run barefoot in every refugee camp and hold every child, cover their ears so they
wouldn't have to hear the sound of bombing for the rest of their life the way I do.

Today, my body was a TV'd massacre.

And let me just tell you, there is nothing your U.N. resolutions have ever done about this.

And no sound bite, no sound bite I come up with, no matter how good my English gets, no sound bite,
no sound bite, no sound bite, no sound bite will bring them back to life.

No sound bite will fix this.

We teach life, Sir.

We teach life, Sir.

We Palestinians wake up every morning to teach the rest of the world life, Sir.

Rafeef Ziadah is a Palestinian spoken word artist and human rights activist based in London.

The Meaning of "From the River to the Sea"

BY MAHA NASSAR

KHALED HOURANI

W hat does the call "From the river to the sea, Palestine will be free" mean to Palestinians? And why do they keep using the slogan despite the controversy that surrounds its use?

As both a scholar of Palestinian history and someone from the Palestinian diaspora, I have observed the decades-old phrase gain new life — and scrutiny — in the pro-Palestinian marches in the United States and around the world during the Israeli bombing campaign in the Gaza Strip following Hamas' Oct. 7 attack on Israel.

Pro-Israel groups, including the U.S.-based Anti-Defamation League, have labeled the phrase "antisemitic." Its use has even led to a rare censure of Representative Rashida Tlaib, the only Palestinian American member of Congress.

But to Tlaib, and countless others, the phrase isn't antisemitic. Rather, it is in Tlaib's words "an aspirational call for freedom, human rights, and peaceful coexistence."

I cannot speak to what is in the heart of every person who uses the phrase. But I can speak to what the phrase has meant to various groups of Palestinians throughout history.

The majority of Palestinians who use this phrase do so because they believe that, in 10 short words, it sums up their personal ties, their national rights, and their vision for the land they call Palestine. And while attempts to police the slogan's use may come from a place of genuine concern, there is a risk that tarring the slogan as antisemitic taps into a longer history of attempts to silence Palestinian voices.

An Expression of Personal Ties

One reason for the phrase's appeal is that it speaks to Palestinians' deep ties to the land. They have long identified themselves — and one another — by the town or village in Palestine from which they came.

Those places stretched across the land, from Jericho and Safed near the Jordan River in the east, to Jaffa and Haifa on the shores of the Mediterranean Sea in the west.

These deeply personal ties were passed down over generations through clothing, cuisine, and subtle differences in Arabic dialects specific to locations within Palestine.

Those ties continue today. Children and grandchildren of Palestinian refugees often feel a personal connection to the specific places their ancestors hailed from.

A Demand for National Rights

But the phrase is not simply a reference to geography. It's political.

"From the river to the sea" also seeks to reaffirm Palestinians' national rights over their homeland and a desire for a unified Palestine to form the basis of an independent state.

When Palestine was under British colonial rule from 1917 to 1948, its Arab inhabitants objected to partition proposals advocated by British and Zionist interests. That's because, buried in the proposals, were stipulations that would have forced hundreds of thousands of Palestinian Arabs off their ancestral lands.

In 1946, the Delegation of Arab Governments proposed instead a "unitary state" with a "democratic constitution" to guarantee "freedom of religious practice" for all and would recognize "the right of Jews to employ the Hebrew language as a second official language."

The following year, the United Nations instead approved a partition plan for Palestine, which would have forced 500,000 Palestinian Arabs living in the proposed Jewish state to choose between living as a minority in their own country or leaving.

The majority of Palestinians who use this phrase do so because it sums up their personal ties, their national rights, and their vision for the land they call Palestine.

It's in this context that the call for a unified, independent Palestine emerges.

During the 1948 war that led to the formation of Israel, around 750,000 Palestinian Arabs fled or were expelled from their villages and towns. By the end of the war, Palestine was split into three: 78 percent of the land became part of the Jewish state of Israel, while the remainder fell under Jordanian or Egyptian rule.

Palestinian refugees believed they had a right to return to their homes in the new state of Israel. Israeli leaders, seeking to maintain the state's Jewish majority, sought to have the refugees resettled far away. Meanwhile, a narrative emerged in the West in the 1950s claiming that Palestinians' political claims were invalid.

Future Vision

Palestinians had to find a way to assert their national rights and lay out an alternative vision for peace. After Israel occupied the West Bank, East Jerusalem, and the Gaza Strip in the so-called Six-Day War in 1967, the call for a free Palestine "from the river to the sea" started to gain traction among those who believed that all the land should be returned to the Palestinians.

But it also came to represent the vision of a secular democratic state with equality for all.

In 1969, the Palestinian National Council, the highest decision-making body of the Palestinians in exile, formally called for a "Palestinian democratic state" that would be "free of all forms of religious and social discrimination."

> The call for a free Palestine "from the river to the sea" came to represent the vision of a secular democratic state with equality for all.

This remained a popular vision among Palestinians, even as some leaders inched toward the idea of establishing a truncated Palestinian state alongside Israel in the West Bank, Gaza Strip, and East Jerusalem.

Many Palestinians were skeptical of this two-state solution. For refugees exiled since 1948, a two-state solution would not allow them to return to their towns and villages in Israel. Some Palestinian citizens of Israel feared that a two-state solution would leave them even more isolated as an Arab minority in a Jewish state.

Palestinians in the West Bank and Gaza Strip — those who presumably stood the most to gain from a two-state solution — were lukewarm to the idea. A 1986 poll found that 78 percent of respondents "supported the establishment of a democratic-secular Palestinian state encompassing all of Palestine," while only 17 percent supported two states.

That helps explain why the call for a free Palestine "from the river to the sea" became popular in the protest chants of the First Intifada — Palestinian uprising — from 1987 to 1992.

Hamas, an Islamist party founded in 1987, did not initially use "from the river to the sea," likely due to the phrase's long-standing ties to Palestinian secular nationalism.

Two States or One?

The 1993 signing of the Oslo Accords led many to believe that a two-state solution was just around the corner.

But as hopes for a two-state solution dimmed, some Palestinians returned to the idea of a single, democratic state from the river to the sea.

Meanwhile, Hamas picked up the slogan, adding the phrase "from the river to the sea" to its 2017 revised charter. The language was part of Hamas' broader efforts to gain legitimacy at the expense of its secular rival, Fatah, which was seen by many as having failed the Palestinian people.

A 2022 poll found strong support among Palestinians for the idea of a single state with equal rights for all.

Offensive Phrase?

Some have claimed it is a genocidal call — the implication being that the slogan's end is calling for Palestine to be "free from Jews." It's understandable where such fears come from, given the Hamas attacks on Oct. 7 during which an estimated 1,200 people were killed, according to the Israeli foreign ministry.

But the Arabic original, "Filastin hurra," means liberated Palestine. "Free from" would be a different Arabic word altogether.

Other critics of the slogan insist that by denying Israel's right to exist as a Jewish state, the phrase itself is antisemitic. Under such thinking, protesters should instead call for a Palestinian state alongside Israel — and not one that replaces it.

But this ignores the current reality. There is

scholarly consensus that a two-state solution is no longer viable — that the extent of Jewish settlements in the West Bank have eaten away at the feasibility of any envisioned Palestinian state.

Further Demonization

There is another argument against the slogan's use: Although it may not be antisemitic in itself, some Jewish people see it that way – and see it as a threat. And that is enough for people to abandon its use.

But this argument privileges the feelings of one group over those of another. And it risks further demonizing and silencing Palestinian voices in the West.

After the assault on Gaza after Oct. 7, Europe has seen an "unprecedented crackdown" on pro-Palestinian activism. Meanwhile, people across the United States report widespread discrimination, retaliation, and punishment for their pro-Palestinian views.

On Nov. 14, 2023, George Washington University suspended the student group Students for Justice in Palestine, in part because the group projected "Free Palestine from the River to the Sea" on the campus library.

Principle, Not Platform

Yes, "From the river to the sea, Palestine will be free" has multiple interpretations.

Palestinians are divided over the political outcome they wish to see in their homeland.

But most Palestinians

using this chant do not see it as advocating for a specific political platform or as belonging to a specific political group. Rather, the majority of people using the phrase see it as a principled vision of freedom and coexistence.

◼◼ ◻

Maha Nassar is an associate professor in the School of Middle Eastern & North African Studies at the University of Arizona.

IDENTITY CRISIS
THE ISRAELI ID SYSTEM

SINCE 1967, THE ISRAELI GOVERNMENT HAS BEEN THE DE-FACTO SOVEREIGN POWER IN CONTROL OF THE WHOLE OF HISTORIC PALESTINE, INCLUDING GAZA, THE WEST BANK AND ISRAEL.

ISRAELI AUTHORITIES CONTROL THE POPULATION REGISTRY AND ID SYSTEM, RESTRICTING WHERE PALESTINIANS CAN LIVE, THEIR ACCESS TO SERVICES AND THEIR PARTICIPATION IN THE POLITICAL SYSTEM.

- POPULATION GROUP
- WHERE YOU CAN LIVE
- WHERE YOU CAN'T LIVE
- CAN VOTE IN ISRAELI PARLIAMENT
- CAN'T VOTE IN ISRAELI PARLIAMENT

ISRAELI POPULATION REGISTRY

JEWISH ISRAELI

PALESTINIAN

VOTE

NO SYSTEMATIC DISCRIMINATION

JEWISH ISRAELI CITIZENS
5.9m

Free to live throughout Israel and **60%** of the occupied West Bank

LEGAL AND DE-FACTO DISCRIMINATION

PALESTINIAN CITIZENS OF ISRAEL
1.3m

Barred from living in **68%** of all towns in Israel by admissions committees

LEGAL DISCRIMINATION AND MILITARY OCCUPATION

EAST JERUSALEM PALESTINIANS
0.3m

Access to most areas, but **ID may be revoked** if living outside of Jerusalem

WEST BANK PALESTINIANS
2.3m

Barred from living in all but **40%** of West Bank due to Israeli settler and military presence

GAZA STRIP PALESTINIANS
1.6m

Barred from living outside of Gaza since 2007

EXCLUDED FROM SYSTEM

PALESTINIAN EXILES
5.7m

Barred from returning to live anywhere in Israel or Palestinian territory

SOURCES
Population estimates for 2011 collated from Israeli CBS, Palestinian CBS, OCHA and Badil. Maps are illustrative, based on data collated from Israeli CBS and OCHA. ID matrix adapted from Helga Tawil-Souri. Additional facts from B'Tselem and Adalah.

Population data http://bit.ly/icbs-pop http://bit.ly/pcbs-pop http://bit.ly/badil-pop
Map data http://bit.ly/icbs-pop http://bit.ly/ocha-maps **Matrix** http://bit.ly/tawil-id
WB areas http://bit.ly/btselem-areas **Israel admissions** http://bit.ly/adalah-areas

REVISION 01
07 JUN 2014

Israeli Apartheid: A Simulation

Orange Bags, Green Bags, Red Bags, Blue Bags

BY SUZANNA KASSOUF

SHERI LAIZER | ALAMY

Like many people I know, I have struggled to navigate the landscape of my grief since Oct. 7, 2023. As I read the news reports of the Hamas attack that killed more than 1,200 Israelis and took 240 hostages, I felt my heart shatter as I imagined the pain and suffering of their loved ones. I was also filled with fear as to what this would mean for the people of Gaza — having witnessed four previous wars and bombardments of the tiny enclave. But my fear paled in comparison to the gruesome reality of Israel's response. Almost a year later, I have been irrevocably changed by the suffering I have witnessed on my screens.

This suffering was not hidden behind the veil of corporate news media. Students saw it every day. Though their individual algorithms on social media determined the degrees and perspectives of their exposure to this violence, almost all students shared one thing in common: They were curious. What is happening? Why? How can this be allowed to happen? What can be done?

As a social studies teacher, it is my responsibility to help students make sense of the world around them — to put this suffering in context. Mainstream news gives us the false impression that the violence in Palestine-Israel began with the Hamas attacks on Oct. 7, but those of us who study history have a different story to tell.

Setup

I teach Inquiry, a 9th-grade introduction to social studies class at Grant High School, a largely affluent, majority-white public school in Portland, Oregon. In 2024, I taught a long unit on Palestine-Israel. The lesson described here attempts to introduce students to the complex systems of fragmentation and dispossession established by the Israeli government to maintain domination and control, and how this system affects the individuals and groups living in the region. It is based on the 2022 Amnesty International report *Israel's Apartheid Against Palestinians*. Like all simulations, it is limited in scope, highlighting some aspects of reality and minimizing others, but is meant to help students gain an overview of the Israeli system of apartheid. We follow up with readings, films, and other activities to flesh out students' experiences in the simulation.

The Simulation

After studying some historical background of Palestine-Israel, students walked into our classroom to the desks pushed to the edges of the room, piled on top of each other, the chairs stacked alongside them.

"Whoa, Ms. Kassouf, what's going on?" Xander asked, as he walked into the room carrying his heavy backpack and Chromebook.

"Hey, Xander! We're doing a simulation today. Find a corner to put your stuff."

More students trickled into the room, looking surprised, apprehensive, excited.

I know that role plays and simulations can be controversial teaching strategies — see the Zinn Education Project's helpful "How to — and How Not to — Teach Role Plays" — but I designed this simulation because I wanted my students to experience firsthand some of the convoluted and unfair dynamics of the system of Israeli apartheid. Just a few months earlier we had wrapped up our Power, Identity, and Culture unit with Bill Bigelow and Norm Diamond's Organic Goodie Simulation, and I thought students would appreciate another everyone-active learning experience.

Once all the students arrived, I projected the ground rules on the whiteboard:

1. Everyone will start by getting a bag, this is your bag for the entire activity — it cannot be switched or changed.
2. Throughout the activity, you will have different opportunities to acquire candy for your bag.
3. IMPORTANT: YOU MAY NOT EAT YOUR CANDY UNTIL THE END OF THE ACTIVITY!
4. I reserve the right to confiscate candy acquired throughout the activity.

I began distributing orange, green, blue, and red bags to students. Unbeknownst to students, each bag color represented a different group with a different ID card under the Israeli apartheid system.

(It's important to be aware of the racial and social-emotional dynamics in class when assigning bags. Because some students with blue bags will have few rights, and students with orange bags will have some power over those with red bags later in the simulation, you'll want to give some thought to which students to assign to which role.)

Orange bags represented Jewish Israelis, who have only one ID card, which endows them with a host of rights and privileges. Palestinians, on the other hand, have four different ID cards, depending on their status, each carrying different rights and restrictions: Palestinians in Gaza (blue bags), Palestinians in the West Bank (red bags), Palestinian citizens of Israel (green bags), and Palestinian residents of East Jerusalem. For simplicity's sake in this first iteration of the simulation, I left out Palestinian residents of East Jerusalem, though next time I conduct this activity, I plan to include them.

For a class of 30, here is the breakdown:

14 orange (for 7 million Jewish Israelis)
5 green (for 2.5 million Palestinian Israelis)
6 red (for 3 million Palestinians in the West Bank)
4 blue (for 2 million Gazans)

Students do not learn what the bag colors represent until the end of the simulation.

Segregation

Once students had their colored candy bags, I told students that the zone where they "lived" in the classroom depended on bag color. I shouted "OK, everyone! Please get into your zones based on your bag color!"

The first lesson students needed to understand was that Palestinians are physically segregated from one another under the Israeli apartheid system — forced to live in certain places according to their ID cards, regardless of history or family ties.

Before students arrived for the day, I had

used blue painter's tape to draw several borders on the classroom floor. Along the left-hand side of the room, I taped a rectangular border encompassing about 18 to 20 percent of the floor space, meant to represent the West Bank. Near the back of the classroom, I taped a much smaller square encompassing about 5 percent of the floor space (just enough space for four students to fit, albeit uncomfortably), representing the tiny area of Gaza. The Palestinian regions of the West Bank and Gaza compose only 22 percent of pre-1948 Palestine, with Israel composing the remaining 78 percent.

I pulled a red marker out of my pocket and scribbled "RED ZONE" within the rectangular border along the left-hand side of the classroom.

"If you have a red bag, please move into the Red Zone!"

Neva, Ryder, Samantha, Josephina, Pierce, and Brennen stepped inside the border, leaning on desks and sitting on the floor.

"If you have a blue bag, please move to the Blue Zone!" I called out, as I scribbled "BLUE ZONE" within the tiny square border taped on the classroom floor. Reese, Madeline, Tristan, and Connor squeezed into the zone, awkwardly adjusting their bodies to fit comfortably.

"Orange and Green, you can't go into the Blue Zone, but you can go anywhere in the Red Zone and anywhere else you'd like in the classroom," I called out, as I walked around the roughly 78 percent of the remaining space.

Both Jewish and Palestinian Israelis can visit the West Bank and enjoy much greater freedom of movement than Palestinians living in Gaza or the West Bank.

Military Service

"Alright, habibis [my dears]! It's time to get some candy! I have four Starburst for anyone willing to do military service."

About 90 percent of the hands in the classroom shot up, waving at me with that desperate "pick me" attitude that only candy can bring out in 9th graders.

"Thank you all so much for wanting to serve your country!" Grabbing my slideshow clicker, I motioned to the projection on the whiteboard.

"Let's see who can do military service . . ."

One at a time, I revealed new rules:

Blue: Barred from military service by law
The students with blue bags dropped their hands in disappointment.
Red: Barred by law
Pierce called out, "Oh, come on!" as he flopped his hand down.
Green: Barred by conscience
Orange: Mandatory

As they are not citizens of Israel, Palestinians in Occupied Territories of Gaza and the West Bank cannot serve in the Israel Defense Forces (IDF). For Palestinian Israelis, it's more complicated. They are considered citizens, but not nationals, and, as such, enjoy different and inferior rights in law and practice. Jewish Israelis face mandatory military service once they turn 18, but Palestinian Israelis are exempt from this requirement. Though they can technically become IDF soldiers, many Palestinian Israelis refuse to participate in the military occupation of their fellow Palestinians. This refusal blocks them from the many benefits and privileges tied to military service in Israel. For students in my class, they missed out on candy for not participating in the military. For Palestinian citizens of Israel, they lose substantial economic compensation, housing subsidies, educational grants, job opportunities, and other benefits afforded to Jewish Israelis. This is one example of the institutional discrimination that Palestinian Israelis face. Students do not learn details like this during the simulation, but their experiences with this blue-red-green-orange inequality lays the foundation for later learning through readings, films, and other activities.

Housing and Permits

"Time to earn more candy!" I called out, holding the bag of Starburst in the air. "You all need shelter, so I'll give some candy to whoever can build a nice house. You can use anything that you find in the classroom to build or draw your home. Of course, we have a few more restrictions . . ." I motioned again to the projection on the whiteboard:

Blue: You can build only in the Blue Zone
Red: You can build only in the Red Zone
Green: You can build only in the Green Zone

Again, I grabbed a green dry erase marker from my desk and walked over to two small boxes I had taped on the classroom floor and scribbled "GREEN ZONE" in their borders.

Though Palestinian citizens of Israel have freedom of movement throughout the country, about 90 percent of them live in 139 densely populated towns and villages as a result of Israeli government policies to deliberately segregate Palestinian citizens of Israel into enclaves.

Orange: You can build anywhere except the Blue Zone

The classroom was electric as students ran around collecting supplies to build and draw their houses. Leo grabbed the Jenga blocks from our game counter and began stacking them into the shape of a small house, Felix and Tom piled together Uno decks, and several students grabbed paper and markers, scribbling drawings of houses.

Though kids in the Red Zone couldn't access the full range of classroom supplies, they got creative, restacking desks and chairs to create their houses. Wanting them to feel involved in this portion of the simulation, I dropped a few pipe cleaners and paper clips into the Blue Zone.

"Ms. Kassouf! I'm done!" Dashiel called out, waving his drawing of a house in the air.

"Nice! Here's two Starburst for your beautiful home!" I said and dropped them into his bag.

I walked around the room, dropping candy into bags for completed homes.

"Can we build a second home?" Sofia asked.

To help students grasp the wealth and income imbalance among Palestinians and Jewish Israelis, I replied "What color bag are you?"

"Orange!"

"Yeah, sure! You're an *Orange* Bagger!"

Sofia and Claire quickly turned my rolling desk chair into a "mobile home" and I plopped a few more Starburst into their candy bags.

To maximize their control of land, the Israeli government gives subsidies to Jewish settlers who buy homes in the West Bank. To illustrate this for students, I called out, "I have four pieces of candy for an Orange Bagger who is willing to build their home in the Red Zone!" The classroom fluttered with waving hands.

In a class of about 30, only one student would represent the roughly 500,000 Jewish Israeli settlers in the West Bank, while about six kids in the simulation would represent the 3 million Palestinians living in the West Bank. The Israeli military guards West Bank settlements, which are often behind walls and fortresses, and take up about 60 percent of the land space of the West Bank — land that the international community regards as belonging to Palestinians.

"Cass, bring your house on over," I said as I directed him to place the drawing of the house he had made in the middle of the Red Zone. "Cass, I know what you're thinking. It's not safe to build your home around all of these Red Baggers. But don't worry," I reached for two free-standing whiteboards and rolled them into the Red Zone, placing them on either side of Cass' home, taking up a little more than half of the taped-off area: "We've got these walls here to protect you. We're going to keep you safe!" I divided the red bag students to each side of the wall, squished now into less than a quarter of their original space.

Once all students had the opportunity to build their home and receive their candy, I yelled, "Oh my gosh! I completely forgot that you need a permit to build a house! How silly of me! I'm going to be coming around now and checking your permits."

As students would learn after the simulation, to interrupt the development of Palestinian communities, Israel has made it almost impossible for Palestinians to acquire building permits for their homes. In 2021, more than 150,000 Palestinians lived under the constant threat of forced eviction and demolition, many of them for the second or third time. In 2020, Israel demolished an average of 18 Palestinian structures every week in the West Bank. The same year, Israel issued 1,094 building permits for Jewish Israelis and only one for a Palestinian.

I grabbed a clipboard and began checking in with students.

"Ah, Felix, beautiful home. Can I see your

bag please?" Felix held out his orange bag. "Nice orange bag, Felix!" I pointed to his bag and then down at my clipboard, "I see your permit here. Great!" I made a mark on my clipboard and moved on to approving the homes of students with orange bags.

I peeked into the Blue Zone and said, "Actually, I don't go into this zone, so for the time being you guys can do your thing here."

Students with red bags representing Palestinians in the West Bank weren't so lucky. Though a few got creative, scribbling paper permits for themselves, as I walked into the Red Zone to "check their permits," I called out "Oh, my god! You have a red bag and built this house without a permit! How dare you?!" I theatrically began tearing down their structures, ripping up drawings of houses, and taking back the candy they had earned from building their house.

Checkpoints

One of the most visible forms of Israeli apartheid is the "security wall" and checkpoints. Though cars with Israeli license plates are often waved right through, Palestinians must wait for hours at these checkpoints, often separating their homes, workplaces, and the homes of families and friends.

To help students experience a fraction of this frustration, I set up a new candy opportunity: Attend your cousin's wedding. This wedding was going to take place in one of the red bag divided sections of the Red Zone — symbolizing Palestinian territory in the West Bank. Students from the other red bag section of the Red Zone, now divided by a "security wall" to protect Cass' house, would need to go through two checkpoints to get to this section of the Red Zone. Students in the Orange/Green Zone would need to get through one. Students with blue bags, representing Gazans, would not be able to attend as they could not leave the Blue Zone.

Before I announced the challenge to students, I told the Orange Baggers in the Red Zone that they should allow people with orange bags to pass through, but that they needed to question those with green and red bags to make sure they actually belonged in this area. I told them to aim for five to 10 questions before they allowed these

colors through. Once I announced the challenge, I clicked play on a large three-minute timer on the projector and announced, "Make sure you are back in your own zone by nighttime — when this timer goes off."

Students lined up at the checkpoints, eager to earn some more candy for their bags.

Andrei, an Orange Bagger, peppered Sam, a Green Bagger, with questions: "Why are you traveling today? Oh, your cousin is getting married? What's his mother's name? How long has he been engaged? What's his wife's name? I thought you said he was getting married, now you're saying he already has a wife?" All the while, Andrei was sending students with orange bags through without questioning them.

By now, students were grasping the fundamental — and complicated — inequality of this system. Life was easier if you had an orange bag. Students in the Blue Zone especially were feeling the raw deal they'd received, unable to step outside of the tiny border taped on the classroom floor. Connor, fed up with his fate as a Blue Bagger, reached out to swipe an orange candy bag from a nearby student.

I confiscated the orange bag candy from the Blue Bagger, along with his candy, reminding him of the activity's Rule #4 — my right to confiscate candy acquired during the simulation.

Of course, in real life, consequences can be dire. As students learn, following the activity, between September 2000 and February 2017, Israeli forces killed 4,868 Palestinians in the Occupied Palestinian Territories *outside* of armed conflict, including 1,793 children. Amnesty International is not aware of *any case* in which an Israeli soldier has been convicted of willfully causing the death of a Palestinian in the Occupied Territories since 1987. In addition, Palestinians are tried in military courts, which have an astronomical 99 percent conviction rate, while Israeli citizens are tried in civil courts.

The Election

Though there are varying levels of autonomy throughout Gaza and the West Bank, in reality, Israel — with its IDF soldiers, tanks, bombs, and guns — controls the entire region. The vast majority of Palestinians under this rule have no say in this authority that rules their daily lives. To demonstrate this, I told students we would have an election and asked who would like to run for office to change how things worked.

I was surprised that in every class I had multiple volunteers from every bag color, including some students who had never volunteered to speak in class before. I am always delighted by the ways simulations and role plays can engage students who often don't feel served by more conventional teaching strategies.

This time, instead of revealing just the rules on who could run and vote in elections, I asked students one at a time:

"Do you think Blue Baggers can run or vote in elections?"

The class responded in unison, "No!"

"Yes, you're right." I clicked the next slide on the projector: *Blue Baggers: Can't vote, can't run for office.* "What about Red Baggers?" I asked.

Again, "No!"

Red Baggers: Can't vote, can't run for office.

"Green Baggers, what do you think? Can they vote? Can they run for office?"

Again, they called out, "No!"

"Ah! They *can!*" *Green Baggers: Can vote, can run for office.*

"What do you think about Orange Baggers?"

"Yes!" they called out, with a mix of exuberance and annoyance.

"Yes, of course." *Orange Baggers: Can vote, can run for office.*

Several students with green and orange bags lined up to give their impromptu election speeches. Importantly, all those with orange bags offered more rights and privileges only to other Orange Baggers in their speeches, the Green Baggers offering similar rights to both Orange and Green Baggers. All but one, that is. Andrei offered more rights to Blue and Red Baggers as well. He didn't earn a single vote.

Throughout our unit, we frequently returned to this election. Yes, this simulation was meant to reveal to students the complex system of apartheid in Palestine-Israel, but it also served to help students understand how we, as individuals, are shaped by the systems we live under. Throughout our unit, we returned, again and again, to a quote by Jewish scholar Michael Brooks: "Be ruthless with systems, be kind to people." In his simulation reflection, Asher wrote, "I think I'm finally beginning to understand this quote."

I have talked with many teachers who are afraid to teach the truth about Palestine-Israel, fearing that criticism of Israel is inherently antisemitic. It's no surprise that so many of us harbor this fear, as Israel — and supporters of Israel, like the Anti-Defamation League (see p. 163) — routinely weaponize accusations of antisemitism to shut down criticism or solidarity with the movement for Palestinian liberation and human rights. Though we cannot bow to this dishonesty, it is our responsibility as educators to ensure that we help students separate the Israeli *government* from being representative of all Jewish *people*. The unjust actions of the Israeli government have nothing to do with their Jewishhness, and everything to do with the corrupting influence of power.

Reflection

With about 20 minutes left in our 90-minute class period, I called the simulation to a close and asked students to grab their notebooks and find a quiet place to reflect, projecting the following prompts on the whiteboard:

> Please take a moment to reflect on the simulation we just did. Share your thoughts and feelings throughout the game. How do you think the students with the other bag colors felt? Be specific. If you'd like, you can make some predictions about what you think the different colors represent.

Once students had time to write and talk in pairs, I asked for a few volunteers to share out.

Lois said, "I had an orange bag and I felt great, because I had all the power. I could basically do anything I wanted — including bullying the Blue and Red Baggers. I imagine it was pretty boring being one of those colors though, especially blue since they couldn't go anywhere for the whole game."

We would talk more about this later, but for

now, I said, "Yeah, when we're the ones in power, it can feel good, and it can feel hard to want to give that up. Especially when we're not seeing firsthand the real suffering of the other groups, or when we've been brought up to believe they are somehow not as valuable as we are, or are our enemies in some way."

No doubt, labeling the experience of Blue Baggers — Gazans — in the simulation as "boring" transforms misery into boredom. But a simulation is not "real life"; it is a simulation. I called on a few Blue and Red Baggers who confirmed feelings of boredom and frustration during the activity. In my classes, there was not much resistance from students with blue or red bags, but if students did resist, I would welcome that. While the main point of the simulation is to help students understand the complex web of laws and policies that make up Israeli apartheid, any instances of defiance can help prompt discussion about the rich and varied traditions of Palestinian resistance.

As we were in the middle of our Palestine-Israel unit, most students guessed that orange represented something to do with Israel and that red and blue represented Palestinians. Green was more of a mystery, as I think most people don't understand that about 20 percent of the Israeli population are Palestinian Israelis (Palestinians who did not flee in 1948 — when Israel became a state — and are sometimes called '48 Palestinians). In fact, Israel often points to these Palestinians, and the superior rights they possess compared to their counterparts in Gaza and the West Bank, to defend themselves against the accusations of apartheid. But, as the simulation shows, the complex laws and policies that form this system inherently rely on this fragmentation of the Palestinian population.

The following class, we confirmed the colors of the bags as students watched *Israel's Apartheid Against Palestinians: Cruel System of Domination and Crime Against Humanity*, the Amnesty International video based on their report. In their reflections, students were able to connect their own experiences during the simulation to what they learned from the video. And students later learned more about the twisted Israeli legal architecture in "The Laws of Israel" see on p. 130.

Amelia, having grasped an essential lesson from the activity, wrote in her notebook, "This class taught me how it is very important to separate the people from the systems. I was a Jewish Israeli in the simulation. I do not believe that what was happening in the simulation was just, but I found myself being influenced. I wanted to keep my power because it was good for me."

Gabe, a Jewish student who had been defensive of Israel throughout the unit, wrote in his reflection: "I learned about the way Israel's laws benefit Jewish Israelis. This connects to my experience during the simulation because I was blue (Gazan) and it was incredibly frustrating. I wasn't able to move out of my little zone. I see how this can relate to Palestinians living in these kinds of conditions. I feel very sad for those families who are split apart because they don't have the same IDs. I think Israel should be a safe place for Jews to go, but that doesn't mean they should get more rights."

I was moved reading Gabe's reflection. I went into this unit knowing that I was gearing up to teach about arguably the most controversial topic of our time, especially for my community. I have many Jewish students with varying perspectives and degrees of knowledge about and connection to the region. During this school year, I had no Arab or Palestinian students, though I myself am Arab American. I felt a strong responsibility to teach this unit from a humanitarian perspective. Gabe's reflection captures this for me. I think that when most young people understand the reality of what is happening in Palestine-Israel, they want a just solution for all people involved. We can't turn back the clock, so the question now is What will we do? How can we teach in a way that builds empathy and compassion for all people, while fiercely opposing unjust and oppressive systems? How can we honor the inherent worth and dignity of every human being? Though a path to peace will be complex, one thing is certain: We can only get there by teaching the truth.

∎ ▪

Suzanna Kassouf teaches at Grant High School in Portland, Oregon. Student names have been changed.

Israeli Apartheid

BY NATHAN THRALL

KHALED HOURANI

What I see when I look at Israel-Palestine is a single sovereign — Israel — ruling over 7 million Jews and 7 million Palestinians. Now, within that system, the Palestinians have variegated rights, and are subjected to different rules depending on where they live.

First of all, it should be said that the majority of those 7 million Palestinians are living without basic civil rights. The worst off are Palestinian refugees who aren't even counted in those 7 million. Those are Palestinian refugees who were not allowed back into Israel or the Occupied Territories.

And the next level are Palestinians in Gaza, who are under a siege, who were under a siege before this war, who could barely leave Gaza, who had to ask for special permission just to travel to the West Bank to study in a West Bank university, to go receive medical care in the West Bank or in East Jerusalem.

And the next level are Palestinians in Area C of the West Bank, and they are the ones who need to go to the Israeli authorities in order to get permission to just build a new shed outside their house, a new floor on top of their home, any kind of structure. And almost all of those requests are denied, and then Israel comes and demolishes anything that these people do wind up building.

The next level are Palestinians who live in Area B and Area A of the West Bank. These are the places that are under some limited Palestinian Authority autonomy. It's very limited, in the sense that Israel is the ultimate sovereign. Israel comes in, and makes arrests, and enters with its forces in Area B and Area A every day.

Just to give some perspective on how much territory we're talking about here, Areas A and B and Gaza, the three places where you have some Palestinian autonomy, all together they make up about 10 percent of the territory under Israel's control. That's all it is, and it's disconnected. Areas A and B are 165 little islands surrounded by a sea of Israeli control.

And then, the next level are Palestinians who live in East Jerusalem, including the parts of the West Bank that Israel annexed in 1967 and unilaterally declared to be part of East Jerusalem, going from the edge of Ramallah in the north to the tip of Bethlehem in the south. And they do not have the right to vote in national elections, but they do have the right to vote in local elections, and they have much more freedom of movement than Palestinians in the West Bank.

And then, the next level are Palestinian citizens of Israel who, as I say, they themselves live in very different circumstances depending on where they are. If they're a Palestinian Bedouin living in an unrecognized village in the Negev, then they're living very much like a Palestinian in Area C of the West Bank, and their citizenship doesn't really get them very much protection. But if you're a Palestinian citizen living in Haifa, it's a very different story. You still don't have all the rights that a Jew does. You don't have the same rights to immigration and land, but it is the most rights that you can have as a Palestinian within the system.

Now, the fact that there are different regulations applied to different groups of Palestinians doesn't negate the notion that this is a single regime. This is Israel controlling Palestinian lives in different ways. It doesn't mean that there's a separate regime in each of these different locations.

And, similarly, in apartheid South Africa, you had a whole host of different rules applying to Black South Africans, "Colored" South Africans, depending on where they lived, if they were in Bantustans, if they were in townships. You even had this tricameral parliament in the 1980s under apartheid South Africa.

So the notion that there's somehow a democratic Israel within its pre-1967 borders, and then there's this temporary occupation that's outside of Israel and separate from Israel, is simply false. And it's an illusion that the world needs to put forward in order to think of Israel as a democracy. Because the only way that you could actually call this place a democracy is if you put up this mental barrier and say, OK, there's Israel within the green line and everything beyond it is no longer Israel, and it's not actually controlled by the same government.

But it is controlled by the same government.

■■ ■

Nathan Thrall is author of A Day in the Life of Abed Salama: Anatomy of a Jerusalem Tragedy, *which received the 2024 Pulitzer Prize for general nonfiction. "Israeli Apartheid" is excerpted from a discussion with Murtaza Hussain, host of the* Intercepted *podcast, July 3, 2024.*

The Laws of Israel: Democracy or Apartheid?

BY BILL BIGELOW

AMMAR AWAD | REUTERS

Fawzia stands on the ruins of her house, destroyed after her ex-husband lost a land ownership case in Israeli courts, 2018.

E very recent U.S. president has celebrated Israel's "democracy" — often adding "vibrant" to the description. Because U.S. leaders have mobilized support for Israel based on the premise that it is a democracy, looking at Israeli laws — and evaluating the extent to which these do or do not embed democratic, egalitarian characteristics — can be valuable.

This activity begins with students reading about some laws of Israel and then deciding whether the actions in several situations are legal, and which laws might apply. After reviewing the situations and attempting to apply actual Israeli laws, students read the definition of "apartheid," as adopted in 1973 by the U.N. General Assembly in the International Convention on the Suppression and Punishment of the Crime of *Apartheid*, and determine whether this could apply to Israel and what more they would need to know to be certain.

Note that the source for many of the laws described here is Adalah – the Legal Center for Arab Minority Rights in Israel. Adalah maintains a searchable database going back as far as 1939 to catalog laws that discriminate against Palestinians. Additional sources for information on laws include Al-Haq, an independent Palestinian nongovernmental human rights organization, and the article "Five Ways Israeli Law Discriminates Against Palestinians" at Al Jazeera, July 19, 2018. Also see *Justice for Some: Law and the Question of Palestine*, Noura Erakat's excellent book that has a broader scope than this lesson, but brilliantly examines the intersection of law and Palestinian rights.

There are of course multiple jurisdictions in Palestine-Israel — for example, the Palestinian Arab residents of the West Bank are officially subject to a different set of rules than Palestinian citizens of Israel. But as Nathan Thrall argues in his summary of "Israeli Apartheid" on p. 128, "the fact that there are different regulations applied to different groups of Palestinians doesn't negate the notion that this is a single regime. This is Israel controlling Palestinian lives in different ways. It doesn't mean that there's a separate regime in each of these different locations."

MATERIALS NEEDED
1. Copies of Student Handout "Some Laws of Israel" — enough for every student in class

2. Copies of Student Handout "Laws of Israel — Situations" — enough for every student in class

3. Copies of Student Handout "International Convention on the Suppression and Punishment of the Crime of *Apartheid*" (Articles I and II) — enough for every student in class

SUGGESTED PROCEDURE
1. Review with students the "Some Laws of Israel" handout. Invite students to share situations they are familiar with in Palestine-Israel, and how these laws might apply. If they engaged in Suzanna Kassouf's "Israeli Apartheid: A Simulation," students are likely to recognize many features they experienced in that activity. As they read, students could generate some hypothetical situations based on the laws.

2. There are many things to draw out in a discussion of these laws. Here are a few:
- "Israel – The Nation-State of the Jewish People" establishes that Israel

is exclusively a Jewish country. Is it possible to be simultaneously a country for one ethnic group and a democracy? (After passage of this law, Prime Minister Benjamin Netanyahu wrote that "Israel is not a state of all its citizens. . . . According to the basic nationality law we passed, Israel is the nation-state of the Jewish people — and only it." But at the same time, he wrote that Arab citizens of Israel, "have equal rights like all of us." If appropriate, share Netanyahu's remarks with students, and ask for their thoughts.)
- What are the implications of this law for those citizens who are not Jewish, or who live in the Occupied Territories?
- How might Israel justify the Absentees' Properties Law, given that this applies to people who are classified as refugees and fled their homes during armed conflict?
- What does the word "return" mean in the Law of Return? Return for whom? What does it not mean?
- What justifications might the state of Israel offer for a "citizenship law" that denies citizenship to people whose families originally lived in the land that became Israel, or who themselves once lived there?
- How might "citizenship," and how it is defined, disrupt families?
- What circumstances of "disloyalty" might lead to one losing citizenship? How might that provision of the law be applied?
- What kind of acts might be defined as "terrorism" under the Anti-Terror (Counter-Terrorism) Law?
- How might one challenge charges under the Anti-Terror Law?
- What kind of literature might be considered "terrorist materials"?
- As of the spring of 2024, about 3,660 Palestinians were being detained without criminal charges by Israel, ac-

cording to Addameer Prisoner Support and Human Rights Association. What are some of the actions that might have led to their detention? How might a detained person challenge one's detention?

- What difficulties would journalists encounter in attempting to document how these laws are being implemented?
- How might the "Nakba Law" affect public school teachers or administrators? How might it affect students?

3. Divide students into small groups to discuss "Laws of Israel — Situations," and determine which laws might apply to each circumstance. As the instructions indicate, for some of these, multiple laws might apply. Brief background on each situation:

1. This happened to Jerusalem teacher Meir Baruchin, on Nov. 9, 2023. It is described in detail in "How Israel Turned a Teacher into a Traitor," a Feb. 9, 2024, article in the Israeli *+972* Magazine. Baruchin was also interviewed on *Democracy Now!*
2. The events in this situation are true, and described poignantly in *The Lemon Tree*, by Sandy Tolan.
3. This situation describes the story of Goldi Mandelbaum, who moved from New Jersey to the Tel Aviv suburb of Ramat Gan in November 2023. The details of an immigration story like this vary from individual to individual, family to family, and place to place, but the choice for Jews to leave the United States (or other countries) and relocate to Israel and become citizens is common. In fact, in Mandelbaum's case, an Israeli nonprofit subsidized her flight from New Jersey to Israel, helped her find an apartment, and pays for her Hebrew lessons.
4. This describes the case of Lara Alqasem, who was detained upon her arrival in Israel in 2018, and held for two weeks before Israel's Supreme Court ordered her release. The Israeli Ministry of Strategic Affairs could not prove that she currently advocated Boycott, Divestment, and Sanctions — only that she had in the past. Hundreds of U.S. and Israeli academics had signed petitions in support of Alqasem, and the Supreme Court found that her case was harming Israel's reputation.
5. The inclusion of the West Bank town of Jericho is added, but all other details in this situation come from those described in *The Lemon Tree*.
6. The situation here is actual, and described in *Jerusalem Story*, Nov. 2022.
7. This is an actual event, described in the *Times of Israel* in Dec. 2023.
8. This is based on a real relationship, described in the *Times of Israel* in Oct. 2021. Although the man's wife did not die and there was no deportation, the *Times of Israel* article points out, "If their Israeli spouse passes away or they divorce, they could be deported — forcing their Arab Israeli children to either leave with them for the West Bank or stay behind without them."
9. There are many cases like this. As mentioned, human rights organizations in Palestine-Israel have identified 3,660 people who are in administrative detention — in prison, but charged with no crime. The specific incident in Situation #9 refers to Hanan Saleh Abdullah Barghouti, also known as Umm Anad. The Addameer website describes her case. (Addameer is Arabic for conscience.)

4. Depending on time, review the situations one by one and solicit students' thoughts on which laws might apply to each situation.

5. There has been controversy about whether or not the term apartheid should be used to describe Israel and its policies toward the Palestinian Occupied Territories. Ask students whether they have heard the term apartheid, and what it means to them. Tell them that apartheid is an Afrikaans word meaning separateness and was the name that the National Party in South Africa used to describe its system of white supremacy following its victory in 1948. Share with students some background on the formal international definition of apartheid. According to Human Rights Watch:

> Two international treaties, the Convention on the Suppression and Punishment of the Crime of Apartheid (Apartheid Convention) and the Rome Statute of the International Criminal Court (Rome Statute), identify apartheid as a crime against humanity. The Apartheid Convention defines the crime against humanity of apartheid in Article II as "inhuman acts committed for the purpose of establishing and maintaining domination by one racial group of persons over any other racial group of persons and systematically oppressing them." The Rome Statute defines apartheid in Article 7, paragraph 2(h) as "inhumane acts . . . committed in the context of an institutionalized regime of systematic oppression and domination by one racial group over any other racial group or groups and committed with the intention of maintaining that regime."

It may be helpful to distribute the Student Handout "Convention on the Suppression and Punishment of the Crime of *Apartheid*" (Articles I and II) for more detail. Ask students to go through each of the items in Article II, which specify "inhuman acts committed for the purpose of establishing and maintaining domination by one racial group of persons over any other racial group of

A playground, located in a Jewish settlement in the West Bank, is divided from Bethlehem by Israel's separation barrier. 2022.

persons and systematically oppressing them," and deciding whether what they know about laws and policies of Israel can be identified as any of these "inhuman acts."

No doubt, students' brief encounter with some important Israeli laws is not enough to equip them to make definitive statements about the nature of Israeli rule in Palestine-Israel. Nonetheless, ask students, "Based on what you have read and discussed in the 'Laws of Israel' and other things we've studied, do you think that the term apartheid could be applied to the Israeli system? Why or why not? What more would you need to know to be more certain of your answer?"

■ ■ ■

Bill Bigelow (bbpdx@aol.com) is curriculum editor of Rethinking Schools.

Some Laws of Israel

The Basic Law: Israel – The Nation-State of the Jewish People: Declares Israel as the nation-state of the Jewish people throughout the world. The law establishes that the ethnic-religious status of Israel is exclusively Jewish. It is the "law of laws," capable of overriding any ordinary legislation. Article 1 states that the Land of Israel ("Eretz Israel") is the historic national home of the Jewish people, in which the state of Israel was established, and in which the Jewish people exercises its natural, cultural, and historic right to self-determination. It adds that the right to exercise national self-determination in the state of Israel is solely for the Jewish people. Article 3 defines the capital of Israel as Jerusalem, which includes occupied Palestinian East Jerusalem. Article 5 establishes that immigration leading to automatic citizenship is a right only for Jews. Article 7 provides that the state views development of Jewish settlements throughout "Eretz Israel," which includes the Occupied West Bank, as a national value, and will act to encourage, promote, and consolidate their establishment. The law nullifies the former status of Arabic, which Palestinians speak, as an official language, leaving Hebrew as Israel's only official language.

Absentees' Property Law: This law defines anyone who was expelled, fled, or left territory that became Israel after Nov. 29, 1947, as "absentee" — including people who were fleeing war or were expelled. This is the case even if Palestinians have retained the deed to their land and house. All property — land, houses, bank accounts, etc. — belonging to absentees was put under the control of the state of Israel, with the Custodian of Absentees' Property.

Law of Return: Allows every Jewish person to immigrate to Israel and automatically become an Israeli citizen. Section 1 of the Law of Return declares that "every Jew has the right to come to this country as an *oleh* [immigrant]." The law also applies to the children and grandchildren of Jews, as well as to their spouses and the spouses of their children and grandchildren. The Law of Return does not apply to Palestinians, even those who were born in historic Palestine, in areas that became the state of Israel. "For the purposes of this Law, 'Jew' means a person who was born of a Jewish mother or has become converted to Judaism and who is not a member of another religion."

Citizenship Law: Article 2(a) of the Citizenship Law says that "Every emigrant under the Law of Return will become a citizen of Israel as a direct result of the return." Article 3 of the law deprives Palestinians who were residents of Palestine prior to 1948 of the right to gain citizenship or residence status in Israel. Amendment No. 9 (Authority for Revoking Citizenship) to Article 11 of the Citizenship Law revokes citizenship in the event of "breach of trust or disloyalty to the state." Note that Jews who immigrate to Israel from the United States can maintain citizenship in both countries. Should a Palestinian living in Palestinian East Jerusalem be allowed U.S. citizenship, Israel takes away the individual's East Jerusalem residency and they will be allowed into Jerusalem only as a visitor.

Citizenship and Entry into Israel Law: This law was passed in 2003 as a temporary order, but has been regularly renewed (with a brief period of expiration from 2021 to 2022). The law denies naturalization to Palestinians from the Occupied West Bank or Gaza who are married to Israeli citizens. All other individuals who marry Israeli citizens can become citizens themselves, but not if they are Palestinians from the West Bank or Gaza.

"Anti-Terror" (Counter-Terrorism) Law: Allows Israeli authorities to detain someone and not bring them before a judge for 96 hours. Detention hearings, reviews, and appeals can be held without the detainee or their lawyer being present.

Secret evidence can be used against a detainee. The law (Article 2A) defines a "terrorist act" as an act or threat to carry out an act with a political, religious, nationalistic, or ideological motive; carried out with the intention of provoking fear or panic among the public or with the intention of compelling a government or other governmental authority, including a government or other governmental authority of a foreign country, or a public international organization, to carry out or to abstain from carrying out any act; and risked serious harm to a person's body or freedom, serious harm to public safety or health, serious harm to religious objects or places of worship, and serious harm to the Israeli economy or environment. The law allows the defense minister to designate a group as a "terrorist organization," if the minister is convinced that it has committed, or intends to commit, terrorist acts as defined above — or assists or finances a terrorist organization.

"Consumption of Terrorist Materials" (amendment to the Counter-Terrorism Law): The law outlaws the "systematic and continuous consumption of publications of a terrorist organization under circumstances that indicate identification with the terrorist organization." The defense minister can designate terrorist organizations — see above.

> **Administrative Detention.** Several laws apply:
> - **Article 285 of Military Order 1651** (military legislation that applies to the West Bank)
> - **Internment of Unlawful Combatants Law** (Unlawful Combatants Law) (Applies especially to Gaza)
> - **Emergency Powers (Detentions) Law** (applies to Israeli citizens)

All three of these laws provide for "administrative detention," which allows the Israeli military to hold prisoners indefinitely on secret information without charging them or allowing them to stand trial. An administrative detention order falls within the powers of the Israeli military commander of the area as well as within the minister of the Israeli security detainees in Jerusalem. Israeli law grants the military commander the power to make any modifications to military orders relating to administrative detention for military necessity. The Israeli military commanders base their decision on secret information, which cannot be accessed by the detainee nor their lawyer. Palestinians wishing to visit their relatives detained in Israeli prisons must apply for a permit from the Israeli security services. With Article 285 of Military Order 1651, military commanders can detain an individual for up to six-month renewable periods if they have "reasonable grounds to presume that the security of the area or public security requires the detention." On or just before the order's expiration date, the detention order may be renewed; there is no limit to the maximum amount of time an individual may be administratively detained. Palestinians may remain in prison for years under this detainee law. There is no requirement that a detainee be informed of the reason for their detention.

"Nakba Law" — (Amendment No. 40 to the Budget Foundations Law): The "Nakba Law" authorizes the minister of finance to withdraw state funds from any institution or body — including school — that commemorates "Israel's Independence Day or the day on which the state was established as a day of mourning," or that denies the existence of Israel as a "Jewish and democratic state."

Regulation 119(1) of the Defense (Emergency) Regulations. Israeli courts have ruled that the military can demolish Palestinian people's homes, farmland, or groves of trees "for military purposes" — or seal off parts of homes. The Israeli High Court of Justice has ruled that Israel has the right to demolish Palestinian homes without granting the residents a right to a court of appeal in the event of "immediate operational necessity."

Laws of Israel — Situations

For each of the situations below, indicate which law or laws might be relevant in deciding what is legal — or not. For some situations, multiple laws might apply. Find as many as you can. The situations described are actual, although some details have been added.

1. An Israeli history teacher in Jerusalem posted on his Facebook page that he opposed the Israeli government's killing of Palestinians. He was arrested and put in solitary confinement for four days. The police seized his two laptops and phone. He was fired from his teaching job in a government school. Was this legal? What laws might the police have used to justify these actions?

2. In the middle of July 1948, the Israeli military forced a family in al-Ramla, Palestine, to leave their home. This was during the Nakba — Arabic for "catastrophe" — when as many as 750,000 Palestinians fled or were forced from their homes by the Israeli military. (Israelis refer to this as the War for Independence.) The Palestinian family had built this home themselves in 1936. They planted a beautiful lemon tree in the backyard. They were able to take only a few suitcases, but were forced to leave everything else behind — their rugs, furniture, family pictures, toys, books, dishes, food, etc. After a long journey, they ended up in the Palestinian town of Ramallah, in the West Bank. They want to return to their home in al-Ramla, which now is in Israel, but a Jewish family lives there. Does the Palestinian family have a legal right to reclaim their home?

3. A 28-year-old Jewish woman from Manchester, New Jersey, wants to move to Israel. She is a social worker, and a U.S. citizen. She grew up in an Orthodox Jewish community and attended an Orthodox day school. When she was younger, her parents took her and their other kids to Israel for vacations, and she has always felt connected to Israel. She came to feel even more attached to Israel after she spent a month there in 2023. She does not speak Hebrew but wants to learn. She has no family in Israel and has never lived there before. She believes that when she arrives in Israel, because she is Jewish, she automatically has the legal right to Israeli citizenship. Does she?

4. A young woman of Palestinian descent from the United States arrived at Israel's Ben Gurion Airport. She had a valid visa and was planning to begin work on a master's degree at Hebrew University in Jerusalem. In the United States, this individual is the former president of the University of Florida chapter of Students for Justice in Palestine, which supports Boycott, Divestment, and Sanctions (BDS) of Israel. Israeli authorities arrested and detained her because of her support for the BDS movement. BDS says it "works to end international support for Israel's oppression of Palestinians and pressure Israel to comply with international law." It is a strategy initiated by Palestinians — inspired by the South African anti-apartheid movement — to get people throughout the world to boycott Israel; to get banks, companies, and pension funds to withdraw investments in Israel; and to pressure governments to end assistance to and cooperation with Israel. The idea is that only when Israel feels pressure from around the world will it recognize Palestinians' rights. Was this a legal arrest and detention of this young woman? If so, how long can she be detained?

5. A Palestinian's parents were born in Lydda, Palestine. They were expelled during the Nakba. This Palestinian now lives in the West Bank, in Jericho, where they have family. But they want to return to Lydda — which the Israelis call Lod. It is now in Israel, but this person says that they have a right to return to where their family lived for generations before the Nakba — that it was Palestine long before it was Israel. Do they have a legal right to return to Lydda/Lod and to become citizens of Israel?

6. The al-Ibrahimiyya College in the al-Suwwana neighborhood in East Jerusalem serves Palestinian high school students. The school uses textbooks that include the Palestinian flag, use the word Palestine, and talk about the Nakba, the catastrophe. Educators there believe that Palestinian children should learn Palestinian history. The Israeli Education Ministry is forcing schools to adopt an Israeli curriculum and to censor the Palestinian curriculum. They insist that students should take the Hebrew bagrut, Israel's high school graduation test. The Israeli authorities arrested the director of the Palestinian Education Ministry. They have threatened Palestinian teachers with firing and even arrest. What laws might Israel use that could affect educators and this school in East Jerusalem?

7. Israeli soldiers demolished the West Bank home of a Palestinian man suspected of killing an Israeli father and son. Troops went into the town of Aqraba in the West Bank and destroyed the home of the man who had been arrested in the killings — although the man had not yet been convicted. Is this legal?

8. A Palestinian man, married to a woman who is an Arab Israeli citizen, has been living in Jerusalem on a temporary pass for more than 20 years. He has repeatedly applied for his Israeli citizenship, citing his marriage to an Israeli citizen as reason for why he should receive citizenship. The authorities denied his plea. In order to legally stay in the country, he needed to regularly apply for temporary permits, which could be denied at any point. Without citizenship, he could not drive or open a bank account. Last year, his wife was killed in an accident and he was deported. His five children were Israeli citizens. Two stayed behind with an aunt, and three followed him to the West Bank. Was his deportation legal?

9. Early one morning, Israeli security forces raided the home of a Palestinian woman living in the West Bank city of Ramallah. They asked for her identification, arrested her, and took her away. They did not tell her why she was being arrested. She has not been convicted of a crime or even charged with a crime. She is being imprisoned in Israel. Many of the people she is imprisoned with have also not been charged with any crime. Israeli authorities have not told her when she will be released, or if she will be released. She had been arrested and held the previous year for four months — also without charge. Is this legal?

International Convention on the Suppression and Punishment of the Crime of *Apartheid*

Article I

1. The States Parties to the present Convention declare that apartheid is a crime against humanity and that inhuman acts resulting from the policies and practices of apartheid and similar policies and practices of racial segregation and discrimination, as defined in article II of the Convention, are crimes violating the principles of international law, in particular the purposes and principles of the Charter of the United Nations, and constituting a serious threat to international peace and security.

2. The States Parties to the present Convention declare criminal those organizations, institutions, and individuals committing the crime of apartheid.

Article II

For the purpose of the present Convention, the term "the crime of apartheid," which shall include similar policies and practices of racial segregation and discrimination as practiced in southern Africa, shall apply to the following inhuman acts committed for the purpose of establishing and maintaining domination by one racial group of persons over any other racial group of persons and systematically oppressing them:

(a) Denial to a member or members of a racial group or groups of the right to life and liberty of person:
(i) By murder of members of a racial group or groups;
(ii) By the infliction upon the members of a racial group or groups of serious bodily or mental harm, by the infringement of their freedom or dignity, or by subjecting them to torture or to cruel, inhuman or degrading treatment or punishment;
(iii) By arbitrary arrest and illegal imprisonment of the members of a racial group or groups;

(b) Deliberate imposition on a racial group or groups of living conditions calculated to cause its or their physical destruction in whole or in part;
(c) Any legislative measures and other measures calculated to prevent a racial group or groups from participation in the political, social, economic, and cultural life of the country and the deliberate creation of conditions preventing the full development of such a group or groups, in particular by denying to members of a racial group or groups basic human rights and freedoms, including the right to work, the right to form recognized trade unions, the right to education, the right to leave and to return to their country, the right to a nationality, the right to freedom of movement and residence, the right to freedom of opinion and expression, and the right to freedom of peaceful assembly and association;
(d) Any measures including legislative measures, designed to divide the population along racial lines by the creation of separate reserves and ghettos for the members of a racial group or groups, the prohibition of mixed marriages among members of various racial groups, the expropriation of landed property belonging to a racial group or groups or to members thereof;
(e) Exploitation of the labor of the members of a racial group or groups, in particular by submitting them to forced labor;
(f) Persecution of organizations and persons, by depriving them of fundamental rights and freedoms, because they oppose apartheid.

BORN UNEQUAL ABROAD

HANNAH

JEWISH AMERICAN
BORN IN THE U.S.

LEILA

PALESTINIAN REFUGEE
BORN IN LEBANON

CAN I VISIT ISRAEL & THE OCCUPIED PALESTINIAN TERRITORY?

YES
You can visit Israel and most of the West Bank, and you'll find programs that may help fund your trip

NO
You are barred from entry to Israel, the West Bank or Gaza

CAN I MOVE THERE?

YES
Because you're Jewish, the 1950 Law of Return guarantees your right to live in Israel. Plus, you'll get a free flight and a bunch of perks if you do so

NO
As a Palestinian refugee, you're barred from returning and denied residency rights, even if you have family living there

CAN I BECOME AN ISRAELI CITIZEN?

YES
The 1952 Citizenship Law entitles you to automatic citizenship, even if you've never set foot in Israel before

NO
You are ineligible if your family became refugees between 1947 and 1949, even if they had lived there for generations before

CAN I PASS ON MY LEGAL STATUS TO MY SPOUSE IN ISRAEL OR THE OPT?

YES
Upon becoming a citizen, you can pass along legal status and even citizenship to your spouse (except if they're Palestinian from the OPT or from several Arab countries)

NO
You have no legal status and cannot gain one, even by marrying a citizen or resident of Israel

HUMAN RIGHTS WATCH

VISUALIZING**PALESTINE**

The individuals depicted above are fictional representations for illustrative purposes only
SOURCES HRW (2021); A Threshold Crossed
WWW.**VISUALIZINGPALESTINE**.ORG

@visualizingpal
/visualizing_palestine
fb.me/visualizingpalestine

APR 2021

The Home Within

BY IBTISAM S. BARAKAT

MOLLY CRABAPPLE

Ibtisam S. Barakat grew up in Ramallah, Palestine, in the West Bank, and attended Birzeit University. She wrote the memoir Tasting the Sky: A Palestinian Childhood. *Barakat studied journalism in the United States and lives in Missouri.*

Once upon a tear
I tired of my fear
And my heart whispered
It's time to return
To my lonesome mommy
And my graying daddy
And the hills of olive
And shimmering dandelion.
So I packed my yearning
And begin my journey
Until I arrived
At the soldiered border
That divides my world.
I handed my card
And stood in prayer
That I'd be allowed inside
Till a cold voice inquired
Didn't you know?
Time has elapsed
And your permit has expired.
Have you business there?
Sir, I don't have a business;
I have my daddy and my mommy
And many people who know me.
But that's not enough,
The guard declared.
His eyes trailed off slowly;
Then he sealed the window
And turned away.
That night I searched
For a refuge from my hurt
But could see no vein
But the path within.
From there I soared
Beyond frontier and guard
And I quickly arrived
At the old stone house
With the green door.
My father's arms
Rushed to surround me
And his thousand tears
Reached to receive me.
They cried in unison
Welcome home.

Uncovering Settler Colonialism: A Concept Formation Lesson

BY JESSE HAGOPIAN

"**E**very empire . . . tells itself and the world that it is unlike all other empires," wrote Palestinian literary theorist and public intellectual Edward Said. "Its mission is not to plunder and control but to educate and liberate." Said's insight encapsulates the deceptive narratives used to justify colonial conquest. This deception has meant that students who live in colonial powers don't often get taught an accurate history of their country in relation to the Indigenous people whose land and lives were taken to build the empire.

To uncover this reality, students need to engage with the concept of "settler colonialism." Colonialism and settler colonialism represent distinct forms of domination and control. Colonialism involves a foreign power exploiting a region for its resources, often maintaining political and economic control over the Indigenous population without necessarily displacing them. The primary goal is the extraction of wealth and resources to benefit the elites of the colonizing country.

By contrast, settler colonialism involves the foreign power not only exploiting but also occupying and settling the land, systematically displacing and often attempting to erase the Indigenous population and culture. Settler colonialism seeks to permanently replace the native population with settlers, establishing a new societal and cultural

RAAFAT ABOU DAKA | ALAMY

order. As Shreya Shah writes, "Settler colonialism . . . is a term for when the colonizer comes to stay and as such the distinction between the colony and the imperial nation is lost. Settler colonialism as a structure requires genocide. . . . It is also distinct from other forms of colonialism because the colonizer comes with the intention of making a new home on the land and as such insists on 'settler sovereignty over all things in their new domain.'"

The primary examples of settler colonialism include European powers occupying North America, Dutch and British occupation of South Africa, British occupation of Australia, and Zionist occupation of Palestine. Comparing these examples helps students better understand them all.

When I first taught this lesson to my 10th-grade world history class, I was struck by their creativity in defining and naming the concept we were exploring. I began by telling the class we would investigate a concept, but I wasn't going to tell them what the concept was. They were going to have to figure it out on their own. I explained that they would uncover and name the concept themselves.

I distributed Handout 1, the "Concept Formation: Historical Examples Graphic Organizer," and Handout 2, the historical example readings. After dividing the class into small groups, I watched as they dove into the readings, discussing and filling out their graphic organizers. As I circulated the room, I overheard insightful conversations. One student said, "In all these examples, the foreign power is trying to replace the native people." Another student added, "Yeah, and they're also bringing their own people to settle on the land."

Once the groups completed their organizers, and came up with a name for their concept, we gathered for a full class discussion. Each group shared their findings and proposed a name for the concept. One group suggested "Domination," while another came up with "Total Control." Another group bluntly suggested "Theft." A group whose members were familiar with the term colonialism decided to call it that. The variety of terms they developed for the concept sparked a lively discussion about the nuances of each term. Many groups made connections between the three historical examples. One student made the connection that the Trail of Tears wasn't that different from the Nakba. Another had heard about the Israeli occupation of homes in the West Bank that the U.N. had deemed illegal and told his group about it.

Whatever name each group ended up giving to the concept, they largely agreed that its critical attributes included a foreign power that exerts political control over Indigenous people, this power relocating its citizens and displacing Indigenous people from their land, and attempting to erase the Indigenous population and culture with violence.

I then distributed Handout 3, the article on settler colonialism, and explained that the concept they had been discussing is known as "settler colonialism." We read through the article together, and it was gratifying to see the students' recognition as they connected their own findings with the scholarly definition. "So, what I called 'domination' is actually called 'settler colonialism,'" one student remarked. I replied that is the term to use when discussing the concept with other people so you can be understood, but that if "domination" helped them remember the concept, that could be useful.

To wrap up, I handed out reflection questions, prompting students to compare their initial thoughts with the scholarly definition. Students expressed a new understanding of how historical events continue to impact Indigenous communities today.

One thing to consider, that isn't raised in this lesson, is that settler colonialism always provokes resistance from Indigenous people. Further lessons on the many forms of Indigenous resistance would be an important follow-up.

I've also included an extension activity to help solidify the concept of settler colonialism in students' minds. Handout 4 asks students to analyze three historical situations that include examples and non-examples of settler colonialism. I then ask the students to determine if the example they read about is colonialism or settler colonialism.

By understanding methods of control that settler colonial societies exert, students can better understand their own country, the ongoing conflict in Israel and Palestine, and the way power has been organized around the world.

◼ ◻

Jesse Hagopian is a Rethinking Schools editor, a high school teacher, and on the staff of the Zinn Education Project. He is the co-editor of the Rethinking Schools book Teaching for Black Lives. *He serves on the Black Lives Matter at School steering committee and is the director of the Black Education Matters Student Activist Award.*

Concept Formation: Historical Examples Graphic Organizer

Instructions:
1. **Read:** Read each of the three short examples about different regions of the world.
2. **Discuss:** Discuss in your group what these examples have in common.
3. **Identify:** For each example, identify three characteristics that each example has in common. At the top of the "concept formation chart" write the name of the characteristic in each box for each one of three.
4. **Explain:** For each characteristic identified, explain how the historical example contains that characteristic.
5. **Name:** Come up with a name for what to call the process described in the examples.
6. **Reflect:** Answer the reflection questions (Handout 4).

Concept Formation Lesson	Characteristic 1:	Characteristic 2:	Characteristic 3:
Example 1: **Native Americans and Europeans**			
Example 2: **Palestine and Israel**			
Example 3: **South African Apartheid**			

The name you chose for this concept: _____

Example 1:
Native Americans and Europeans

In the 16th and 17th centuries, European nations such as England, France, and Spain began to control parts of North America. They occupied land of the Indigenous peoples who had lived there for thousands of years. European governments sent the military and administrators to enforce their rule.

European settlers were encouraged to move to North America through promises of land, resources, and economic opportunity. Incentives such as land grants, the promise of religious freedom, and economic prospects like the fur trade and agriculture drew settlers in large numbers.

Beginning in the 1820s the white "settlers" and the U.S. government forcibly removed thousands of Cherokee, Creek, Seminole, Chickasaw, and Choctaw people from their ancestral lands in the southeastern United States to so-called Indian Territory west of the Mississippi River. One of these forced relocations became known as the Trail of Tears and resulted in the deaths of thousands due to disease, lack of adequate shelter and clothing, and starvation. The U.S. government's promotion of Manifest Destiny, the idea that Americans were destined by God to expand westward across the continent, further fueled expansion and the seizure of more Indigenous peoples' lands. The Homestead Act of 1862 promoted more white settlement. This act provided 160 acres of public land — land occupied or formerly occupied by Indigenous peoples — to settlers for a small fee, provided they improved the land by building a dwelling and cultivating crops. Hundreds of thousands of settlers moved west, further displacing Indigenous people.

The settlers established farms, towns, and cities. The new, predominantly European population undermined Indigenous people's culture through policies and practices that sought either to eliminate Native peoples or assimilate them into European ways of life. Indigenous languages, religions, and social structures were suppressed, with children being sent to boarding schools designed to erase their Native identities. Legal systems and property rights favored the European settlers, marginalizing Indigenous traditions and authority.

Example 2:
Palestine and Israel

The early Zionist movement advocated for the establishment of a Jewish homeland in Palestine. In 1917, the Balfour Declaration was issued by the British government, expressing support for "the establishment in Palestine of a national home for the Jewish people." This declaration from the most powerful empire in the world encouraged Jewish immigration to Palestine. Following World War II and the Holocaust — when Nazi Germany systematically murdered more than 6 million Jews — international support for a Jewish state in Palestine grew stronger. In 1947, the United Nations approved a plan to partition Palestine into separate Jewish and Arab states. The land of Palestine had been inhabited by Indigenous Palestinian Arabs for generations, forming a rich and continuous cultural and historical presence. In 1948, the state of Israel declared independence, leading to a war with neighboring Arab countries and the removal of many Palestinians. This event, known to Palestinians as the Nakba — catastrophe in Arabic — resulted in the forced displacement of approximately 750,000 Palestinians from their homes.

After 1948, Israeli political and military authorities took control over large areas that had previously been inhabited by Palestinians, creating a new government. The Israeli government and Zionists around the world encouraged Jews from Europe and other parts of the world to immigrate to Israel, and to settle. These settlers established communities and cities on land that had been inhabited by Palestinians, resulting in the displacement of the existing population. Settlement policies included incentives such as citizenship, housing assistance, and economic opportunities, which aimed to increase the Jewish population and help make Israel more secure. Palestinians faced restrictions on their movement, land ownership, and political participation. The Israeli government destroyed many Palestinian villages, and cultural sites were often neglected or destroyed. The Zionists created a legal system to support their settlements, further entrenching their dominance.

Example 3: South African Apartheid

Before European settlement, South Africa was inhabited by various Indigenous groups. These included the Khoe-San (or Khoisan, which comprises the San and the Khoekhoe), and later, Bantu-speaking peoples. In the 17th century, Dutch settlers, known as Afrikaners, arrived and began to establish control over parts of the region. They created farms and towns, often displacing Indigenous communities. In the 19th century, British colonists arrived and further expanded European settlement in South Africa. White settlers, both Afrikaners and British, occupied the most fertile and valuable lands.

In 1948, the apartheid era began when the National Party, dominated by Afrikaners, came to power and implemented policies to enforce racial segregation and economic discrimination. The government enacted laws that restricted the rights of the non-white majority and centralized political control in the hands of the white population. Whites received incentives such as land grants, favorable economic conditions, and support for agriculture and mining. Through a law called the Group Areas Act, Black people were banned from living in cities, which were reserved for white South Africans; Black people were allowed to live only in areas called townships, outside the cities. Many Black South Africans were not even allowed to live in townships and were forced into areas known as bantustans, often in regions with poor-quality land.

This apartheid government sought to suppress the cultures and languages of non-white South Africans. Education for Black South Africans was poor, and designed by the white government to prepare Black people only for manual labor, to restrict their cultural practices, and attempted to teach them to accept apartheid. The legal system enforced segregation and economic inequality, ensuring that white settlers ruled political and economic life.

What Is Settler Colonialism?

BY SHREYA SHAH

Settler colonialism is a term for when the colonizer comes to stay and as such the distinction between the colony and the imperial nation is lost. It is enacted through practices like the creation of reserves, residential schools, and abduction into state custody as well as practices like the extraction of natural resources through mining, pipelines, and more. In settler colonialism, "colonizers impose their own cultural values, religions, and laws, make policies that do not favor the Indigenous peoples. They seize land and control access to resources and trade."

Settler colonialism involves the total appropriation of Indigenous life and land rather than the selective appropriation for profit (as is the case in other forms of colonialism). The colonizer comes with the intention of making a new home on the land and as such insists on "settler sovereignty over all things in their new domain."

In settler colonialism, the most important thing is land (water, earth, and air), because it is the source of capital and the new home of the settlers. . . . Beyond this, the colonizers, in the process of settler colonialism, redefine the relationships between people and land as only being those of an owner to his property. All other relationships and connections to land are made to be pre-modern and backward as land is recast as property, a resource, and nothing more. The settlers do this through the destruction of Indigenous peoples, Indigenous communities, and Indigenous peoples' claims to land under settler regimes. For settler colonialism to occur, land is seen as a "resource" and Indigenous peoples are erased so that the settlers can "truly claim ownership" of the land.

Settler colonialism as a structure requires genocide: the removal and erasure of Indigenous populations, communities, and nations that pre-exist the arrival and creation of the settler nation. Understanding settler colonialism can help non-Indigenous folk better support the global movements for Indigenous sovereignty that are central to dismantling settler colonialism and replacing this structure with something more just and sustainable.

This is excerpted and adapted from the Indigenous Foundation. The original can be found at
theindigenousfoundation.org/articles/what-is-settler-colonialism.

Extension Activity

Instructions: Read these three historical examples and determine which, if any, qualify as settler colonialism.

British Colonial Rule in India

The British East India Company began establishing trading posts in India in the early 17th century and gradually expanded its control through military force and alliances with local rulers. By the mid-19th century, following the Indian Rebellion of 1857, the British Crown took direct control of India, marking the beginning of the British Raj. The British exploited India's resources for the benefit of Britain, viewing India as a source of raw materials like cotton, tea, spices, and as a market for British manufactured goods. British governance often relied on local power structures, using Indian princes and landlords to administer regions. This allowed the British to maintain control with relatively few British officials. They introduced English education, legal systems, and cultural norms, often undermining Indian institutions and practices. However, there was no large-scale permanent settlement of British people in India. British rule led to significant economic changes, social upheavals, and resistance movements, ultimately culminating in India's independence in 1947.

Belgian Colonial Rule in the Congo

King Leopold II of Belgium claimed the Congo Free State as his personal possession in 1885. The area became a Belgian colony in 1908, following international outrage over Leopold's brutal exploitation. The Belgians' main goal was the extraction of valuable resources, particularly rubber and ivory. They subjected the local population to extreme violence and forced labor to meet production quotas. The Belgian administration was harsh; they had direct control over the Congolese people, including severe punishments for those who did not meet labor demands, leading to millions of deaths. The Belgian administration did not send large numbers of Belgians to the Congo. Instead, they focused on resource extraction and economic gain. The exploitation under Belgian rule led to profound social and economic disruptions, terrible human rights abuses, and trauma for the Congolese people. The Congo gained independence in 1960, but the legacy of colonial rule has continued to affect its development.

Aboriginals and the British

In 1788, the British established a penal colony at Sydney Cove in Australia, marking the beginning of British control over the continent. The British government declared the land "terra nullius" (land belonging to no one) despite the presence of Aboriginal Australians who had lived there for tens of thousands of years. British authorities established colonial administrations to govern the new settlements and impose British law. British settlers, including convicts, free settlers, and later waves of immigrants, moved to Australia in large numbers.

The British government gave incentives for settlement. The British transported convicts, and gave land grants for free settlers. They established farms, ranches, and towns, often displacing Indigenous communities. The settlers took land for agriculture and mining, changing the landscape and creating economic systems based on European models. To assimilate Aboriginal Australians into British culture, the settlers removed children from their families to be raised in institutions that taught European customs and languages. Indigenous spiritual practices and social structures were disregarded, and European settlers took many traditional lands without compensation. The British rulers designed legal and social systems to benefit the settlers, leading to the marginalization and impoverishment of Indigenous peoples.

Determined to Stay:
Palestinian Youth Fight for Their Village

BY JODY SOKOLOWER

The *Determined to Stay: Palestinian Youth Fight for Their Village* curriculum is based on my book of the same name about Silwan, a Palestinian community just south of the beautiful Old City of Jerusalem. Like virtually every West Bank Palestinian community, Silwan is under constant threat of house demolition, house theft, imprisonment, and attack by Israeli forces and Israeli settlers. And, like virtually every other Palestinian community, Silwan is filled with creative, courageous, and indomitable resistance. As teachers search for ways to introduce students to the historical context for what's happening in Palestine, Silwan is a good place to start.

I went to Silwan in 2012. I could see the conflict as soon as I walked out the Mughrabi Gate of the Old City, wove through Israeli tour buses and yelling tour leaders, and walked down Wadi Hilweh Street. The first thing I saw was King David National Park — a sprawling museum that's a monument to why Israel thinks it can throw Palestinians out of Silwan. El Ad, the Israeli development company behind the park, spearheads the campaign to ethnically cleanse Silwan. They've built miles of tunnels under Silwan, destroying houses, schools, a mosque. The park has an amphitheater, Segway tours, movies, a party room. King David Park is an archeological Disneyland with villainous goals.

A few doors down from King David Park is a small building with a red metal door. It's the home of Madaa Creative Center for Kids and the Wadi Hilweh Information Center. There I met Jawad Siyam, who started both centers — to unite community resistance, to support children and their families, and to give kids the chance to experience "a little of their childhood."

Jawad showed me around: We saw kids working in the computer center, practicing hip-hop, reading in the tiny library. We visited the women's workshop, where they were making mosaic table tops. Jawad took me to a new project — a beautiful cultural center with a sports field, murals, a whole schedule of community events. We had coffee and pastries in the café. I was awed by the creative, vibrant resistance to the efforts by Israel to erase both Palestinian history and the Silwani community living there now.

Two weeks after I got back to the United States, Israel demolished the café for a parking lot. I couldn't believe it. I was so angry, I didn't know what to do. So I wrote a book. I decided to use the story of Silwan to illuminate Palestine's history and current reality.

When I went back to Silwan to interview youth and their families, I asked Jawad what I should focus on.

"Focus on three things," he told me:

1. The criminalization of Palestinian children to force their families to leave
2. The demolition of Palestinian houses and Israeli settlers' theft of Palestinian houses
3. The City of David National Park and the use of archeology as a tool of continuing colonial conquest

"And be sure," he reminded me, "to put our resistance, our determination to stay in Silwan, in the center."

Those topics resonate with how racism and colonialism continue to work in the United States. I knew students here would make connections.

So in *Determined to Stay*, I center the voices of Silwani youth. And I weave in stories like that of Yacoub Odeh, 8 years old when his family was pushed out of Lifta, a village close to Silwan, in 1948. And Corrina Gould, who tells the story of her people, the Ohlone, and their fight to save the West Berkeley Shellmound in California's Bay Area.

History needs to be grounded in resistance, or it can breed alienation and hopelessness. Once we recognize injustice, what do we do? I stress resistance, both in Palestine and in the United States, to provide examples students can draw from.

Samia Shoman, co-coordinator of the Teach Palestine Project, and I created two lessons as an introduction to *Determined to Stay: Palestinian*

The Lesson

Divide the class into five groups, representing each of the five individuals in the activity. Students learn about one of the people in *Determined to Stay* and tell their story to classmates. Each group reads about their individual, then meets with other individuals around the class to discuss: How does this person define "home"? Why were they forced to leave their home or why is their home at risk? How has that affected their identity, their sense of who they are in the world? What are their hopes for the future in terms of home? A full lesson description with worksheets and slide decks is available at TeachPalestine.org. The longer lesson includes 11 narratives.

Youth Fight for Their Village, or as part of a unit on Palestine. We begin with the idea of home — asking kids what home means to them, whether their home or the home of someone they know has ever been threatened and what impact that had. The central activity is a jigsaw activity based on narratives from the book. The shorter lesson, included here, uses five narratives: 14-year-old Sara, whose Silwan home was destroyed when she was 8; Hatem, a teenager from Hebron, precariously living and working in Jerusalem without legal papers, although his home is less than 20 miles away; Yacoub, who was 8 during the 1948 expulsion of everyone from his village; Corrina, whose Ohlone people's history in the San Francisco Bay Area parallels that of Yacoub; and Ayesha, a Palestinian American teenager.

■■ ■

Jody Sokolower is co-coordinator of the Teach Palestine Project at the Middle East Children's Alliance. A former managing editor of Rethinking Schools, she is the author of Determined to Stay: Palestinian Youth Fight for Their Village, *editor of* Teaching About the Wars, *and co-editor of* Rethinking Sexism, Gender, and Sexuality.

Sara

I'm a 14-year-old Palestinian girl. I live in Silwan, a village just south of the Old City in Jerusalem. Silwan used to be a Palestinian village, but now more and more Israeli settlers are moving in and forcing us out. We are getting more crowded, and the Israeli government won't let us build new houses or even additions onto our houses.

When I was 8 years old, we tried to build another floor on our house so my brother Ali could get married. One morning, I woke up and there were Israeli soldiers and dogs at the door. I asked my older sister what was going on. She told me to be quiet. "They have come to bulldoze our house," she said. "If you don't stop talking, they will hit you."

They locked us in a room downstairs, and we could hear them tearing our house apart over our heads.

If you are Palestinian, they will not give you a building permit, even to add on one room. If you do it anyway, they use it as an excuse to demolish your whole house. That's what happened to us. Afterward, I kept having the same nightmare about that day. Sometimes I still see it in my dreams. For a long time, I felt afraid. But I am not afraid anymore. I go to demonstrations to protect al-Aqsa Mosque in the Old City, I practice dabke, our traditional dance, to keep our culture alive, and I learn about our history from my parents.

We Palestinians are patient. Even if it hurts, we have to stay determined and strong to fight the enemy who wants to take our village and our country. We believe we will get our rights back. What they are doing to us — the occupation — doesn't make us weak. It makes us stronger.

. . . .

Hatem

According to the Israelis, I'm an illegal immigrant, even though this is my country and I'm only 20 miles from where I grew up.

I'm 16 years old and my family lives in Hebron, in Palestine's West Bank. Last year, my father got really sick and he can't work. I dropped out of school to work full-time. It's hard to make money in Hebron, so I came to East Jerusalem. Even though the cities are so close, if you're Palestinian, you need a residency permit to be in Jerusalem, and I don't have one. There are checkpoints everywhere. If I get caught again, they will put me in prison.

I'll tell you how I got caught. A few months ago, I went home to see my family and I was coming back to Jerusalem. There was a group of us; we had a ladder and a rope to climb the wall near the Qalandia checkpoint. I jumped the wall and hid in a mosque. Then I started walking. But a Jeep full of Israeli soldiers grabbed me, tied my hands behind my back, put my jacket over my head, and threw me in a car.

They forced my head down. Every time I tried to raise it, they pushed it down again. They took me to a prison. They hit me and asked me a lot of questions: Who is your father? What is your address? Who else climbed the wall?

After many hours, they took me to the checkpoint and sent me back to Hebron. After a few days, I paid someone to help me get back to Jerusalem. Now I'm scared to go back home to visit my family.

Ayesha

I'm a Palestinian American. I just graduated from high school in San Francisco. I've been to Palestine twice. I felt like I was home there. Don't get me wrong: San Francisco is my home, but Palestine is my actual home. I felt like I belonged.

My dad is from a small village near Bethlehem. It's tense there because there's an Israeli settlement across the street. Just to get to my grandpa's land, where he grows vegetables and fruit, we had to go through an Israeli checkpoint. My grandpa was excited to show us what he was growing: tomatoes, cucumbers, all kinds of vegetables. That's really "farm to table." They pick vegetables that they grow on their land, and that's what is for dinner. My grandpa had so much joy on his face when he talked about his land.

It is hard to be Palestinian in school here. We never studied about Arab history, Arab Americans, or Palestine. And then there are ignorant comments, like "all Palestinians are terrorists" or "it's not their land anyway." When you're the one targeted, it's hard to even comprehend what's happening.

It would have made such a difference if our history was taught. Another thing that would help is more Arab teachers. Last year, I had a Palestinian teacher. I connected with her so much and I felt secure in her class.

The other thing that helps is allies. I hope kids get educated about Palestine, speak up, and help us get curriculum in our schools about Palestinians, Arabs, and other folks who are ignored. Being an ally, that's the first step to being amazing.

. . . .

Corrina Gould

Palestine isn't the only place where settlers have forced people out of their homes and off their land. I am Indigenous Chochenyo/Karkin Ohlone. My ancestors created the first village along the San Francisco Bay in California, more than 5,700 years ago. Before the European conquest, there were grizzly bears, forests everywhere, and so many shellfish you could eat as much as you wanted.

We lived peacefully for thousands of years. Then, at the end of the 18th century, the Spanish conquerors and the Catholic Church brought the mission system to California. They enslaved my ancestors in those missions. Later, we went from being enslaved at the missions to being enslaved on Mexican ranches. After the U.S. war with Mexico came the Gold Rush, which made things even worse for us. Some people say that 95 percent of our people died.

I started to learn about this from my mother, who as a child was sent to an Indian boarding school. Now I work to make sure that our history isn't forgotten. Before the European settlers came, there were 425 shellmounds in the San Francisco Bay Area. They were ceremonial and community centers. The biggest one was the West Berkeley Shellmound. Today that shellmound is buried under a parking lot. We're fighting to save it — to turn it into a place where Ohlone people can have ceremonies, and where everyone can learn about the true history of this part of California. A lot of healing has to happen, and we hope that the West Berkeley Shellmound can be part of that. People don't tell the truth about history in this country, that we are always on occupied territory of Native people. It's all stolen land.

Yacoub Odeh

I'm an old man now, but I grew up in Lifta, a Palestinian village of about 3,000 people near Silwan. When I was a child, Lifta was a wonderful place. We had two pools that brought water to the gardens. The people in the village divided the garden among the families who lived there according to how big the family was, and everyone planted as they liked. Our houses were old and beautiful, with carved entrances to the windows and walls.

In February 1948, when I was 8 years old, the Zionist gangs forced us to leave Lifta. I still remember that terrible day. My father carried my younger sister and I followed with my older sister. My parents found someone driving a truck. In the back were children from three families and we were the fourth family. We escaped in the truck with my mother. My father and the other men returned to Lifta to try to save the village. After there was a massacre at a nearby village, they realized they couldn't save our village and my father joined us. He was so sad. My mother was crying. She showed him the oranges she brought from our orange tree and the key to our house. We lost our house, we lost our village. We had nothing. We had left without packing anything because we thought in a day or two we would return.

For a long time, we had to live outside, under a fig tree. Then we moved into one small room. I lost two years of schooling, and had to change schools many, many times. These things shaped who I was and my way into the future. When I was a teenager, I began to participate in the Palestinian movement that said "We will struggle to go back home, we will return." We are still struggling to go back to our homes.

After they kicked us out of our villages, they blew them up. More than 70 years later, I take visitors back to see the ruins of Lifta so they will know our history. On some of the destroyed houses, you can still see the beautiful carving above the doors and windows.

Borders and Walls
Stories that Connect Us to Palestine

BY JODY SOKOLOWER

Note: PDFs of graphic organizers, articles, and other materials described in this unit are in the "Resources" column of the Borders and Walls Unit Outline at teachpalestine.org.

My mixed-grade class of high school English language learners traveled around the room, participating in a Borders and Walls Gallery Walk. Carla, a 10th grader who immigrated to the United States from Mexico, had just finished looking at photos of the Berlin Wall coming down, and now she stared at images of the U.S./Mexico border wall.

"What would it take," she asked, "to make this wall come down too?"

That's exactly the kind of question I hoped to provoke in this unit on two of the most signif-

icant wall systems in the world: The first is one that many of my students were familiar with, the U.S./Mexico border. The second is Israel's apartheid walls — the wall that snakes through the West Bank, cutting Palestinians off from their neighbors and families, their farmland, schools, hospitals, and places of worship; and the one that encloses the Gaza Strip, creating the world's largest open-air prison.

I started with walls and then expanded our exploration to include a critique of settlers/pioneers and raise questions about borders in general: Who draws border lines? Why? What is the impact on the people living there and on the environment?

Borders and Walls Gallery Walk

The Borders and Walls Gallery Walk was the first activity. My goal was to catch the students' interest and get them generating questions that we could pursue throughout the unit. I pick walls based on who is in the room and what is happening in the world, then look for three or four evocative images of each, balancing images of oppression with those of resistance. I always start with photos of the U.S./Mexico border wall and of the apartheid wall system in Palestine. One of Carla's classmates was from Germany, so for this class I included the Berlin Wall (always a good choice because it got torn down, a clear illustration that borders aren't necessarily permanent). Because I had students from China, Tibet, and Nepal in that class, I included the Great Wall of China. I usually have four groups of photos.

As students looked at the photos posted around the room, they filled out a graphic organizer:

- What do you see? Be specific.
- Where do you think this is?
- What does it make you think about? How does it make you feel?
- What questions do you have?

Once students analyzed the photos, they returned to their seats and we discussed their responses. I charted their questions and comments for further discussion as the unit unfolded.

Then I asked them to answer a prompt in their journals:

> What impact have walls/borders had on your life or that of someone close to you? Think about walls/borders in the broad sense (prison walls, gang territory, gentrification, structural racism, and/or sexism as well as geopolitical borders). If you crossed borders in an airplane instead of on the ground, that still counts.

To make sure that students understood the question, I offered a few examples from my own life: In high school when I decided not to take physics because "boys don't like smart girls"; how I felt, visiting a loved one in prison, when I had to walk out of the visiting room and leave them behind the concrete walls; the first time I saw Israel's apartheid wall snaking through Bethlehem.

I gave the students about 15 minutes to write. I told them: "When you think you're done writing, you'll probably put down your pen and wait for other folks to finish. Once you get tired of waiting and pick your pen back up to start writing again, that's the real journaling. You've gotten past the surface answer and now you're exploring your deeper feelings."

When everyone finished writing, I asked for volunteers to share what they wrote. Because this was a class of immigrants, everyone had crossed borders. A student from Oaxaca described her father's treacherous journey through Mexico and across the Rio Grande. Several students described the invisible walls in their neighborhoods, making some blocks safe and others dangerous. Jorge

said: "The English language test that keeps us out of regular classes is a wall, too."

I told the students that in this unit we would focus on two sets of borders and walls: The U.S.-Mexico border wall, and the ever-changing borders in Palestine-Israel and what Israel calls their "security walls." We would look for patterns and also differences. Looking at these two situations would give us a stronger understanding of the international and historical role of borders and walls.

Manifest Destiny and the Promised Land

The goal of the next lesson was to explore the similarities in ideology behind the conquest of what is now the United States and that of Palestine. We read two original source documents about Manifest Destiny — one by President John Quincy Adams in 1811:

> The whole continent of North America appears to be destined by Divine Providence to be peopled by one nation, speaking one language, professing one general system of religious and political principles.

And one by newspaperman John O'Sullivan in 1845. O'Sullivan is credited with coining the term "Manifest Destiny":

> The right of our manifest destiny to overspread and to possess the whole of the continent which Providence has given us for the development of the great experiment of liberty.

I projected the texts so we could look at them together. "'Manifest' means clear or obvious," I explained. "'Destiny' means fate; something that is definitely going to happen in the future. Are there other words you need definitions for?"

Once everyone was comfortable with the words in the quotes, we read them aloud. I asked students to discuss the following questions in pairs, and then again as a whole group:

- What do these quotes mean? How would you put them in your own words?

- Why do you think Adams and O'Sullivan said these things? What did they want people to believe?
- What is Manifest Destiny?
- What effect do you think the idea of Manifest Destiny had on immigrants to the United States in the 19th century? On folks who worked for low wages on other people's farms? On people hoping to get rich quick?
- What is a settler? What are the good things about being a settler? What are the bad things about being a settler?

Then I explained: "When a more powerful country conquers other places and takes control of their land, resources, and people, it's called colonialism. There are different kinds of colonialism. The kind of colonialism here in the United States, where Indigenous lands have been stolen and occupied by settlers, is called **settler colonialism.**

Because almost everyone in this class came from a country that had experienced colonial conquest, I asked: "What are some similarities and differences between settler colonialism and colonialism where the rulers are far away — like colonial control of India or the Philippines?" This was an exciting discussion for these students; we created a Venn diagram to record ideas. (In a class in which few students have direct experience to call on, it may be more of a distraction from the main idea.)

Next I projected an interactive map to demonstrate the rapidity of the conquest of North America. I asked students:

- What was the impact of Manifest Destiny on Indigenous peoples and cultures?
- What was the impact for European settlers?

We read "We Exist," a poem by Janice Gould, a member of the Maidu Tribe of Northern California, as a recent expression of Indigenous feelings about Manifest Destiny. Another option is "This Poem Is Taking Place on Stolen Land," by Cahuil-

la Native American poet Emily Clarke.

Then we repeated the process with two texts about Palestine. The first was a 1971 quote by then-Prime Minister Golda Meir: "This country [Israel] exists as the fulfillment of a promise made by God Himself."

The second was by David Ben-Gurion, who became prime minister of Israel from 1949 to 1954 and 1955 to 1963. He wrote this in a letter to his son in 1937 (before the Holocaust):

We will expel the Arabs and take their place. In each attack a decisive blow should be struck resulting in the destruction of homes and the expulsion of the population.

After we read both quotes aloud, the students discussed the following questions in pairs, and then we compared notes as a whole class:

- What do these quotes mean?
- How are they similar or different from the U.S. quotes?
- What questions do they raise in your mind?
- Why do you think these quotes — and this attitude — was so important? How do you think they have affected Palestinians? Jews in Israel? Jews in other parts of the world?

I explained to the students that Meir's statement is an expression of Zionism, the belief that the Jewish people are historically and/or religiously entitled to a Jewish state on all the land within the current borders of Israel plus Gaza and the West Bank (including all of Jerusalem) — and sometimes parts of Lebanon, Syria, Jordan, and Egypt as well. We then looked at a series of maps that illustrate the progressive conquest of Palestinian land by the Zionists.

I asked students: What has been the impact of the so-called Promised Land on Palestinians? What has been the impact for Zionist settlers?

This lesson often leads to deep discussions. In some classes, students have argued about our responsibility to the Indigenous people on the land that is now the United States. In this class, students got into a far-ranging discussion about the use of religion to justify colonial conquest.

To finish this introduction to parallels between settler colonialism in the United States and Palestine, we read Palestinian poet Mahmoud Darwish's beautiful poem "I Come from There."

Filling in the History

At this point, I provided some historical context. I used a brief history I wrote and stories of three Palestinians who were children or teenagers in 1948. My students are fortunate that I have a Palestinian colleague who comes into class and tells the history of the Nakba and its aftermath, using the story of his own family. Other possibilities include reading *The Lemon Tree* by Sandy Tolan or the multiple narratives approach to studying the Nakba from Samia Shoman's unit. (See "Independence or Catastrophe? Teaching Palestine Through Multiple Perspectives" on p. 41.)

Because most students have been taught that the formation of Israel was a reaction to the Holocaust, it's important to cover the pre-World War II history of Zionism. (See "Teaching the Seeds of Violence in Palestine-Israel" on p. 33.) For teachers interested in more background, *The Ethnic Cleansing of Palestine*, by Israeli historian Ilan Pappé is an excellent source. The four-part Nakba series on the Palestine Remix site contains a detailed history of the events leading up to and including 1948. (See the Resources section for more possibilities, p. 202.)

Voices of Palestinian Youth

Now it was time to look at the current impact of the walls and borders on Palestinian youth. We used five short videos created by teenage girls at Shoruq, a community center in Dheisheh Refugee Camp near Bethlehem. (See "Palestinian Girls Make Videos About Their Lives" in the video resources section of the Teach Palestine Project website.) I would add Farah Nabulsi's short film *The Present* (available on Netflix, see Resources). All of these resources are in Arabic with English subtitles. My Arabic-speaking students were excited to hear their home language as an expert voice; this experience is far too rare in most U.S. schools.

Afterward, I assigned journal writing and then we talked about what they learned:

- What surprised you?
- What is similar about being a youth in Palestine and in the United States? What is different?
- What do you think and feel about all of this?

Indigenous Peoples and the U.S.-Mexico Border

Next we explored the impact of the U.S.-Mexico border wall on people and the environment. I started with a journal-write and discussion:

- When you think about the U.S.-Mexico border, what images come to mind?
- Where do you get your ideas about the border — from personal experience? experiences of friends and/or family? The media?

Then we turned to research. "Border Wall Scars" by Alisa Reznick (*High Country News*, 2021) explores the environmental and human impact of the expansion of the border wall, from the perspective of the Tohono O'odham Nation, which has been torn in two by the border in Arizona. *American Scar: The Environmental Tragedy of the Border Wall* by Daniel Lombroso (New Yorker Documentary, 2022) is a moving video about the destruction of the desert and the impact on animal routes. "Nature Interrupted: Impact of the U.S./Mexico Border Wall on Wildlife" by Iván Carrillo (*Knowable Magazine*, June 2024) is an in-depth investigation of the impact of Trump's border wall expansion.

In terms of the impact of immigration across the border and the struggle for legal documentation, I would ask: What are the crossing-the-border stories in your classroom, school, and/or community? Otherwise, I can suggest excerpts from the young reader's edition of Reyna Grande's *The Distance Between Us* (for upper elementary and middle school) and Javier Zamora's *Solito: A Memoir* for high school.

Putting It All Together: Final Project

To get students thinking about the final project, I asked:

> When you think about everything we've learned about borders and walls in Palestine and at the U.S.-Mexico border, what patterns emerge? What's similar? What's different between the two situations? What do you think about the whole idea of borders and walls? Has your thinking changed from the beginning of the unit? In what ways?

This time, I gave them the choice of expressing their thoughts and feelings as a journal entry, a piece of art, or a brainstorming map. The next day, they shared and discussed their responses. Then I offered students three choices for a final project:

1. Create a children's book about borders and walls
2. Answer a set of specific questions on the unit (see Final Project handout)
3. Develop your own essay on some aspect of the material

I offered a number of choices for the final project because students' reactions to the unit were so varied. For example, Thomas, a recent immigrant from China, was a strong and conscientious student, one who helped others with their work. When my Palestinian colleague visited our class to describe his family's experience being forced from their village during the Nakba and his own experience growing up in a refugee camp, Thomas kept falling asleep. Three times, I woke him up and asked him to pay attention, but to no avail.

The next day, I asked him what happened: "What was the problem?"

He told me that in his English class they had been reading Elie Wiesel's *Night* and talking about the Holocaust. Thomas was confused about how Jews, who had been the victims of such horrible oppression, could be oppressors themselves. He couldn't take it in and fell asleep instead. I agreed that it was both confusing and upsetting.

"That's a huge contradiction, isn't it?" I said. "That a group of people could go through something so horrible and then do something so similar to another group of people. And you know, everyone who experienced the Holocaust didn't think the same way about it afterward. A few Holocaust survivors went on to fight for Palestinian rights — they didn't want what happened to them to happen to anyone else, ever again.

"Holding all that in your mind at the same time and trying to make sense of it, that's an important thing to be able to do. Maybe you could write your essay about how confused and upset this made you feel, and what you've learned from that."

Taking me up on the suggestion, he used his final paper to work through his thoughts and feelings.

I was impressed by how engaged students were throughout this unit, but I shouldn't have been surprised. The specifics of settler colonialism — and how it underlies everything that has followed in U.S. history — are critical to understanding our world today. Seeing Zionism as a more recent version of settler colonialism, this time on steroids, clarifies the ties between the United States and Israel — and the strong links between the struggle for justice here in the United States and in Palestine.

When I first taught this unit, other teachers would often say, "Palestine is so far away and isn't that relevant to our students. It's not a priority to teach it." Today, as we watch in horror the unfolding genocide in Gaza and the determination of the Palestinian people to hold onto their land and their future, it's never been clearer why we need to teach this, now and every year.

■■ ▪

Jody Sokolower is co-coordinator of the Teach Palestine Project of the Middle East Children's Alliance. She is a former managing editor of Rethinking Schools.

5

Challenging Zionism
and Antisemitism

Anti-Zionist Abecedarian

BY SAM SAX

ERIK RUIN | JUSTSEEDS

after you've finished
building your missiles & after your borders
collapse under the weight of their own split
databases
every worm in this
fertile & cursed
ground will be its own country.
home never was a place in dirt or even
inside the skin but rather
just exists in language. let me explain. my people
kiss books as a form of prayer. if dropped we
lift them to our lips &
mouth an honest & uncomplicated apology —
nowhere on earth belongs to us.
once a man welcomed me home as i entered the old city so i
pulled out a book of poems to show him my papers — my
queer city of paper — my people's ink
running through my blood.
settlers believe land can be possessed —
they carve their names into firearms &
use this to impersonate the dead — we are
visitors here on earth.
who but men blame the angels for the wild
exceptionalism of men?
yesterday a bird flew through an airport & i watched that border
zone collapse under its basic wings.

■ ■

Sam Sax is a queer, Jewish writer and educator. They're the author of Yr Dead
(McSweeney's, 2024). This poem originally appeared in the Washington Spectator.

What Antisemitism Is and What It is Not

BY NINA MEHTA AND DONNA NEVEL

To challenge antisemitism effectively, we need to know what antisemitism is — and what it is not. Knowing what antisemitism is not helps us resist false accusations of antisemitism directed at those fighting for Palestinian liberation.

What Is Antisemitism?

Antisemitism is discrimination, targeting, violence, and dehumanizing stereotypes directed at Jews because they are Jewish.

There are two distinct views of the history of antisemitism. One views antisemitism as eternal, as a natural phenomenon, and in isolation from other forms of oppression. It puts forth that antisemitism is never-ending, can't be understood, and can't be stopped. The Anti-Defamation League (ADL) and other conservative and right-wing Jewish organizations rely on the eternalist perspective, which sees Jews as always under threat — it is "us" (the Jewish people) against "them" (the rest of the world).

The other perspective — the one we adhere to — understands antisemitism as historically contextual, situated amidst interrelated conditions and struggles. That is, antisemitism interacts with specific political, social, and economic realities as well as with different targets of systemic violence and injustice. When looking at Jewish experience and the realities of antisemitism in different locations, context is critical.

Current Manifestations of Antisemitism

An extreme manifestation of antisemitism today is white nationalist violence. We have witnessed horrifying white nationalist violence directed at many of our communities — against immigrants, Muslims, Black, Queer and trans people, and Jews. Antisemitic white nationalist violence has included, among others, the 2018 murder of 11 congregants at the Tree of Life Synagogue in Pittsburgh; the 2019 shootings at a Chabad synagogue in Poway, California; antisemitic hate groups and rallies; the desecration of cemeteries; and bomb threats in Jewish spaces.

White nationalists employ conspiracy theories about Jewish power and control and about Jews as untrustworthy and sinister. These stereotypes and tropes have been used historically and continue to appear in images that recirculate. Here are two examples:

- Greed: the false beliefs that all Jews are rich, good with money, stingy, cheap, selfish, or obsessed with gaining more wealth. This stereotype originated in the Middle Ages, when money lending and tax collection were among the available occupations for many Jews.
- Global Domination: a false narrative that Jews are global puppet masters who control the media, the economy, and governments. This trope originated in *The Protocols of the Elders of Zion*, which claimed to document the secret meeting of powerful Jews conspiring to take over the world. This trope has circulated in terms like "Globalists" and "the Rothschilds," and today in the depiction of George Soros as an all-powerful "puppet master."

While we highlight places where antisemitism is most present and concerning, we recognize that antisemitic attitudes, views, and actions — like all forms of injustice — can show up among anyone who lives in our society.

What Antisemitism Is Not, and Why It Matters

Organized campaigns in support of Israel derail and mis-state the meaning of antisemitism and conflate it with criticism of Israel and Zionism. The Israeli state and its supporters have long hurled false accusations of antisemitism at supporters of Palestine, but this has intensified as the movement for Palestinian justice has grown and as more people protest displacement, oppression, and genocide.

Accusations of antisemitism related to Palestine and Israel take different forms. In our K–12 schools, high school students have been suspended for hanging Palestinian flags (including in schools with Israeli flags). Teachers have been disciplined for wearing keffiyehs and investigated for demanding that school officials recognize Israel's violence against the Palestinian people in public statements or for simply teaching Palestinian history.

We have seen resolutions — such as HR 894 — that state that anti-Zionism is antisemitism. Congressional hearings with university presidents have condemned anti-Zionist protests as antisemitism. These aim to penalize actions in support of justice for Palestinians and to criminalize those speaking out in universities and schools, workplaces, and communities against Israel's ongoing violence. These attacks have nothing to do with the fight against antisemitism, but rather are designed to destroy our movements for justice and harm those who speak out and take action.

Zionism and Anti-Zionism

Given the common conflation of anti-Zionism and antisemitism, it is important to understand what Zionism and anti-Zionism are. Zionism is the primary ideology that drove the establishment of Israel in the land of historic Palestine. Beginning in the late 19th century, as nationalism rose in Europe and as antisemitism intensified, the Zionist movement advocated, in word and action, for a Jewish state. Zionism resulted in the establishment of a Jewish-majority, supremacist nation-state in the land of historic Palestine and the expulsion of approximately 750,000 Palestinians from their land and homes, known as the Nakba, catastrophe in Arabic.

Anti-Zionists oppose the ideology of Zionism. Anti-Zionists stand against a nation-state with exclusive rights for Jews above others. Anti-Zionists support liberation and justice for the Palestinian people, including their right to return to their homes and land. Anti-Zionists believe in a future where all people on the land of historic Palestine live in freedom, safety, and equality.

Safety and Solidarity

An attack directed at Jews for being Jewish (which makes Jews unsafe) is different from a political position that challenges injustice in relation to Israel or Zionism (which does not make Jews unsafe). Someone may feel uncomfortable with that position but that is different from being unsafe. It is a crucial distinction.

When people refuse to push back against the conflation of antisemitism with opposition to Israel's policies or ideology, they end up privileging the uncomfortable feelings of some Zionists over the actual safety of Palestinians and those standing with the Palestinian people. As Palestinians and advocates for Palestinian liberation lose their jobs, are doxxed and harassed online, attacked physically, and face congressional censure for trying to save lives, it is clear who is made unsafe.

It's simple: Safety never grows from guns, checkpoints, walls, and a police state. True safety is built through forging solidarity with those fighting for a more just world. Working for Palestinian freedom and against antisemitism and all forms of injustice are intertwined. We must be committed to all of it.

■ ▪

Nina Mehta, an educator and researcher, and Donna Nevel, a community psychologist and educator, are co-directors of PARCEO, a resource, research, and education center that works with universities, schools, and community groups to strengthen their educational work and organizing for justice. PARCEO co-created two curricula: Project48's Palestinian Nakba curriculum and Challenging Antisemitism from a Framework of Collective Liberation.

Educators Beware:
The Anti-Defamation League Is Not the Social Justice Partner It Claims to Be

BY NORA LESTER MURAD

The Anti-Defamation League (ADL), calls itself "the leading anti-hate organization in the world." But it is not the social justice educational partner it claims to be. The ADL is a divisive political advocacy organization, and a leader among Zionist organizations — like the Jewish Community Relations Council (JCRC), American Jewish Committee (AJC), the Institute for Curriculum Services (ICS), and the Jewish Federations of North America — that reinforce unconditional support for Israel and erasure of Palestinians in schools across the United States.

The ADL's programs are widespread, with wholesome names like "No Place for Hate" and "A World of Difference." According to their website, in 2023 alone they reached 7 million students and provided professional development to 24,000 educators. The ADL makes it easy for districts and schools to partner with them: They provide free, ready-made materials, from lesson plans on antisemitism and the Holocaust, to professional development on anti-bias for educators, administrators, and even school police.

But the ADL's unfounded attacks on groups working for Palestinian rights, and the ways it undermines BIPOC communities have made it unwelcome among social justice groups. More than 300 organizations — from the Movement for Black Lives to the National Lawyers Guild to Red Nation — have signed on to the #DropTheADL campaign, which reminds progressive organizations that "the ADL is not an ally."

Inciting Fear Based on Unreliable and Manipulated Data

From news outlets to school officials, many people in the United States rely on the ADL for information about antisemitism. The ADL presents a terrifying picture of a crisis that escalates year over year. Speaking about the ADL's 2023 audit of antisemitic incidents, its CEO, Jonathan Greenblatt warned: "Antisemitism is nothing short of a national emergency, a five-alarm fire that is still raging across the country and in our local communities and campuses."

For decades, the ADL's statistics have been repeated by mainstream media without scrutiny. In the past few years, though, multiple analyses have pointed out the ADL's reliance on vague reports, lack of verification, and the lumping together of weighty and trivial incidents. *Jewish Currents* points out this "makes it more difficult to measure antisemitism in American life." The ADL also includes what they call "anti-Israel rallies" in their database of antisemitic incidents. In fact, the *Jewish Forward* newspaper reported that of the 3,000 "antisemitic incidents" recorded by the ADL in the first three months after October 7, 1,317 were rallies where activists expressed hostility toward Zionism, not Jews. These practices led to Wikipedia's recent designation of the ADL as a generally unreliable source. Wikipedia editors took this stance, they wrote, "due to significant evidence that the ADL acts as a pro-Israeli advocacy group and has repeatedly published false

and misleading statements as fact, unretracted, regarding the Israel/Palestine conflict. The general unreliability of the ADL extends to the intersection of the topics of antisemitism and the Israel/Palestine conflict."

ADL statistics are based on conflating criticism of Israel or the political ideology of Zionism with hatred of Jews. One way that the ADL promotes this conflation is by advocating to codify the International Holocaust Remembrance Alliance's (IHRA) working definition of antisemitism. The IHRA definition includes 11 examples, seven of which shut down criticism of Israel and Zionism. One example says that it is antisemitic to: "[deny] the Jewish people their right to self-determination, e.g., by claiming that the existence of a State of Israel is a racist endeavor." This enables the ADL to label as "antisemitic" any discussion of the more than 700,000 Palestinians expelled during Israel's founding as well as discussion of Israeli and international human rights organizations' finding that Israel is an apartheid state. The IHRA definition is the basis for a spate of laws against BDS (Boycott, Divestment, and Sanctions). These laws aim to control speech of public employees and contractors, including educators like Bahia Amawi, the Austin, Texas, public schools speech therapist fired for refusing to sign an anti-boycott pledge. It is also the basis of proposed bills that would deport immigrants without trial if arrested at Palestine-supporting events, strip funding from public schools if they fail to impose repressive measures on teachers or students who criticize Israel or uplift Palestinians.

The reality of antisemitism is more nuanced. On the one hand, antisemitism, along with other forms of racism, has clearly increased with the Trump-era emboldening of right-wing actors. Antisemitism has gained new visibility in chilling scenes like the 2018 Tree of Life Synagogue shooting in Pittsburgh that killed 11 people and wounded six, and the 2017 Charlottesville rally of white men marching through the streets chanting "Jews will not replace us!" Yet U.S. Jews no longer experience the discrimination (in housing, jobs, etc.) they did in previous periods, and they enjoy a relatively high standard of living on average,

having become integrated into the economic and political structures.

Israel's claims to act on behalf of world Jewry, even as it slaughters Palestinians, complicate matters. Peter Beinart, a prominent commentator on Jewish politics, notes that "three academic studies — one in the U.S., one in Belgium, one in Australia — over the last 20 years all show a strong correlation between substantial Israeli military operations that kill a lot of Palestinians and rise in reported antisemitic incidents." So, there may be a connection between Israeli violence against Palestinians and anger toward Jews. But how do we parse out what is and isn't actual antisemitism when both the Israeli government and the IHRA definition consider it hateful to use certain words and phrases to protest human rights violations against Palestinians?

The ADL's framing makes it difficult to see the role antisemitism and its weaponization play in upholding white supremacy. Instead, they falsely smear social justice movements, including those organizing against genocide, Islamophobia, and police violence — and they erase the Jewish communities who support and participate in those social justice movements. And when it misreports acts against Zionism as discrimination against Jews, it blurs the distinction between political disagreements and hatred against a group.

The ADL's conflation of anti-Zionism and antisemitism is racist because it implicates Palestinians, and supporters of Palestinian human rights, as antisemites who commit "hate acts" merely for talking about their own life experiences as refugees, living under Israeli occupation, or fighting colonialism.

Claiming to Support Students and Educators but Actually Bullying Them

The ADL leverages its reputation and relationships with policymakers and funders to rail against groups with whom it disagrees politically. Its CEO Jonathan Greenblatt characterized Black Lives Matter as "wrong on the facts and offensive in tone" when the Movement for Black Lives 2016 policy platform recognized links between U.S. policing and Israeli militarism. In 2022, the ADL declared Jewish Voice for Peace, Students for Justice in Palestine, and the Council on American Islamic Relations to be antisemitic. In November 2023, the *Intercept* reported that the ADL labeled Jewish organizations calling for a ceasefire "hate groups."

In schools, the ADL works with partners to bully educators and students by disparaging their reputations, calling for disciplinary action against them, and submitting formal complaints that subject schools, educators, and students to invasive and exhausting investigations.

For example, the ADL has played a leadership role in the right-wing opposition to liberated ethnic studies. In February 2024, in cooperation with the Louis D. Brandeis Center, the ADL filed a complaint with the U.S. Department of Education's Office for Civil Rights against the Berkeley Unified School District alleging that administrators failed to take action to stop the "nonstop bullying and harassment of Jewish students by peers and teachers." Civil rights organizations like Palestine Legal say the ADL and its partners are increasingly weaponizing Title VI of the Civil Rights Act of 1964, which bars discrimination based on race, national origin, and shared ancestry. By claiming that schools that allow criticism of Israel create a "hostile environment," they essentially argue that students who support Zionism — a political ideology — are a protected class under the law.

In response, some schools are clamping down on educators' freedom to teach and students' right to learn. After two high school students in Philadelphia made a podcast comparing the art of Palestinians with the art of enslaved people, it was selected by their teacher and vetted by their principal to be played at the school's week of Black History Month assemblies. But another teacher claimed the podcast was antisemitic and forwarded it to a local Zionist organization. The organization led a campaign that successfully pressured the school district to remove the podcast from the remaining assemblies. Although the podcast did not mention Jews or Zionism, the ADL nonetheless joined a call to pressure the school district to investigate the students' teacher Keziah Ridgeway, an award-winning anti-racist educator.

Months after joining the call to fire Ridgeway, the ADL brought a Title VI complaint against the School District of Philadelphia. In the complaint, the ADL advocates for the "suspension and expulsion" of students and the "suspension and termination" of teachers, who under the IHRA definition — which they encourage the district to adopt — have engaged in "discriminatory conduct" for being publicly critical of Zionism. With this approach, schools cannot cultivate space to untangle antisemitism from anti-Zionism and grapple with real antisemitic (and other racist) incidents in meaningful, restorative ways.

The ADL uses anti-critical race theory rhetoric to derail anti-racist curriculum, promoting a watered-down anti-bias pedagogy that hides rather than explores power, systemic analysis, and historic context. It denounces DEI programs in education and the private sector, including in a February 2024 appearance by Greenblatt on CNBC's *Squawk Box*, where he asserted the need to "overhaul DEI," because these programs, according to Greenblatt, "perpetuate the exclusion of Jews." Meanwhile, anti-racist educators argue that while all forms of bigotry and discrimination have their own histories and manifestations, they must all be understood in the context of white supremacy and fought together in a framework of collective liberation. The ADL's cynical efforts to privilege the comfort of some Jews over the human rights of Palestinians, and above the right of all students to learn in a safe and uncensored environment, should disqualify them from participating in any aspect of U.S. education.

■■ ▪

Nora Lester Murad is a writer, educator, and activist. Her young adult novel Ida in the Middle *won a 2023 Arab American Book Award, a 2024 Middle East Book Award, and a 2023 Skipping Stones Honor Award, and was a finalist for the 2024 Jane Addams Peace Association Children's Book Award. From a Jewish family, Murad raised three daughters in the West Bank with her Palestinian husband. She shares teaching and advocacy resources at www.IdaInTheMiddle.com and can be reached through her blog at www.NoraLesterMurad.com.*

The initiative to Drop the ADL from Schools, droptheadlfromschools.org, is part of the national #DropTheADL campaign, droptheadl.org.

No, Anti-Zionism Is Not Antisemitism

BY BILL BIGELOW

In 2023, the U.S. House of Representatives overwhelmingly passed a resolution — 311 to 14, with 92 voting "present" — that "clearly and firmly states that anti-Zionism is antisemitism."

It is not.

Yes, there are examples of the entanglement of anti-Zionism and antisemitism. But this resolution is an effort to silence critics of Israeli aggression and U.S. complicity by insisting that opposition to Zionism is — and has always been — antisemitic. Jewish Voice for Peace and IfNotNow activists featured in the film *Israelism* demonstrate how wrong this conflation is. But so does knowing some history of Zionism and Palestine.

The "Seeds of Violence" mixer described in *Teaching Palestine*'s history chapter (p. 33) covers early Zionist immigration to Palestine during the Ottoman period — late 19th, early 20th century — up through the first years of the British Mandate in the 1920s. In the activity, students attempt to "become" individuals whose lives intersected with one another — and who sometimes clashed over whether or not Palestine should become a "national home for the Jewish people," as Lord Balfour wrote in the fateful Balfour Declaration in 1917.

I include roles on Theodor Herzl, the "father of Zionism"; an idealistic young radical Zionist of the Second Aliyah Jewish migration to Palestine, which began about 1904; and Arthur Ruppin, the prominent Zionist land agent of the Jewish Agency in Palestine. As Herzl writes in his seminal *The Jewish State*, the Zionists' mission was to establish a Jewish "national homeland" in Palestine: "a rampart of Europe against Asia, an outpost of civilization as opposed to barbarism."

One role features Elias Sursuq, a wealthy absentee Beirut landlord who owned vast tracts in

MOLLY CRABAPPLE

Palestine and was happy to profit from land sales to the new arrivals from Europe. Landlords like Sursuq sold prime agricultural land to Zionists who had no place for Palestinians in their planned national homeland and expelled peasants — *fellahin* — who'd lived on and farmed the land for generations. As Ruppin wrote, "We are bound in each case of the purchase of land and its settlement to remove the peasants who cultivated the land so far, both owners of the land and tenants."

Palestinians resisted their displacement by Zionist settlers. Peasants organized and fought to hold on to their land, supported by journalists, who wrote articles and editorials warning about the Zionists' ultimate plans for Palestine. As editor 'Isa al-'Isa wrote in 1914: "[We are] a nation threatened with disappearance by the Zionist tide in this Palestinian land . . . a nation that is threatened in its very being with expulsion from its homeland."

But here's the thing: In the world — and in the individuals students encounter in the role play — some of the fiercest critics of Zionism were other Jews. Students meet Yosef Castel, a Sephardi Jew whose family had lived in Jerusalem since King Ferdinand and Queen Isabella expelled the Jews from Spain in 1492. He and other Sephardi Jews lived contentedly, as Jacob Yehoshua wrote, in "joint compounds of Jews and Muslims. We were like one family. . . . Our children played with their [the Muslim] children in the yard, and if children from the neighborhood hurt us, the Muslim children who lived in our compound protected us. They were our allies." Many Sephardi Jews, like Castel, opposed the ethnic separatism that Zionists were so militantly committed to. In 1921, Castel wrote, "Both sides [Palestinians and Zionists] are fighting each other over a single land [Palestine], and they must, as a matter of historical necessity, live in it together and peacefully develop their national homes in the same land, which is destined to be one state."

Another anti-Zionist Jew who students encounter is Pati Kremer, a member of the socialist Jewish Bund in what was then Russia. As her role indicates, "Working-class Jews had a choice: socialism or Zionism." The Zionists urged flight instead of fight. While members of the Bund were committed to the struggle for Jewish cultural rights and socialism in Eastern Europe, Zionists saw hope only in immigration to Palestine. As Kremer's role articulates, working-class Jews should have "no desire to go to Palestine, where Jewish capitalists would continue to exploit us."

Also featured in the role play is the Christian Zionist President Woodrow Wilson, who in 1919 was petitioned by prominent anti-Zionist U.S. Jews — congressmen, former ambassadors and consuls, surgeons, businessmen, rabbis, professors, attorneys, and even Adolph Ochs, publisher of the *New York Times*. The March 5, 1919, *Times* published the full text of the anti-Zionist petition, "setting forth our objections to the establishment of a Jewish State in Palestine . . . and to the segregation of the Jews as a nationalistic unit in any country." Petitioners wrote that "The American Zionists represent, according to the most recent statistics available, only a small proportion of the Jews living in this country . . ."

The petition offered four arguments against Zionism: 1. The "establishment of a sovereign state in Palestine" implied that Jews in other countries held a "double allegiance." Zionists are "under the spell of an emotional romanticism or of a religious sentiment fostered by centuries of gloom." 2. Not all Jews will be able to immigrate to Palestine, and in many countries, Jews will be branded as aliens, it will put their safety at risk, and justify more repressive legislation. 3. There are other people living in Palestine, and Zionist settlement will "provoke bitter controversies." These "bitter and sanguinary conflicts . . . would be inevitable . . ." 4. "[T]he reestablishment in Palestine of a distinctively Jewish State is utterly opposed to the principles of democracy . . ."

Finally, it is worth remembering, that there were — and are today — Zionists who are antisemitic. For example, as students learn in the role play, Lord Balfour himself was both a Zionist and an antisemite who pushed the 1905 Aliens Act in Great Britain, expressly to keep out Jews — "undesirable immigrants" — fleeing the horrors of Eastern European pogroms.

In the role play, students have conversations that surface different perspectives on Palestine, Zionism, and justice. The seeds of today's violence were planted in those turn-of-the-century years — by the choices made and the alternatives left on the table. Students can see it themselves as they encounter conflicting visions for the future of Palestine.

It is not simply my opinion that anti-Zionism is not necessarily antisemitism, as the U.S. House of Representatives insists. That's what history teaches. And this is as true today as it was 100 years ago — as mentioned, witness the inspirational anti-Zionist activism of groups like Jewish Voice for Peace and IfNotNow. Educators should not be bullied by politicians — or by their own administrators — who use phony claims about anti-Zionism in their attempt to suppress a curriculum that seeks to honestly understand the dynamics that led to today's tragic events in historic Palestine. Zionism needs a critical look in our classrooms — it's sound history, it's good teaching.

◼◻

Bill Bigelow (bbpdx@aol.com) is curriculum editor of Rethinking Schools.

The Antisemitism Awareness Act Bars the Teaching of Modern Jewish History

BY BENJAMIN BALTHASER

SEAN GALLUP | GETTY IMAGES

The writer Mike Gold, whose *Jews Without Money* was arguably the most influential literary novel by a Jewish American in the mid-20th century, was a committed anti-Zionist.

His funny and often tragic tale of working-class Jewish immigrants in New York City cheers early 20th-century Jewish life, celebrating Jewish gangsters, prostitutes, revolutionaries, peddlers, house painters, doctors, Hasidic rabbis — all but a lone figure: a "Zionist dry goods merchant" who rigs votes, undermines labor unions, and engages in racist real-estate deals.

Gold, who was the editor of the influential left-wing arts and culture journal *New Masses*, published other Jewish writers in the 1930s who shared his disdain for the Jewish nationalists in Mandatory Palestine, referring to Zionists as "fascists" and to the Revisionist Zionist Vladimir Jabotinsky as a "Jewish Mussolini."

I mention Gold as his novel and many essays would be all but inadmissible in my classroom and in Jewish Studies classrooms under the Antisemitism Awareness Act.

This law, requiring the Department of Education to adopt the definition of antisemitism put forth by the International Holocaust Remembrance Alliance, says antisemitism is not only "hatred of Jews" but prohibits criticism of Israel.

Declaring Israel a "racist endeavor," or "applying double standards" to Israel that one would not apply to "any other democratic nation," or "drawing comparisons of contemporary Israeli policy to that of the Nazis" are, according to this act, equivalent to discriminating against or defaming Jewish people.

There is no other definition of bigotry in the world that equates criticism of a state, even harsh and unfair criticism, with discrimination or bigotry against the state's people. If one claimed that denunciations of the Russian empire are "anti-Slavic" or "racist against Russians," we would immediately see through that as just a defense of Russian state interests.

Perhaps the strangest part of the push for the government to adopt the IHRA definition of antisemitism as part of federal civil rights law is just how much Jewish history and culture would be banned from classrooms. Hannah Arendt, one of the most important Jewish philosophers of the 20th century and herself a Holocaust refugee, abandoned Zionism by the mid-1940s to become one of Zionism's most scathing critics when it became clear that Israel would become not a state for all its people but only for Jews.

Rabbi Elmer Berger, head of Reform Judaism's American Council for Judaism, went even further in the 1950s to state that there is nothing in the Jewish tradition suggesting that Jews had a special ethnic right to a nation at all. Sigmund Freud referred to Zionism as "baseless fanaticism"; Albert Einstein referred to the Irgun, the pre-state Zionist paramilitary organization, as "Nazis."

Tony Kushner, Noam Chomsky, Howard Zinn, Abbie Hoffman, Lenny Bruce, Philip Roth, Grace Paley, Jonathan Glazer, Walter Benjamin, Adrienne Rich, Wallace Shawn, Daniel Boyarin, Shaul Magid, Judith Butler and Ed Asner are among countless Jews who are considered "antisemitic" under the new law, despite many being not only key figures in Jewish arts and letters, but leaders in the field of Jewish studies.

The critique of Zionism among American Jews is not mere opinions of isolated Jewish individuals, but rather a strong, living current in American Jewish secular and religious life. It represents long-standing Jewish traditions that criticize militarism, the violence of nation-states, and racial exclusion. One-third of American Jews under 40 consider Israel's assault on Gaza to be a "genocide" and two-fifths of American Jews of the same age range consider Israel to be an "apartheid state." The new antisemitism law could silence vast swaths of Jews within educational institutions. It would in some ways be the most punitive law against Jews to be enacted in the United States since the Immigration Act of 1924.

Of course, many Jews believe that Israel represents them, and is inseparable from their form of Jewish religion or cultural practice. There are also many Jews who have signaled that Israel does not represent them or their conception of Jewish life and identity.

Congress has no business defining what it means to be Jewish.

Of course, this is not only a Jewish question. Silencing critics of Israel is a violation of free speech and academic freedom, ignores Palestinian narratives, and threatens voices calling for a peaceful future for all in the Holy Land. The appearance of the U.S. government taking sides in a contentious debate will only inflame those who feel Jews have too much power and are unfairly favored by the last global superpower.

There is something just very un-Jewish about such a law. Jewish custom is alive with debate, dissonance, disagreement. "Two Jews, three opinions" is a well-known Jewish maxim describing a shared culture of robust, vigorous disagreement.

Freedom of speech is a sacred principle of Jewish life, and American life. This is why it's essential to oppose efforts to silence the movement for justice in Palestine by equating criticism of Israel with antisemitism.

Benjamin Balthaser is an associate professor of Multi-Ethnic U.S. Literature at Indiana University South Bend. A version of this article was originally published in the Hill.

We Are American Jewish Educators, and We Demand Justice for Palestinians

BY HANNAH KLEIN AND JAKE ROTH

JOE BRUSKY

The majority of the dead in Gaza are civilians; far too many are children. We are Jewish educators, and we refuse to remain silent in the face of these atrocities. As teachers, we work with children every day, and our love and care for them extends beyond our classrooms.

We call for justice in Palestine because we are educators, but also because we are union members with the United Teachers Los Angeles (UTLA), who are part of a movement for social and economic justice in Los Angeles and beyond. As union activists, the right of all people to a safe place to call home is one of our most deeply held beliefs, along with our faith in the power of solidarity and collective action to change the world.

As Jews, we know that our people's safety is bound up in the safety of all people. We also come from a tradition that empathizes with the struggles of all oppressed people — we refuse to make an exception for Palestinians just because their oppressors are Jewish.

Our Jewish Values

We were brought up with strong Jewish identities, attending synagogue, celebrating Jewish holidays, and immersing ourselves in Jewish culture, community, and history. As children we learned about the value of Tikkun Olam — "mending the world."

Our people participated in the Civil Rights Movement, the anti-Vietnam War movement, the feminist movement, the movement for LGBTQ liberation, and the labor movement. To be Jewish means to come from the tradition of Jewish volunteers for the registration of Black voters during the Civil Rights Movement, who made up nearly a third of white volunteers, and who sometimes paid for their dedication with their lives. Being Jewish means to come from the tradition of the Jewish workers who helped build the U.S. labor movement into an engine for transformative social change, winning the eight-hour workday, Social Security, and other reforms that make life more bearable for working people.

But to be Jewish also means that we came from generations of traumatic experiences of exclusion, dehumanization, and dispossession. Many Eastern European families came to this country after being expelled from their homes in pogroms. Many in our communities survived the Holocaust, and we carry the names and memories of those who didn't. We cannot forget the horrific pain our people have endured, caused by racialized hatred and empowered by complacency and ignorance, and it calls us to fight bigotry wherever we see it. Never again means never again for anyone, not just our people.

> As Jews, we know that our people's safety is bound up in the safety of all people.

Refusing the Palestinian Exception

We have been told that Israel is a safe haven for Jews, a homeland to protect us from antisemitic hatred. We were taught about kibbutzim where people modeled cooperative economic systems, about trees planted in the desert, and about folk dances joyously revived.

But we weren't taught about the oppression, dispossession, and dehumanization that the Palestinian people endured as Israel was created, and that continues to this day. We weren't taught about the Nakba, the ethnic cleansing of Palestine between 1947 and 1949, in which 15,000 people died and 750,000 were displaced. We weren't taught about the apartheid system that confers lower status and fewer rights to Palestinians living in Israel and the Occupied Palestinian Territories. We weren't taught about the settlements, the checkpoints, the prisons, the raids, the evictions, or the bombs.

We learned what Israel has meant for Palestinians outside of mainstream U.S. Jewish institutions, as we pursued deeper understanding — another important Jewish value conferred onto us in our upbringing: the value of inquiry, debate, and dissent. We were taught not to accept what we were told as absolute truth, but to learn more, to look at situations from different perspectives, ask questions, and think for ourselves.

What we learned about Israel produced a cognitive dissonance with our Jewish values and led us to seek out other Jews and allies in social justice movements who saw the oppression of the Palestinian people, carried out supposedly in our name. It led us to organizations like Jewish Voice for Peace and IfNotNow, Jewish-led organizations that oppose U.S.-backed Israeli occupation and apartheid. We are part of a growing current within the Jewish community that does not adhere to Zionism, the ideology that supports an exclusivist Jewish ethnostate in Israel. This alternative current sees our liberation as bound up in the liberation of Palestinian people and all people.

A Wave of Opposition

The cognitive dissonance of Israel's stated claims as a bastion of security against genocide — while simultaneously carrying out the systematic destruction of Palestinian life, infrastructure, and history — has saddened and bewildered us. We are haunted by the horrific images of human destruction, news of attacks on hospitals and refugee camps, and genocidal rhetoric from members of the Israeli government.

As U.S. Jews, it's impossible to see how anybody can square the concept of Tikkun Olam, mending the world, with the atrocities carried out by the Israel Defense Forces.

We know we are not alone in this frustration. In 2005, 170 Palestinian civil organizations — including teacher and other unions, medical associations, and religious and humanitarian organizations — called for an international movement to boycott, divest from, and sanction Israel. That movement has grown tremendously during the 2023–24 Israeli assault on Gaza.

We have seen huge demonstrations around the world, including in the United States. We have seen direct actions led by fellow Jews, including an occupation of the U.S. Capitol organized by Jewish Voice for Peace and a highway shutdown here in L.A. led by IfNotNow. Growing numbers of Jews refuse to support the ethnic cleansing of the Palestinian territories in our name.

We have seen the argument that the genocidal assault on Gaza must continue for the safety of Jews in Israel, as well as Jews globally. We reject this framing as it ignores the obvious: the oppression of Palestinians endangers Jews living in or near the conflict zone and stokes antisemitism and anti-Jewish violence worldwide as legitimate criticism of Israel collides with old tropes and hatreds. Israeli apartheid may exist for the purpose of Jewish safety in theory, but in reality its consequence is the opposite.

There Is Power in a Union

In our time as UTLA rank-and-file members, we have organized for the schools our students deserve and for social and economic justice. This includes our Beyond Recovery contract campaign that culminated in the 2023 solidarity strike with SEIU 99 and led to monumental wins for our schools and communities. We know that it is not enough to change the conditions for students inside our buildings — our schools exist in a larger social context. Injustice and oppression outside our school walls follows us and our students into our classrooms. This is why we fight for housing justice and to mitigate the impacts of climate change in our contract campaigns. This is why we must also advocate for those affected by Israel's siege on Gaza, including our Palestinian, Muslim, and Jewish students who should not be expected to bear the burden of these injustices alone.

We still hear that there's not enough money to realize the promise of public education in Los Angeles and other districts around the country. Meanwhile, our country sends billions of dollars of weaponry to Israel. We need to fund our schools, not destroy Palestinian ones.

As a union of educators, we have a responsibility to model a commitment to justice for our students and their families, many of whom look to us for moral clarity in response to what they see on the news. Furthermore, this issue directly affects our members and our students, some of whom have lost family members in Israel, Gaza, and surrounding areas, and all of whom attend schools starved by austerity.

Every day more lives are lost. Today, in Gaza, children are alive who may not be alive tomorrow. Let's get on the right side of history, demand, and take action for justice in Palestine.

■■ ▪

Hannah Klein and Jake Roth are teachers in the Los Angeles Unified School District and members of United Teachers Los Angeles. An earlier version of this article appeared in Jacobin.

6

Solidarity with Palestine

"If I Must Die"

BY REFAAT ALAREER

If I must die,
you must live
to tell my story
to sell my things
to buy a piece of cloth
and some strings,
(make it white with a long tail)
so that a child, somewhere in Gaza
while looking heaven in the eye
awaiting his dad who left in a blaze—
and bid no one farewell
not even to his flesh
not even to himself—
sees the kite, my kite you made, flying
up above
and thinks for a moment an angel is there
bringing back love
If I must die
let it bring hope
let it be a tale

Refaat Alareer was a professor of world literature and creative writing at the Islamic University of Gaza and the editor of Gaza Writes Back: Short Stories from Young Writers in Gaza, Palestine. *He was killed by an IDF airstrike on Dec. 6, 2023, along with his brother, nephew, his sister, and three of her children.*

Teaching Solidarity: The Black Freedom Struggle and Palestine-Israel

BY HANNAH GANN, NICK PALAZZOLO, KEZIAH RIDGEWAY, AND ADAM SANCHEZ

"**S**olidarity with #Ferguson. Remember to not touch your face when tear-gassed or put water on it. Instead use milk or coke!" tweeted Ramallah-based Mariam Barghouti in 2014. When protests of the police murder of Michael Brown in Ferguson, Missouri, were brutally repressed by the National Guard during the first wave of the Black Lives Matter Movement, Palestinians like Barghouti took to Twitter to advise U.S. protesters on how to deal with the tear gas unleashed on them. After all, the tear gas used on Palestinians in the Occupied Territories, is made in the United States. This moment and countless expressions of solidarity since have reignited ties between the Black and Palestinian struggles for freedom.

How Black people in the United States should respond to Israel and to Palestine became contentious in the 1960s and '70s. There had been a long-established Black-Jewish Civil Rights coalition in the United States. Religious Black Americans identified with the story of enslaved Hebrews fleeing Egypt for "the promised land." Jewish experiences of antisemitism made many particularly sensitive to the oppression of others. Several Jewish Americans were founders of the NAACP. The Holocaust, and the white supremacist ideology that drove it, further cemented bonds between Black and Jewish communities, while also increasing support for Zionism amongst Jews in the United States. As the Civil Rights Movement emerged, many Jewish Americans donated time and money to the cause, and some expected Black Americans to reciprocate with support for Israel.

SAFIA LATIF

But the Black freedom struggle took a decisive anti-imperialist turn in the late 1960s, as many, including Martin Luther King Jr., began speaking out against the U.S. war in Vietnam. Black American activists increasingly drew inspiration from and influenced the burgeoning anti-colonial resistance across Africa and the Global South.

As Israel became central to U.S. foreign policy in the Middle East, many Black leaders began to investigate the plight of Palestinians. Israel's strikes against its Arab neighbors in the June 1967 (Six-Day) War and its subsequent occupation of Palestinian territories encouraged many to speak out for the first time. Black Power activists increasingly saw the Palestinians as allies in a common struggle against a global U.S. empire driven by and for racial capitalism. They attempted to build solidarity to highlight what they viewed as the racism inherent in the occupation of Palestine and the colonialism inherent in the subjugation of Black Americans. It is in this context that Palestine-Israel became a major focus of Black organizers.

This lesson highlights the complexity and diversity of thought as Civil Rights and Black Power leaders and organizations developed their views on Palestine-Israel. Students work in groups to examine how six different leaders and organizations (Malcolm X, Martin Luther King Jr., Bayard Rustin, the NAACP, the Student Nonviolent Coordinating Committee, and the Black Panther Party) articulated their solidarity with Palestine, their support for Israel, or their attempt to strike a balance between. Students become experts on one perspective and then share their knowledge with others. In seeing how Black Americans recognized common connections and shared struggle with people of different nationalities, we hope students will deepen their own global curiosity and empathy.

After exploring Black views on Palestine-Israel in the 1960s and '70s, students join this complex conversation through role play. They imagine themselves as part of a U.S. organization fighting for racial justice in 1975, when the United Nations passed Resolution 3379, declaring that Zionism is a form of racism. Then, drawing on arguments they read previously from Black leaders and organizations, students craft an argument about whether the United States should support U.N. Resolution 3379.

Although this is a history lesson, some students will see parallels to current debates. There have been powerful expressions of solidarity with Palestinians from Black intellectual and political leaders such as Angela Davis, Alice Walker, Michelle Alexander, Cornel West, and Ilhan Omar, as well as organizations like the Movement for Black Lives. At the same time, other Black leaders, like those in the Congressional Black Caucus who visited Israel on a delegation organized by the lobbying group the American Israel Public Affairs Committee, continue to support what they call "Israel's right to self-defense." As history teachers in Philadelphia, the first and still one of the few places that requires high school students to take an African American history course, we aimed to build on Dr. Martin Luther King Jr.'s assertion that "No one is free until we all are free" and create a lesson to deepen students' understanding of Black internationalist perspectives — perspectives key to shaping the struggle for collective liberation.

Hannah Gann is a teacher at the Workshop School in Philadelphia and a founding member of Philly Educators for Palestine. She is also an active part of the Racial Justice Organizing Committee, West Philly Participatory Defense Hub, and Food Not Bombs Solidarity.

Nick Palazzolo coordinates the International Baccalaureate Diploma Program at Central High School in Philadelphia and teaches History for the IB, Queer Studies, and African American History. He was a Zinn Education Project 2022–2023 Prentiss Charney Fellow and serves on the leadership team of Building Anti-Racist White Educators.

Keziah Ridgeway is an educator, author, activist, mother, and wife born and raised in Philadelphia. She is a member of the Racial Justice Organizing Committee, a curriculum writer, professional development coordinator, and a 2020 Lindback Distinguished Teacher Award Winner.

Adam Sanchez is the managing editor of Rethinking Schools.

Visit zinnedproject.org/solidarity to access the full lesson plan, handouts, and student readings. Below are excerpts from the student readings in this lesson, which draw from Michael Fischbach's *Black Power and Palestine.*

Malcolm X and Palestine-Israel

Malcolm X was assassinated in 1965, two years before the war between Israel and the surrounding Arab nations would compel Black leaders in the United States to respond to the Israeli-Palestinian conflict. But Malcolm's early pro-Palestinian, internationalist perspective paved the way for the Student Nonviolent Coordinating Committee's and the Black Panther Party's wider popularization of support for the Palestinian struggle.

Malcolm's introduction to the Palestinian cause was rooted in his conversion to the Nation of Islam (NOI). Between 1952 and 1964, Malcolm served as a minister and national spokesperson for the NOI. The NOI encouraged Black people to connect with their African heritage and called attention to international events. They maintained contact with Muslims throughout the world, including Palestinians.

As a member of the Nation of Islam, Malcolm advocated for Black people in the United States to separate from white people and create their own nation. In discussing Jewish nationalism, Malcolm combined affirmation of Jewish aspirations for their own country, with condemnation of Zionism. After a discussion at Boston University, Malcolm referenced Israel to justify why Blacks asking for their own land was reasonable and not anti-white. "Look at Israel. Israel has a nation of her own," Malcolm asserted. "They don't call Jews anti-anything because they have Israel. They want a nation of their own, the same way we do."

While using Jewish nationalism to explain Black nationalism, Malcolm was nevertheless intensely critical of the Zionist project, and increasingly so after he broke from the Nation of Islam and moved away from their perspective of building "a nation within a nation."

Student Nonviolent Coordinating Committee (SNCC) and Palestine-Israel

In August of 1967, Ethel Minor published an article in the Student Nonviolent Coordinating Committee (SNCC) newsletter criticizing Israel. Though intended to educate SNCC activists and not as an official statement, it launched the Black Power movement's growing solidarity with Palestinians into public life.

Minor met Palestinians while studying at the University of Illinois and worked with both the Nation of Islam and Malcolm X's Organization of Afro-American Unity. She joined SNCC in 1965 and organized a Middle East study group on understanding Palestine-Israel.

In the months leading up to the 1967 Arab-Israeli War, staff at SNCC's Atlanta headquarters began working on background papers to educate SNCC activists about the region. When the war began, SNCC's research department issued news summaries alongside a four-page section titled "History of Zionism and the Israeli-Arab Conflict."

When SNCC's central committee met that month to discuss a position on the war, they could not agree. Some were concerned that such a position would harm their fundraising efforts, since many Jews financially contributed to SNCC. Ethel Minor's article was a response to the committee's request for more information.

Minor listed 32 statements under the title "The Palestine Problem: Test Your Knowledge" in response to the question "Do you know?" All criticized Zionism and Israel.

Martin Luther King Jr. and Palestine-Israel

In the years after Martin Luther King's assassination, champions of both Israel and Palestine have claimed King's support for their cause. This is both because King's position on the conflict was complex and deliberately careful and because King's politics were radicalizing in response to the growing militancy of young Black activists — particularly in the Student Nonviolent Coordinating Committee (SNCC).

King worked closely with Jews and Jewish organizations in the United States — many of which were steadfast supporters of Israel. Jews were also disproportionately represented among contributors to King's organization the Southern Christian Leadership Conference (SCLC). And as a Christian minister, King was intimately familiar with the biblical justifications that were used by Israel's supporters to stake claim to the land: that God gave the ancient Hebrews the Promised Land in ancient Canaan (land that today encompasses Israel, the Occupied Territories of the West Bank and Gaza, Jordan, and southern portions of Syria and Lebanon). Comparisons of Black suffering with that of the Hebrew slaves were commonplace in Black Protestant churches and were made by King himself in the speech he gave the night before his assassination.

In this light, it is no surprise that on multiple occasions King asserted that "Israel's right to exist as a state in security is incontestable" and that he considered Israel to be "one of the greatest outposts of democracy in the world."

But King was also not oblivious to the Palestinian perspective. In his only trip to the biblical Holy Land in 1959, King met with Palestinian dignitaries after hearing about the plight of Palestinians directly from a doctor in the West Bank whose family had been ordered to evacuate from West Jerusalem in 1948.

Most of what King said about Palestine-Israel came in the last few years of his life in response to the so-called Six-Day War. King had come out forcefully against the war in Vietnam previously that year and was worried about being associated with Israel's war and military occupation. He told his advisers that Israel "now faces the danger of being smug and unyielding."

Bayard Rustin and Palestine-Israel

Though not as well known as Martin Luther King or Malcolm X, Bayard Rustin was a key Civil Rights Movement leader. He co-founded the Congress of Racial Equality and was the main organizer of the 1963 March on Washington and the 1964 New York City school boycott, the largest civil rights protest of the decade.

In 1965, Rustin transitioned from "protest to politics" as he put it in an essay published in *Commentary* magazine. He argued that after desegregating public accommodations and achieving voting rights, the movement's ability to address the "social and economic welfare" of Black people depended on building "a coalition of progressive forces" that would amass influence within the Democratic Party.

As part of this new strategy, Rustin worried that growing Black critiques of Israel would ruin the Black-Jewish coalition he had worked to build. Fellow pacifist David McReynolds recalled that Rustin also felt deep empathy with Jews, rooted in his identification with them as an oppressed people. Finally, Rustin believed that U.S. support for Israel would go a long way in promoting democracy by countering the Soviet Union.

Rustin sprang into action when President Nixon held up the sale of U.S. military aircraft to Israel in an effort to broker a peace deal between Egypt and Israel in 1970. Israel and U.S. Jewish organizations viewed Nixon's efforts for Israeli withdrawal from Sinai as a policy of appeasement of the Arab states. Rustin agreed.

On June 28, 1970, he took out a full-page advertisement in the *New York Times* and *Washington Post* titled "An Appeal by Black Americans for United States Support to Israel." He mobilized 64 signatures from politicians, athletes, clergymen, and civil rights leaders.

NAACP and Palestine-Israel

When the Six-Day War began in 1967, the Conference of Presidents of Major American Jewish Organizations asked Roy Wilkins, executive director of the National Association for the Advancement of Colored People (NAACP), to issue a statement of support for a pro-Israel rally.

The NAACP board of directors could not agree on how to respond. Some wanted to maintain the NAACP policy of avoiding issues unrelated to civil rights. The NAACP had not taken a stance on the Vietnam War. Others said that the board should consider the financial contributions of Jewish Americans. In addition, Jews were among the founders of the NAACP and the organization had praised the formation of Israel at its convention in 1948.

Wilkins did not issue a statement. In the end, 20 NAACP board members approved issuing a supportive statement, 14 voted against. Although never published, Wilkins wrote: "A people persecuted down through the centuries has been returned to its motherland and through sacrifice, industry, knowledge, and ingenuity has made a land bloom and has built a bastion of democracy." Unwilling to recognize Arab grievances as anything other than a hatred of Jews, Wilkins used Islamophobic rhetoric: "Never again must it be possible for 14 nations, united only in a common and fanatic hatred of a people and its religion, to surround, militarily, another nation and announce brazenly to a stunned world that their concerted mission is one of extermination."

At the end of the summer, developments within the burgeoning Black Power movement provided Wilkins and the NAACP the opportunity for a more public defense of Israel. The Student Nonviolent Coordinating Committee (SNCC) published a newsletter critical of Zionism and Israel. The NAACP received angry letters from Jews indicating that they would no longer donate to Black causes.

Wilkins was concerned about the long-standing Black-Jewish coalition for civil rights.

The Black Panther Party and Palestine-Israel

In July 1967, only nine months after the Black Panther Party for Self-Defense formed in Oakland, California, the BPP newspaper published an article condemning Israel's preemptive attack on Egypt and Syria, in what became known as the Six-Day War. The war led to Israel's annexation and occupation of the Sinai Peninsula, the Gaza Strip, the West Bank, East Jerusalem, and the Golan Heights. In 1968, the Black Panther newspaper condemned camps for Palestinian refugees as "concentration camps," championed the Palestinian guerrilla fighters in Fatah, and proclaimed that "Israel IS because Palestine's right to be was canceled."

Over the next two years, the Black Panther paper published 33 articles supporting Palestinian liberation and criticizing Israel. At a 1970 press conference, BPP co-founder Huey P. Newton said that Minister of Information Eldridge Cleaver and Field Marshall Donald Cox were "in daily contact with the Palestinian Liberation Organization" at the BPP embassy in Algeria. BPP Communication Secretary Kathleen Cleaver, who largely ran the Panthers' office in Algiers, worked to forge links between Palestine Liberation Organization leaders and the Panthers.

The Black Panthers saw themselves in a global revolutionary struggle against capitalism, imperialism, and white supremacy directed against peoples of color, including Palestinians. The increasingly strong military, economic, and diplomatic support for Israel by the United States connected the fight for Palestinian liberation to the Black freedom struggle. "The link between America's undercover support of colonialism abroad and the bondage of the Negro at home becomes increasingly clear. . . . [Our] fight is one and the same," Eldridge Cleaver stated in 1968. "It is at this point, at the juncture of foreign policy, that the Negro revolution becomes one with the world revolution."

Black Panther Party Captain Aaron Dixon on Internationalism, Black Freedom, and the Palestinian Liberation Struggle

BY JESSE HAGOPIAN

BY JOE MABEL | COMMONS.WIKIMEDIA.ORG

Aaron Dixon is an activist and author. He co-founded the Seattle chapter of the Black Panther Party — the first chapter outside of California — in 1968 when he was 19 years old. In 1972, Dixon moved to Oakland to work with Huey P. Newton and Bobby Seale, and serve as a bodyguard for Elaine Brown, who became chairperson of the Black Panther Party in 1974. In 2006, Dixon ran for a seat in the U.S. Senate on the Green Party ticket in opposition to the Iraq War. In 2012, following the publication of his memoir My People Are Rising, *Dixon traveled to Palestine to stay with Palestinian families in Jerusalem and the West Bank and learn more about their culture and their struggle for justice.*

On May 29, 2024, I spoke to Dixon about Israel's genocide in Gaza and the connection between Black and Palestinian liberation. This interview has been edited for clarity.

JESSE HAGOPIAN: Tell me more about how you came to develop your understanding of Palestine and Israel. When did you first become aware of the struggle for a free Palestine?

AARON DIXON: I only vaguely remember those things that happened in 1967. I didn't really get clued in about Palestine until after I joined the

Black Panther Party and started reading the international section of the Black Panther Party newspaper. Weekly, there were articles in the *Black Panther Intercommunal News Service* talking about the Palestinian struggle.

JH: The internationalism of the Black Panther Party is an inspiration to me. How did that perspective develop in the Panthers?

AD: Most of that can be attributed to Huey [Newton], because he just devoured books, and he read a lot of different kind of books from all over the world — he wasn't reading books just about the struggle in America. He had the wisdom to know the importance of having a newspaper and the newspaper was developed as soon as the [Black Panther] Party started. He knew we had to have our own news media so we could define what was happening, not just in America, but internationally.

JH: And it wasn't only the BPP that supported Palestine. Many of the Black Power organizations and leaders of 1960s and '70s did. Why has the Black freedom struggle and Palestinian liberation movement been so intertwined?

AD: Because we are all people of color, and we are all suffering from the same things. From the same guns and the same bullets. The IDF [Israel Defense Forces] has been training police departments in America that brutalize Black people for a while now. They use the same tactics against Palestinian people, so we can't help but support our Palestinian brothers and sisters. They are suffering tremendously from the same imperialists who cause our suffering. We have suffered in this country for hundreds of years. Native people have suffered. That is why, for the most part, I find that Black people and people of color support Palestine.

JH: You had a chance to visit Palestine. Tell me about who you went with and what you learned.

AD: Yes, the organization that sponsored my trip was the Interfaith Peace-Builders — now they're called Eyewitness Palestine. It was one of the most significant things I've done in my life.

We went to a lot of different places. We went to Hebron. Oh my God, Hebron is a heartbreaker. You know what they did to Hebron? It was a Palestinian city known for their ceramics and other crafts. The Israelis went in there with 4,000 soldiers and took over 400 homes and created an apartheid system where Palestinians can't even walk down the main street. They can't own any weapons, which means they have to get a permit in order to buy a butcher knife. They allowed a Zionist to go into the mosque there and murder many Palestinians. [On Feb. 25, 1994, Baruch Goldstein, a member of the far-right, ultra-Zionist Kach movement, opened fire on Palestinian Muslims praying in the Ibrahimi Mosque in Hebron. He murdered 29 people. Itamar Ben-Gvir, currently the Israeli Minister of National Security, had a portrait of Goldstein in his living room prior to entering government. —*editors*]

Our experience in Hebron started with meeting an Israeli settler from Brooklyn. When he showed up, he's got a gun on his hip. And so I said, "Why do you have a gun? You know, we don't have guns. Why do you?" I told him, "You're going to take your gun off." He said, "No, I'm not going to take it off." And so me and a young sister from Chicago, we decided to walk out. We were not going to participate. So we waited outside.

Next, we went to visit a market in Hebron where there were a lot of Palestinian shops. That's where a lot of tourists came, so that's where they made their money. But Israel shut down half of the market, and the market that was left, the Israelis who had taken over the buildings above were throwing garbage down on the Palestinians at the market. They were throwing acid. They were throwing urine. Just horrible. The Palestinians had to put up a chicken wire screen above them to keep all that stuff from raining down on them.

There, we met a Palestinian girl. It was obvious that she was traumatized, but she was a freedom fighter and she talked about how they went and tried to keep this building from being taken away from them and how brutal the Israeli soldiers were. As we were walking, we had a crowd of Palestinians walking with us. When we got down to the main street, we saw some barricades there. Our delegation kept on walking, but then we realized when we turned around that all the Palestinians were back at the barricade. We said, "Come on." They said, "No, we can't walk on this street. We can't walk on this main street." [Israel has designated several streets in Hebron as Jewish settler-only streets, where Palestinians are prohibited. —*editors*]

I mean, I saw so many things in Palestine. Many places we went you could see the giant apartheid wall. We saw how they built the wall around one Palestinian man's house so he couldn't get to many of his olive fields. We went out and we helped him to harvest olives that we could get to. But that wall is so ugly, and it has taken up a lot of the Palestinians' water resources. The Palestinians don't have control over their water because the wall was built in such a way that it included the Palestinian rivers and streams. The Palestinians were telling us, don't forget what you saw, and I could never forget because I felt it so deeply.

JH: The Israeli attacks on schools have been happening for a long time. And It's been a horror to see all the schools blown up in Gaza. And teachers who want their students to discuss and debate these issues in the United States are being persecuted. There are lots of teachers being driven out of the classroom for trying to teach the truth about Palestine.

AD: It's unbelievable. To think we still can't teach the truth. We already experienced that during my generation. Native Americans experienced their history being erased, Black history being erased, and here we are, still not being able to teach the truth.

The truth is the most important thing. And courageous teachers are teaching the truth. But our enemies have always tried to hide the truth. Like that fool [Florida Gov. Ron] DeSantis, trying to ban teaching about racism — he's a dangerous person. We have to be in the struggle to teach the truth, and my hat is off to the teachers teaching the truth about Palestine, especially in those places where they're faced with this intense Zionism and racism.

JH: Yes, and also the students fighting back. It's amazing to see students rising up, occupying their campuses, disrupting graduations, raising their voices against Israeli occupation and genocide, and calling for their colleges to divest from Israel. I wanted to ask you what you thought of these protests.

AD: When I first started seeing students protesting, I thought of the student movement against the war in Vietnam. That lasted over 10 years. That was a constant struggle. We watched the atrocities being committed by the U.S. Army in Vietnam. We saw all these people on the news in villages being massacred. The students protesting the war faced a lot of violence. Those college kids at Kent State were shot by the National Guard. But eventually, you know, they helped turned the tide against war, and hopefully this will be the same thing with Gaza.

The students today have been attacked by the police. And just like the anti-Vietnam war struggle, the longer it goes on, the more people are siding with the students. The genocide in Gaza has awakened people throughout the world. Several countries have recently recognized Palestine. Zionism is being exposed.

They try to say if you say anything against Israel, or if you challenge any of their policies, you're anti-Jewish. This has been exposed by the thousands of Jewish students involved in this movement for a free Palestine. They don't want to be associated with that racist regime in Israel. And they have had some important victories getting some of their colleges to divest from Israel.

All of our struggles — whether for Palestine, or economic justice, or against racism — are stronger because of the determination of the Palestinians to survive. They have faced so many obstacles, and if they haven't given up, how can we?

■■ ▪

Black Solidarity with Gaza — #CeasefireNow

CHRISTOPHER HAZOU

Members of the Dream Defenders delegation to Palestine play with Palestinian children, 2015.

EDITORS' NOTE: *Following the Ferguson Uprising in response to the police murder of Mike Brown and the 2014 Israeli bombardment of Gaza, several organizers formed Black for Palestine, a network of Black activists committed to supporting the Palestinian struggle for freedom, justice, peace, and self-determination. Below, we reprint their statement released in November 2023, one month into Israel's brutal assault on Gaza.*

We make this statement as Black people in solidarity with Palestinian people, committed to our collective liberation, in grief and in outrage at the catastrophic violence that the state of Israel is enacting on Gaza. As we write, Israel has killed more than 15,000 Palestinians in Gaza — including 6,000 children. Over 30,000 people are injured.

We are coming together to demand:

- an immediate ceasefire
- the unimpeded entry of humanitarian aid and services, medical teams, supplies, and trauma care
- the immediate restoration of water, food, fuel, electricity, and internet
- ending the U.S. obstruction of Palestinian protections against genocide under international law
- the prevention of forced displacement of Palestinians in Gaza outside of Palestine
- an end to the siege on Gaza and the occupation of Palestine, including U.S. support

We refuse to remain silent or inactive as 2 million people in Gaza — half of whom are children — are fenced into an open-air prison, facing the bombs and barricades of the Israeli military. We condemn the displacement of more than a million Gazans who have nowhere to run as their homes, shelters, evacuation routes, and border crossings are bombed. We cry out as Israel continues to target hospitals, mosques, churches, schools, bakeries, entire neighborhoods, and entire families — the lifeblood and foundations of community.

We name the murderous responsibility of the United States government in particular, which is supplying aircraft, weapons and diplomatic cover to Israel as its forces commit these atrocities. After the Israeli minister of defense called the Palestinians of Gaza "human animals" on Oct. 9 and announced that they would be denied life necessities — the U.S. secretaries of state and defense and President Biden himself went to Tel Aviv to only affirm their support of Israel's genocidal actions. We are angered that the U.S. was the sole country to veto the U.N. Security Council resolution for a humanitarian ceasefire.

All life is precious, we reject the targeting of civilians, and we mourn the loss of all civilian life. The Israeli government, its allies, and Western media have tried to isolate, demonize, and dehumanize the people of Gaza to provide a false justification for Israel's unjustifiable mass killing. Our solidarity is in defiance of those efforts and against the Israeli occupation of Palestine, which perpetuates a cycle of violence and death.

Israel is an occupying power engaged in countless violations of international law toward its occupied population. Our demands in solidarity with the Palestinian struggle for self-determination and freedom are for more than the basic necessities under war. We stand with the Palestinian people who have been struggling for their land, their homes, their families, and their future for a century and who remain steadfast in the face of the ongoing catastrophes and atrocities committed against them. We honor the strength, the resilience, the commitment, the love, the memories, and the songs of our kin in liberation.

We make this commitment in a long tradition of Black people standing with other peoples around the world in our shared struggle against oppression, racism, and colonialism. This includes calling for an end to U.S. aggression in the Vietnam war, standing with anti-colonial struggles around the world, and most recently with the Black uprising of 2014 and building solidarity with Palestinians over our shared terrain of U.S. and Israeli state violence and disregard for our lives.

We call on Black youth, elders, students, artists, workers, people of faith, activists, teachers, and politicians to fearlessly mobilize and speak out for Palestinian freedom, to organize our communities and institutions to do the same. Our collective demands are stronger than any attempt to silence or attack us. We will meet those challenges together and united, we will overcome them.

We stand in solidarity with Palestinians and we will stand here until Palestine is free.

Signed by more than 6,000 individuals and organizations, including Mumia Abu-Jamal, Michael Bennett, Angela Davis, Marc Lamont Hill, Mariame Kaba, Robin D. G. Kelley, Noname, Cornel West, Saul Williams, the Dream Defenders, and the Movement for Black Lives. For the full list of signatories, visit BlackForPalestine.com.

What We Learned from Our "Oakland to Gaza" K–12 Teach-In

BY MEMBERS OF THE OAKLAND EDUCATION ASSOCIATION FOR PALESTINE GROUP

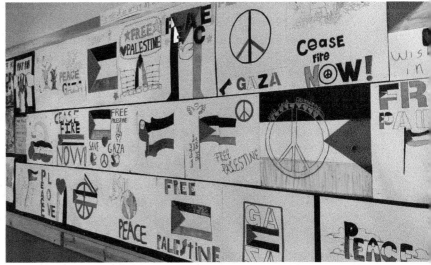

More than 20 U.S. educator unions have passed resolutions calling for a ceasefire in Gaza, some labeling Israel an apartheid state and an occupying force. Our own union, the Oakland Education Association (OEA), also passed a resolution in November 2023, calling for an immediate ceasefire and an end to the Israeli occupation and encouraging union members to show their support by attending marches, contacting elected officials, and teaching about Palestine.

After the resolution passed by almost a two-thirds margin, a group of rank-and-file organizers (of which we are a part), involving educators of all grade levels, formed OEA for Palestine to consider next steps. It was clear to us that educators must offer more than official union statements. We must encourage co-workers and students to think deeply about the humanitarian crises unfolding in the world and the role of the United States and others in creating and sustaining them.

Over about a month of meetings, a core group of 10 grew to a network of 50 teachers, and generated the idea of organizing a teach-in. Knowing that our ability to navigate complex issues with our students is one of educators' greatest strengths, we reasoned that educators could organize a teach-in to apply our labor toward encouraging critical discussion and global political consciousness. Oakland teachers had begun teaching about Palestine long before the teach-in. Oakland educators and students were already participating in marches and protests for a ceasefire. We hoped the teach-in could bring the energy of this activism into our classrooms and encourage more interest in the movement.

OEA has a history of supporting districtwide teach-ins, including a 1999 teach-in about the political prisoner Mumia Abu-Jamal and the death penalty, one in 2003 about the war on Iraq, and in 2011 about state-imposed austerity measures in education. After debate centering around whether a teacher union should "take a side" in global political affairs, the OEA endorsed the "Oakland to Gaza Teach-In" by a two-thirds majority.

Organizing the Teach-In

The December 2023 teach-in had three elements: a collection of curricular resources, a virtual panel of Palestine activists, and guest speakers from the Oakland community to speak in person in classrooms. We used social media to spread the word and circulate the resources but mostly relied on the OEA for Palestine network that we had built and other connections we had at school sites. We had one-on-one conversations with colleagues about the seriousness of the crisis and the importance of taking collective action as teachers.

The resources — organized as a non-exhaustive bank of suggested materials rather than a single curriculum — included everything from read-alouds to art projects to math lessons to critical examinations of the conflict's history. They came from a variety of sources, including the Abolitionist Teaching Network, PBS, Teach Palestine, and UNICEF. In the spirit of liberatory pedagogy, we sought to center voices and stories of Palestinian people. For example, some upper elementary school students read Palestinian artist Malak Mattar's *Sitti's Bird: A Gaza Story* (see p. 87) to learn about the reality of war for Gazan children in 2014 and created artwork and writing on the meaning of "liberation" — libertad — in a Spanish immersion classroom. One middle school lesson encouraged students to study and discuss the role of art in Palestinian resistance movements. Many teachers also created their own Palestine-related materials, such as one computer science teacher who created a lesson on technology access and restrictions in Palestine and a Spanish teacher who taught a lesson about the Palestinian and Jewish diasporas in Latin America.

The curricular resources we assembled emphasized the complexity of the historical context and the need to present multiple perspectives — including the violent history of antisemitism and its catalyzing role in the Zionist movement. A group of 10th-grade English students, for example, produced voice memos reflecting on their study of excerpts from ABC's 1988 "Nightline in the Holy Land" broadcast (during the First Intifada), which presents side-by-side interviews from "everyday" Israelis and Palestinians on how they see the history of the same land. Another example is Samia Shoman's "Independence or Catastrophe? Teaching Palestine Through Multiple Perspectives" (see p. 41), which prompts students to analyze both Palestinian and Israeli perspectives on key historical events and culminates in a mock U.N. conference negotiation.

While many teachers, as well as the virtual panelists and community guests, publicly presented their pro-ceasefire stance, the teach-in was focused on providing tools to think through the history of the conflict and analyze the current crisis. The organizers of the teach-in had different opinions on the conflict and the best path toward its resolution, but we shared the conviction that the biased messaging of mainstream curricula (and corporate media) calls for an urgent correction by educators. Students should know that Palestinians are a people, and their century-long struggle for liberation deserves to be recognized and studied.

The Palestine Curriculum War Raging in Oakland

In the weeks leading up to the teach-in, we found ourselves immersed in the nationwide debate on how — or whether — Palestine should be taught in schools. Many Oakland teachers were already including the assault on Gaza and its history in their lessons.

On Oct. 31, OUSD's chief academic officer called on teachers to "support our students in learning about the human tragedy in Gaza and Israel" and sent out resources and sample lesson plans on the Israel-Palestine conflict and the Oct. 7 attack. There were major gaps in the district's resource list. The district included little information about Israel's bombardment and invasion of Gaza that by then had killed 17,000 Palestinians and displaced 1.8 million. The only reference to this U.S.-backed military campaign was added on Oct. 11 and used loaded media language, such as a timeline noting that 1,200 Israelis "have been killed by Hamas," but that 1,055 Gazans simply "have died." More importantly, the official resources did not represent the more than 100-year-long Palestinian resistance to occupation and dispossession. None of the provided material was authored by Palestinians, yet the school district included lessons by two Zionist lobbying groups, the Anti-Defamation League and the Institute for Curriculum Services. The former is well known for insisting that anti-Zionism is antisemitism and the latter for lobbying to remove mention of Palestinians and Palestine from ethnic studies curricula. Finally, the district did not provide any materials for elementary classes.

These biases and omissions are what prompted us to assemble our own resource bank to supplement the school district's limited offerings. Through union-related chat groups, email lists, and social media, OEA for Palestine members encouraged educators to submit relevant curricular materials for us to review. We also enlisted the support of a few experts from organizations like Teach Palestine. As the introduction to the resource bank explained, our goal was "to introduce our students to a range of perspectives and equip them with the tools to engage critically, participate in the discourse, and draw their own conclusions."

On Dec. 2, following the announcement of the teach-in, Oakland's superintendent sent an email to all educators and families stating that she was "deeply disappointed" by "the harmful and divisive materials being circulated and promoted as factual." She also dusted off a rarely cited 2004 board resolution with a lengthy list of expectations for teachers tackling controversial topics in class. The school board president escalated the superintendent's "disappointment" by effectively threatening to fire anyone who participated in the teach-in, saying to the press "you can't show up and do whatever you want and not face any consequences." Their intimidation tactics and media strategy made it clear that our district sided with those seeking to suppress Palestinian perspectives in the curriculum.

We noted two types of criticism of the teach-in: Some critics raised concerns about individual resources. We took this critique seriously and viewed the curriculum bank as a living document. Based on feedback, we edited documents for vague language and corrected inaccuracies, especially anything that ran the risk of being interpreted as antisemitic. But some critics sought to frame Palestinian-centered study as inherently antisemitic. Following the Oakland superintendent's email expressing "disappointment" and the board president's threat to punish educators, the Deborah Project, a pro-Israel law firm, sent every principal in the district a cease and desist letter, stating that teachers have no legal right to exercise free speech in the classroom. Media outlets cherry-picked quotations from teach-in resources to make it seem as if the lessons and materials underplayed antisemitism or the interests of Jewish people. For example, a Fox News report falsely claimed that the teach-in resources "don't mention the Holocaust by name," and cited one quote, "During World War II, many Jewish people were killed and mistreated," taken from a worksheet for elementary students.

We vehemently oppose antisemitism. Several of the teach-in organizers are Jewish, even Israeli, and are from Holocaust-surviving families. We also oppose the weaponization of antisemitism against Palestinians, who are denied human and civil rights and are murdered by the Israeli military. We reject the idea that critique of political Zionism and of Israel as a de jure Jewish state is antisemitic, as well as the idea that winning Palestinian civil rights would negate the rights of Israeli Jews.

How It Went

Despite the school district's intimidation tactics, nearly 100 teachers across 30+ schools indicated an intent to participate on our registration form, which was circulated via school site email listservs, regional site reps' WhatsApp groups, at union meetings, and on our Instagram account. Several hundred students viewed the livestream panel. Across the district, students made connections from Oakland to Gaza, as they participated in seminar-style discussions, analyzed data and graphs, folded paper cranes, produced argumentative writing to defend their claims, created multimedia art projects, made audio recordings of their reflections, asked questions of guest speakers, and so much more — all in English, Spanish, and Arabic.

Secondary students were engaged during the virtual panel, which included speakers from the Palestinian Youth Movement, Jewish Voice for Peace Bay Area, and the Black Alliance for Peace and was moderated by a parent. Panelists spoke about their relationship to the Palestinian struggle for freedom and how it connects to issues students face in the Bay Area. A Palestinian American panelist shared that "for me, being engaged in the Palestinian freedom struggle means rejecting .

. . the separation of my land and my people that has been forced on me because of the massacres my grandparents faced." And a Jewish panelist shared that to him, engaging with the Palestinian freedom struggle means "rejecting Zionism's attempt to say that the only way Jewish people can be safe is through . . . militarized violence."

Students showed their curiosity, asking follow-up questions: "How can we educate our peers about the matter without overwhelming them?" "How can we help or get involved in the Palestinian struggle?" and "Are people in Israel protesting against the war?"

While a few parents expressed disapproval of the teach-in, stating that it would be "divisive" or "too complex" for children, many students, parents, and community members reached out via email to express gratitude for the teachers who participated. With their permission, we shared snippets from their messages on our Instagram. One parent wrote:

> As an Arab Muslim who was born and raised in Oakland, I experienced the aftermath of 9/11 as a 3rd grader, enduring negative treatment from both teachers and peers, and bullying during my middle school years. Now, as a parent with two children in OUSD schools, I am disheartened to learn that my son has been facing similar challenges. . . . As I review the resources provided, I am overcome with emotion. I am immensely proud of your courage, true leadership, and advocacy for the voiceless. . . . Thank you for your unwavering commitment and for being a beacon of hope in our community.

Looking Forward

In the face of attacks, we recognized that our safety as activists is not guaranteed (especially for non-tenured teachers). Nevertheless, it is our responsibility to reject the normalization of oppression. Though we have received no reports of teachers and staff receiving official retaliation for participating in the teach-in, the district faces allegations of discrimination and antisemitism from Zionist parents and organizations. The U.S.

Department of Education's Office of Civil Rights is investigating a complaint against OUSD alleging that the teach-in "discriminated against students on the basis of national origin (shared Jewish ancestry)."

Many teachers were supportive but fearful of being called antisemitic for participating in the teach-in or felt that the issue was "too political" for classrooms. With the climate of backlash, we understood why our co-workers had concerns, and we sought to engage with them. We facilitated schoolwide meetings and held one-on-one conversations at our schools about why it is important for educators to express solidarity with Palestine.

Some critics of the teach-in wrongly but sincerely feared that our support for Palestinian liberation meant that we did not care for Jewish safety or that we urged the expulsion of Jews from the land. We learned that we needed to explicitly state our support for the equal right of Palestinians and Jews to live on the land of Palestine/Israel.

The teach-in strengthened relations between educators and other community and social movement organizers, while putting into practice our union's commitment to international solidarity. Across the country, we want to help spread and strengthen this work to combat those who pit Jews against Palestinians to suppress liberatory education. We aim to build on the success of the teach-in and organize further events, bringing more teachers and organizers together in support of Palestine. We hope to hear about future teach-ins and labor actions that advance the struggle for Palestinian freedom.

■ ▫

The authors wish to remain anonymous because Palestine education efforts have been targeted by groups seeking to punish and silence educators. The Oakland Education Association for Palestine Group is made up of rank-and-file teachers in the Oakland Education Association who came together during Israel's assault on Gaza to organize support for a ceasefire and Palestinian freedom from occupation. The group includes teachers at the elementary, middle, and high school levels who come from a variety of ethnic and religious backgrounds, including several Jewish members. To contact the organizers, email oeaforpalestine@gmail.com.

Educators:
Support Boycott, Divestment, and Sanctions

BY LARA KISWANI

NIKKOLAS SMITH

Dear Educators,

We live in a world where everyday people are often convinced they have limited power to change their conditions, or to shape the future. History itself teaches us something very different. In every major movement for justice, collective mobilizations to raise awareness, disrupt business as usual, advocate for policy changes, and challenge existing power structures are what created the changes we often celebrate today. From the Montgomery Bus Boycotts, early abolitionists boycotting products produced by enslaved people, Gandhi's Salt March, the United Farm Workers grape boycott, to the anti-apartheid movement of South Africa, these collective actions remind us of what is possible today.

The power of workers through the utilization of tactics such as boycotts, divestments, and sanctions has often been the tipping point for change. Labor power can interrupt systems of harm, and potentially transform them. It deepens the wedge between the corporate elite, and all working people, and provides us with avenues to not only put pressure on decision makers, but also move the masses toward a shared vision and project where all people can live free of exploitation. In the case of Palestinian solidarity, as was the case with the movement against apartheid South Africa, the Boycott, Divestment, and Sanctions (BDS) movements offer everyday people a vehicle to engage in the work of social change.

In 2005, 170 Palestinian civil organizations, including teacher unions, issued a historic call to boycott, divest from, and sanction Israel. The Palestinian call for BDS is inspired by the South African anti-apartheid movement that, through international cultural, economic, and political boycotts, helped isolate apartheid South Africa, and aided in the ending of the apartheid regime. The successes of the movement spanned globally and had deep economic and political impact — from governments banning South African imports, to ordinary people pressuring supermarkets to stop selling South African products, musicians refusing to perform in the apartheid state, South African sports leagues being suspended from international competitions, and governments, including the United States, imposing economic sanctions on the country. Today, people in the United States not only have an opportunity to build on this history and contribute to the movement for Palestinian freedom, but we also bear a responsibility to do so as the U.S. government facilitates the ongoing genocide through its financial and political support of apartheid Israel.

We are witnessing the largest movement of trade unions in solidarity with Palestine in U.S. history. In late July 2024, a coalition of unions representing more than half of organized labor called for the United States to stop arming Israel. From local teacher unions passing resolutions in support of BDS, to national unions of educators calling on the government to shift foreign policy, there is potential and a critical need for educators today to translate this solidarity into material action. Everyone should examine their pension funds, and organize to divest from corporations with direct ties to apartheid Israel and military contracts profiting from war. Doing so is not only a gesture of solidarity with Palestine, it is also a teaching gesture, demonstrating to students that we do not only educate about social justice in the classroom, we do not only encourage our students be agents of change, but we too practice those values outside the classroom. And after all, divesting from genocide, racism, militarism, and violence is not only a moral imperative, it is necessary for the future of humanity.

In struggle,
Lara Kiswani

■ ▪

Lara Kiswani is the executive director of the Arab Resource and Organizing Center (AROC), which is committed to fighting for racial and economic justice and the dignity and liberation of Arab and Muslim communities. She is also a lecturer in the Ethnic Studies Department at San Francisco State University.

Things You May Find Hidden in My Ear

BY MOSAB ABU TOHA

For Alicia M. Quesnel, MD

I

When you open my ear, touch it
gently.
My mother's voice lingers somewhere inside.
Her voice is the echo that helps recover my equilibrium
when I feel dizzy during my attentiveness.

You may encounter songs in Arabic,
poems in English I recite to myself,
or a song I chant to the chirping birds in our backyard.

When you stitch the cut, don't forget to put all these
    back in my ear.
Put them back in order as you would do with
    books on your shelf.

II

The drone's buzzing sound,
the roar of an F-16,
the screams of bombs falling on houses,
on fields, and on bodies,
of rockets flying away —
rid my small ear canal of them all.

Spray the perfume of your smiles on the incision.
Inject the song of life into my veins to wake me up.
Gently beat the drum so my mind may dance with yours,
my doctor, day and night.

RAWAN ANANI

*Mosab Abu Toha is a Palestinian poet, short story writer, and essayist
from Gaza. Abu Toha is the author of* Things You May Find Hidden in
My Ear: Poems from Gaza, *which won a 2022 Palestine Book Award.*

Teachi
history
protec
the
future

OP
ON
RIGHT
E OF

7

More Teaching Ideas
and Resources

Poetry Teaching Guide

BY LINDA CHRISTENSEN

Gate A-4
by Naomi Shihab Nye, p. 17

Naomi Shihab Nye is a Palestinian American poet who grew up in both Jerusalem and San Antonio, Texas. Nye has said that, for her, "the primary source of poetry has always been local life, random characters met on the streets, our own ancestry sifting down to us through small essential daily tasks." In this lovely prose poem, Nye brings the kindness of the world into focus while describing an incident at an airport. Through the poem, she also explores Palestinian culture.

Consider watching Naomi Shihab Nye reading the poem in a National Endowment for the Arts YouTube video before discussing the poem with students. After they've listened and read the poem on their own, ask what they learn from this moment of kindness, what they think it reveals about Palestinian culture.

Nye writes, "This is the world I want to live in. The shared world. . . . This can still happen anywhere. Not everything is lost." Invite students  to write about a time they witnessed kindness. Begin by asking them to list moments of kindness and generosity. These might include incidents they experienced personally or that they watched unfold. Share those incidents to encourage more memories to surface. These are often small moments, so they need time to bubble up. Once students have lists, ask them to choose one and write. These may be in the form of a prose poem or a narrative. After they write, share these pieces and discuss what they have in common.

How can they make these moments happen more frequently? What needs to change in our society — and in the world — to make these more common?

But I Heard the Drops
Sharif S. Elmusa, p. 32

Tell students: Given what you've learned about Palestine-Israel, think about why the poet's father cries. On your own, make a list of reasons a Palestinian might cry. Share reasons with the class. With a partner, write a poem that may begin "For 30 years, I cried" and tell who, what, or why they cried. You may choose to use lines from the original poem to move your poem forward, e.g., "They trickled down . . ."

Born on Nakba Day
by Mohammed El-Kurd, p. 51

For students to understand and appreciate this poem, they need to know the history of the Nakba. El-Kurd's poem would make an excellent follow-up to Samia Shoman's lesson, "Independence or Catastrophe? Teaching 1948 Through Multiple Perspectives." (See page 41.) Begin by reading the title of the poem. Ask students to close their eyes and think about what they learned about what happened during the Nakba. Encourage them to think about verbs they might use if they were a poet. What scene might they describe? Ask them to open their eyes and make a quick list of everything that came to mind, then share.

Once students have shared ideas, read "Born on Nakba Day" out loud or listen to El-Kurd read the poem on YouTube, as his voice and the music make the poem more accessible. Throughout the poem, he uses violent imagery to underscore the violence of the Nakba. Discuss the images he uses and compare them to the ones students imagined.

El-Kurd repeats the line "I was born on the 50th anniversary of the Nakba." Discuss the differences between the two stanzas. Note how the second stanza creates a scene, using all the senses.

Drawing on their knowledge of the Nakba, students may choose to write a poem, depicting a scene they imagined as El-Kurd does in "Born on Nakba Day." Or students may choose to write a persona poem. In an article about persona poems in my book *Reading, Writing, and Rising Up*, I describe how persona poems lead "with heart and imagination, asking students to find that place inside themselves that connects with a moment in history, literature, life — and to imagine another's world, to value it, to hold it sacred for a moment as a way of bearing witness for another human being. This poem demands emotional honesty, intellectual curiosity, poetic craft, and the ability to imagine stepping into someone else's life at the moment when their life changes."

My student Khalilah Joseph created the following poem after learning about the incarceration of Japanese Americans during World War II. Khalilah wrote from a segment in Monica Sone's *Nisei Daughter* where the family burned their Japanese possessions because neighbors warned them about "having too many Japanese objects around the house." Ask students to think about details Khalilah used from Sone's book. How did she take that scene and make a poem?

Becoming American

I looked into the eyes of my Japanese doll
and knew I could not surrender her
to the fury of the fire.
My mother threw out the poetry
she loved;
my brother gave the fire his sword.

We worked hours
to vanish any traces of the Asian world
from our home.
Who could ask us
to destroy
gifts from a world that molded
and shaped us?

If I ate hamburgers
and apple pies,
if I wore jeans,
then would I be American?

Returning to the images they created about the Nakba, students may choose to write a poem from the point of view of someone who experienced the Nakba. Students have also written from the point of view of an object from a particular moment in history — a dead student's shoe after the Soweto Uprising, a cherished baby rattle brought by a mother on the Cherokee Trail of Tears.

After students have written their poems, share them in a read-around to solidify students' visual impression of the Nakba and its meaning for those who were affected.

Writing My Own Book, by Dandara, p. 70

The young poet/songwriter addresses their song to "you." Who is the "you" in this piece? Who is the "we"? This song is written almost like a letter of defiance. Notice that the first half is written as a list of questions. The second half is written as statements.

Using Dandara's style and tone, write a letter of defiance to a person or group who has wronged you or your people. What questions might you ask? What might you say?

rice haikus
Suheir Hammad, p. 72

What is a "meal of resistance"? Describe the big and small injustices suffered by the Palestinians. Some described by Hammad, others recalled from what you've learned about the history. Who is the "they" who poured sugar into rice to ruin them both?

Haikus, the poetic style Hammad uses in this poem, are three-line poems that have 17 syllables in total, with five syllables in the first and third lines and seven syllables in the second line. Using what you know of the history of Palestine-Israel, write a haiku. You might focus on history, injustice, a particular individual, or you might focus, as many haiku poets do, on what is loved about the landscape and people of these lands.

Gaza Chapter

The YouTube clip "Palestinian Poet Mosab Abu Toha Is Documenting War in Verse" is a great preface for the poems in this chapter. Toha speaks of Gazan poets' role of bringing their experiences to the world. "What poetry is trying to do is invite people to feel and experience what we are experiencing in Gaza. [Poetry is] putting other people in our feelings, inviting them to be part of what is happening to us." We encourage watching this short clip with students before immersing them in the poetry from Gaza.

Because of Us
by Em Berry, p. 76

Em Berry's opening "This morning I learned . . ." is an evocative first line to pull students into their own writing. Ask students to write the words, "This [morning/week/year/month/] I learned . . ." and then quick-write what they have learned. If

they are deep into learning about Palestine-Israel, they may write a list of what they have learned from the unit. If the lessons are in their infancy, they may choose to write about what they have learned about another subject — baseball, their family, school, etc. After they have written, and depending on the topic, students may pair-share or do a quick read-around to collect group knowledge of their learning.

Read the poem aloud. Discuss the poem with students. Allow them time to sit with the poem by answering these questions: In this poem, Em Berry uses the word "gauze" to make a statement about the attacks on Gaza. Berry begins the poem "This morning I learned . . ." Who is the "our" and "us" in the poem? Who is "they/their"? What does the poet learn? How does she employ the word "gauze" to describe the war in Gaza? Quick-write a response to the poem and then discuss.

After students have read and discussed the poem, they may return to the opening line or choose another line like "because of us" or "I wondered" and write a poem using what they have learned about the history of Palestine and Israel, Gaza, etc.

Before I Was a Gazan
by Naomi Shihab Nye, p. 93

Naomi Shihab Nye wrote her powerful poem "Before I Was a Gazan" from the point of view of a young boy. She uses everyday language to capture the boy's excitement about his math paper before his world is shattered by loss.

Read the poem aloud. After reading, allow a moment of silence for the impact of the poem to settle in. Ask students to write about the poem before opening the class for discussion. Move into feelings, rather than analysis. Ask, "What moved you about the poem?"

As a follow-up, students may choose to write their own persona poem from the point of view of someone they have studied during this unit. Tell students that Nye's poem is a persona poem. Using her poem as a model, ask them to define what that means. Who is the "I" in the poem? Why does the poet use someone else's voice?

Then ask students to make a list of the people or places they could write a persona poem from. After they have shared their lists, encourage them to choose one person and write from that person's voice. A second listing and sharing might include moments they could write about, places their persona could describe.

On Politics and Poetry
by Marwan Makhoul, p. 89.

Makhoul's short poem begins "In order for me to write poetry that isn't political . . ." And then Makhoul describes what must happen before he can write non-political poetry. Ask students to use Makhoul's first line and to finish it, beginning with "I must . . ." Have students do a quick read-around to hear each other's vision of peace.

What a Gazan Should Do During an Israeli Air Strike
by Mosab Abu Toha, p. 101

To better understand the poet and his knowledge of life in Gaza, students might read Mosab Abu Toha's essay "A Palestinian Poet's Perilous Journey Out of Gaza" in the *New Yorker* before reading the poem. Toha captures the urgency and fear of the moment in his poem "What a Gazan Should Do During an Israeli Air Strike." Partly this is achieved by using short, clear, concise instructions. This is not a pretend list, this list reveals the knowledge gleaned by someone who takes on these tasks, packing the practical — tiny toys, IDs, money — but then he veers into the items that ground his life: photos of late grandparents, his grandparents' wedding invitation, a packet of strawberry seeds, and dirt.

Read the poem aloud. (If students read his essay ahead of the poem, ask where his experiences with attempting to flee Gaza show up in the poem.) Ask students to write a quick-write response to the questions: What does Toha's list and instructions tell you about leaving Gaza? Share students' responses.

Ask students to imagine that they are forced to flee their home: What would they take and why? What would their eyes linger on? What would they want to do one last time?

Droughts and Floods
by Jesse Hagopian, p. 106

Jesse Hagopian calls his poem "Droughts and Floods." Ask students: What are the droughts and floods described in the poem? Ask students to list the contrasts and contradictions that Hagopian articulates. Imad al-Maqadmeh, a Palestinian survivor of a bombing Hagopian describes in his poem, asks: "Why did they bomb us? Why? I want to know why. Why? We are all children in the school." Hagopian's poem suggests that the "they" here is not just Israel, but also those who make and profit from the weapons used. How might a Boeing executive respond to al-Maqadmeh's question? According to the poet, what prevents sufficient resources to "water the garden of learning and love"? Hagopian is a teacher in Seattle. What connection does he see between young people in Seattle and young people in Gaza? The poem expresses hope for a global "intifada." Intifada is a word that at times has been misrepresented. It is Arabic for a "shaking off," a getting rid of, and describes uprisings against oppression. What is the nature of the "global intifada" the poet imagines — what needs to be shaken off, what needs to be created?

We Had Dreams
p. 108

Before students arrive in class, cut the passages apart and either arrange on the wall or on desks. Tell students that these are passages written from Gaza after the Israeli bombardment began shortly after Oct. 7.

Ask students to walk around the room, pausing to read each dream. When they find one that speaks to them, tell them to write the passage down and return to their desk. Ask them to write a response to their chosen piece. This may be written in many ways:

1. Why this passage matters
2. What this passage makes me understand about Palestinians living and dying under siege in Gaza
3. A letter back to the person, responding to their text
4. What echoes of this passage they feel in their own lives

After students finish writing, ask them to stand by the passage they wrote about, read the passage and then their response. It is OK if multiple students chose the same passage. Share them all at one time. After everyone has read, discuss the impact of the passages on their understanding of what's happening in Gaza.

"We Teach Life, Sir"
by Rafeef Ziadah, p. 114

This poem is Rafeef Ziadah's response to a question asked by a journalist: "Why don't you stop teaching your children hatred, and this will be all over?" Her answer to the question is a spoken word poem. Throughout the poem, Ziadah inserts other questions from journalists that illustrate the news media's ongoing portrayal of Palestinians as "terrorists." She counters the questions with descriptions of what is happening to Gaza. She also counsels herself to remain calm and polite throughout the poem while she is screaming inside about the world of Palestine that she witnesses.

Listen to or watch Rafeef Ziadah recite the poem to get the full effect. After listening to the poem through the first time, encourage students to find the questions journalists ask or the stories they want to hear about Palestine and underline or highlight them. For example, "Why don't you stop teaching your children hatred, and this will be all over?" Then ask them to mark her answers. (Recall the journalist's question to Palestinian Abu Samir in Fawaz Turki's "Why Must You Go Back to Palestine?" on p. 71: "But why, why must you go back to Palestine? Why Palestine specifically? There are many Arab countries you can be resettled in.")

Once students have examined the poem, the content, and the structure, ask them to write a paragraph discussing her anger and frustration about the media's portrayal of Palestine.

The poem may also be used as a model for students' own frustration at the media's focus on some aspect of their lives that they understand to be skewed or incomplete. Brainstorm a class list together. Think about questions that might be asked and answered. As they work toward their own poem, point out the use of poetic devices in the poem, like the repetition of the phrase "we teach," which provides a throughline from the initial question.

The Home Within
by Ibtisam S. Barakat, p. 140

Why can't the poet return home? What lines provide clues? Imagine reading this poem to a friend who doesn't know the history of Palestine-Israel. Describe what might have happened to your friend. Why might the poet have left? Why does he want to return? What does the "soldiered border" refer to? Where does the poet find "refuge from my hurt"?

Using words from "The Home Within," write an "I miss" poem from the poet's perspective. Who or what does the poet miss? Add other details that you might imagine the poet using.

Anti-Zionist Abecedarian
by Sam Sax, p. 160

Sam Sax is a queer Jewish writer and educator. They have won numerous awards, including the James Laughlin Award and the National Poetry Series award. They are a two-time Grand National Bay Area Slam Poetry award winner.

Sax's poem is not an easy poem to read because it demands a lot of background knowledge. Some of this information, of course, can be found in lessons and readings in *Teaching Palestine*. In this poem, Sax employs the abecedarian poetry format where the first letter of each line or stanza follows sequentially through the alphabet. Prior to reading, students may need help wrestling with the title: What does Anti-Zionist mean? What is an abecedarian poem?

After reading the poem, ask students to go back through and think about the pronouns Sax uses. Who is the "you" Sax is writing to? Who are the "we" and "us"? Who are the "my people" Sax refers to in the poem? Once students have peeled back the pronouns, ask them to look again at the poem. Sax's poem is an extended argument. Tell students to use the margins to grapple with Sax's poetic argument. What points are they making? Encourage students to gather their marginal notes and write an interpretation of the poem. Share these in class.

As a follow-up, students might try writing their own abecedarian poems. Using Sax's poem as a model, this assignment might tie up their study of antisemitism or they might write their poem as an argument about a topic they are passionate about.

If I Must Die
by Refaat Alareer, p. 176

Refaat Alareer, a prominent Palestinian professor, poet, and writer, was killed in an airstrike in northern Gaza, on Dec. 6, 2023. His brother, his sister, and her four children were also killed. In interviews before his death, he discussed the inhumane choices he and his wife and their six children faced: Stay in Gaza and risk death or flee without anywhere to go that was safe. "It's an archetypal Palestinian image of a discussion, a debate on should we stay in one room, so if we die, we die together, or should we stay in separate rooms, so at least somebody can live?"

In interviews, in writing, in his work with youth, Alareer attempted to bring the humanity of Palestinians to the world: "Feel their pain. Put yourself in their shoes." He edited *Gaza Writes Back: Short Stories from Young Writers in Gaza, Palestine* (2014), a collection of 15 stories written by young Gazans living under Israeli occupation  since 2009. He also co-edited *Gaza Unsilenced*, a 2015 collection of essays, photos, and poetry. He was a co-founder of We Are Not Numbers — a nonprofit organization that aims to amplify the voices of Palestinian youth living in Gaza and the refugee camps. Anticipating his death, he wrote the poem "If I Must Die." The poem is read by Scottish actor Brian Cox on *Democracy Now!*; images of air strikes play alongside the poem.

To understand the heartbreak of writing a poem in anticipation of death, students need to know about the author, his life, and his work. The best place to learn about him is at the We Are Not Numbers website, where students can read tributes to him from his students.

Lift Refaat Alareer's work of making Gaza visible by directing students to read the stories and poems he helped students construct. Ask students to wander through both the stories section of the We Are Not Numbers website and the poetry section of the website and read a few stories and poems. At the website, encourage students to note lines or phrases or entire pieces to share with the class. What do they learn about conditions in Gaza? What else do they want to know? After students share their findings in small groups or the whole class, ask them to write a one-page commentary about what they learned: Encourage them to include lines from the pieces as well as their own feelings. What should people know about living in Gaza?

Things You May Find Hidden in My Ear
by Mosab Abu Toha, p. 193

Toha dedicated this poem to Dr. Alicia M. Quesnel, an otologist and neurotologist in Bos-

ton. The speaker of the poem talks directly to the doctor as she sutures his head wound and damaged ear, describing the different sounds she might find there. In the first stanza, the speaker details what is left when earthly possessions disappear, the sounds he wants her to save: memories of his mother's voice, songs in Arabic, poems in English. In the second stanza, he describes the sounds he wants her to "rid my small ear canal of them all": drones, F-16s, bombs, screams.

If they have read or listened to Toha writing/speaking about his experiences, in Gaza, they will enter the poem with greater background knowledge.

First, read the poem aloud to students and ask them simply to listen to the poem. The second time through, ask students to read for "content and structure," then to mark up the poem, making notes in the margins: What is the poem about? What do we learn about the speaker of the poem? If students don't notice that it is written to a doctor or that the speaker gives instructions, encourage them to think about why Toha constructed the poem this way. Discuss the poem after students and read and marked it up.

As an extension to this poem, students might write about what sounds are hidden in their ears, what do they want to keep? What do they want taken away? Consider this an opportunity for students to sit with their own lives for a moment. This can be a brief quick-write, a verse poem, or a direct address poem like Toha's. They may use the poetic "hooks" from Toha's poem:

When you open my ear
You may encounter

End the session with a pair-share or a full-class read-around.

■ ■

Linda Christensen is a Rethinking Schools editor and author of Reading, Writing, and Rising Up *and* Teaching for Joy and Justice: Re-Imagining the Language Arts Classroom. *She co-edited* Rhythm and Resistance: Teaching Poetry for Social Justice. *For many years Christensen directed the Oregon Writing Project at Lewis & Clark College in Portland, Oregon.*

Resources for Teaching Palestine

There are many wonderful resources for teaching about Palestine — and more being written and produced all the time. Materials in the pages that follow include our attempt to describe some books, films, and a few websites that we know have been used by teachers around the United States and Canada. Most of these we have collected from *Rethinking Schools* and Teach Palestine. Following each entry are initials of the source for that write-up. Contributors include TeachPalestine.org (TP), Nadine Foty, Palestine in Our Schools (NF), Nina Shoman-Dajani (NSD), Katharine Davies Samway (KDS), Deborah Menkart (DM), Samia Shoman (SS), Adam Sanchez (AS), Jesse Hagopian (JH), Keziah Ridgeway (KR), Bill Bigelow (BB), the Institute for Palestine Studies (IPS), and the Zinn Education Project (ZEP).— *editors*

Children's Books

Sitti's Secrets
By Naomi Shihab Nye
Illustrated by Nancy Carpenter
(Aladdin Publishing, 1997)
32 pp.

In 1994, Naomi Shihab Nye released *Sitti's Secrets*, a story about Mona's trip to Palestine to see her grandmother or Sitti, and the loving bond that they share for each other and for Palestine, despite living in different places. Nye published one of the first books on Palestine in English. Growing up as a Palestinian-Egyptian American, I was well aware of my multifaceted identity but also my difference, which as a child made me feel left out at times, and as if I needed to constantly explain myself to my peers and teachers. *Sitti's Secrets* delves into the complexities of having a dual identity like Mona, and is particularly important for our students who may be reluctant or nervous about sharing their differences at such a young age when they are just beginning to navigate school, making friends, and developing confidence. *NF*

These Chicks
By Laila Taji
Palestine Museum
2018

Laila Taji's *These Chicks* is a board book for early childhood learners based on an old Arabic nursery rhyme. This work acknowledged the importance of language as a way of preserving our historical memory. *These Chicks* offers many Palestinians and Arabs living in the diaspora a way to teach their children Arabic so they might feel connected back to "home." The book contains both Arabic transliterated text as well as English translation so this folk song of our parents' childhood can be passed on to future generations in the diaspora. As a baby, my father would sing to me in my crib many Arabic tunes that allowed the love of the Arabic language to grow in my heart and make me feel more connected to my Arab identity. As I grew older, my family and I toured schools, churches, and rallies to educate people about Palestine through music. An important piece of this work was translating Arabic lyrics to English so the audience could grasp the meaning of traditional Palestinian songs. Simply hearing the Arabic language allowed these primarily non-Arabic-speaking U.S. audiences to appreciate a bit more about our culture and experience. That is precisely what Taji's work can do for our students. *NF*

P Is for Palestine
By Golbarg Bashi
Illustrated by Golrokh Nafisi
(PM Press, 2024)
72 pp.

Golbarg Bashi's *P Is for Palestine* (2018) is an early childhood alphabet book that highlights the rich culture and history of Palestine from falafel sandwiches, to the birthplace of Jesus in Bethlehem, near Jerusalem, to the keffiyeh, our scarf that is a symbol of Palestinian resistance. I remember being ridiculed for bringing hummus in my lunch to school. Now it is a fashionable treat, but not necessarily associated with Palestine. My classmates laughed at me, saying that my lunch was weird and smelled bad. When I tried to educate my peers and school about Palestinian culture through international day festivals, teachers did not allow me to bring Palestinian food, wear our traditional dress, and perform a traditional folk dance called dabke. *P Is for Palestine* is a great book to introduce these elements of Palestinian culture in early childhood classrooms so that awareness can more easily become a part of the larger school culture preventing a silencing of Palestinian representation. *NF*

The Boy and the Wall
By Amahl Bishara
Illustrated by Lajee Center
(2005)
24 pp.

Amahl Bishara's *The Boy and the Wall*, in English and Arabic, is about life in Aida, a Palestinian refugee camp near Bethlehem, where the lives of Palestinians were turned upside down when Israel built a huge concrete separation wall (called an apartheid wall by former President Jimmy Carter and Archbishop Desmond Tutu, among others). In a rhythmic speak-and-respond structure modeled on Margaret Wise Brown's *The Runaway Bunny*, a Palestinian child talks with his mother about what he can do to help his community overcome the impact of the wall and all that it brings, including soldiers with guns and tear gas canisters. His mother's responses underscore her love for him and Palestinian traditions and culture, and the resilience of Palestinians under occupation. For example, when the boy says, "Or maybe I will become a mountain so that I can be bigger than the wall, and see over it," his mother replies, "If you become a mountain and become bigger than the wall . . . I will become a farmer and plant olive trees and tend to you and live from the olives you bear." An introduction provides information about the Aida Refugee Camp and life under occupation, including how the apartheid wall affects Palestinians (e.g., separating Palestinians from family members and friends, their land, their work, medical care, religious sites, and open land where children can play). The illustrations are by children from Aida. *KDS*

Homeland: My Father Dreams of Palestine
By Hannah Moushabeck,
Illustrated by Reem Madooh
Chronicle Books (2023)
40 pp.

Hannah Moushabeck uses the stories her Palestinian father told about his childhood to introduce children to life in Jerusalem before the Nakba, when her family was forced to leave their homes and ended up scattered across the globe. Despite the sad end, it's a joyous book, filled with Reem Madooh's lively illustrations of daily life in the Old City, family celebrations, and mischievous children. (Preschool and up.) *TP*

Olive Harvest in Palestine
By Wafa Shami
Illustrated by Shaima Farouki
(Gate Advertising, 2019)
34 pp.

Olive Harvest in Palestine is a picture book that shows a beautiful slice of Palestinian life as it relates to olives. The story follows two Palestinian girls, Manal and Noor, as they participate in their community's tradition of harvesting and processing olives into olive oil. The girls have fun as they follow the lead of their community in this collective effort, and they learn from their father the ancestral and cultural importance for Palestinians of harvesting olives and producing olive oil. (5 years and older.) *TP*

Salim's Soccer Ball: A Story of Palestinian Resilience

By Tala El-fahmawi
Illustrated by Neveen Abu Saleem
(Tablo Publishing, 2022)
50 pp.

Salim's Soccer Ball conveys, in simple rhyming stanzas, the resilience and strength that Palestinians find in each other and in the land. Salim loses his soccer ball. As he asks the adults in his community for help, each one shares how they have persevered in their contributions to the community despite living under occupation. Author Tala El-fahmawi creatively helps children think about loss, grief, and the healing that can be found amongst loved ones and in community. *Salim's Soccer Ball* is an age-appropriate introduction to the concepts of apartheid and occupation, as well as Palestinian cultural practices as a form of resilience. (5 years and older.) *TP*

Baba, What Does My Name Mean?

By Rifk Ebeid
Illustrated by Lamaa Jawhari
(Rifk Ebeid, 2020)
32 pp.

Rifk Ebeid's *Baba, What Does My Name Mean?* follows Saamidah's magical journey through Palestine to discover the true meaning of her name: patient, persistent, and one who perseveres. She visits different Palestinian cities, learning their ancient history, geography, and the deep roots of her Palestinian ancestors on this land. When she returns home from Palestine, she understands why her parents named her Saamidah and the role she must play in helping to free Palestine. As a child, I remember feeling like I didn't belong because I could never walk over to a map in my classrooms and see my father's home, Palestine. When I asked, I was met by responses that Palestine didn't exist. Most world maps in our schools do not include Palestine, further erasing Palestine from students' consciousness and denying Palestinian children their sense of belonging in the classroom. By reading Ebeid's book that reframes Palestinian geography and history, students can learn about these Indigenous communities and the land they originally inhabited. *NF*

Sitti's Bird: A Gaza Story

By Malak Mattar
(Crocodile Books, 2022)
32 pp.

Malak Mattar's *Sitti's Bird* is a touching story about a budding artist from Gaza named Malak, who dreams of showing her artwork to the world. (See Donnie Rotkin and Jody Sokolower's teaching article, "*Sitti's Bird: A Gaza Story*, p. 87.) Her grandmother's bird, trapped in a cage, teaches her about her own life as a child in Gaza, unable to fully pursue her dreams. As a child, my Egyptian mother always talked with me about Gaza because it is the Palestinian region that shares a border with Egypt, my other home. Yet, she was careful and thoughtful in the way she chose to expose me gradually to the reality of Israeli brutality and occupation for many Gazan children. My mother, an Egyptian artist, used the healing power of the arts to teach me about Palestine as a child. *Sitti's Bird* exhibits how the arts can teach children about sensitive topics related to injustice and brutality in an age-appropriate way, particularly through Malak's inspiring story as a Gazan artist. *NF*

The Mouse Who Saved Egypt

By Karim Alrawi
Illustrated by Bee Willey
(Crocodile Books, 2011)
26 pp.

This picture book is a translation of an ancient Egyptian folktale. A young Egyptian prince stumbles on a mouse trapped in a thorn bush and sets him free. When the prince becomes pharaoh of

Egypt, he is a kind and generous leader. Suddenly, the kingdom is threatened with attack. The mouse he rescued saves the day by mobilizing all the mice of Egypt to eat through the enemy army's clothing, straps, saddles, and armor. Instead of Arab cultures stereotypically portrayed as barbaric and violent, here children are exposed to a better introduction. The prince helps out a little mouse because of his kind heart; through doing good, good is brought back to him. *The Mouse Who Saved Egypt* is a great way to open dialogue about kindness and the good you put out into the world without expecting anything in return. (Preschool and early elementary.) *TP*

Rest in My Shade:
A Poem About Roots

By Nora Lester Murad and Danna Masad
(Olive Branch Press, 2019)
46 pp.

Rest in My Shade is a poem from the perspective of an olive tree. The tree grows from an abandoned olive pit to become part of a Palestinian olive grove. After many years, it is violently uprooted by an Israeli bulldozer, thrown on a truck, and eventually replanted in a public square. The

poem focuses on the pain and longing of displacement and the importance of resilience. Because of the thematic focus on displacement, *Rest in My Shade* can open discussions about the reasons why people are displaced, and how that feels. The poem only alludes to the occupation in Palestine and the forced exile of Palestinians. So, for example, there is no explanation of why the bulldozer uproots the tree. It is left to educators to provide context. Each page of *Rest in My Shade* is illustrated with the work of a different Palestinian artist, providing opportunities for comparison and art projects. More resources for teaching: https://www.restinmyshade.com/teaching-resources/(Early elementary and up.) *TP*

We Are Palestinian: A Celebration
of Culture and Tradition

By Reem Kassis
Illustrated by Noha Eilouti
(Crocodile Books, 2022)
105 pp.

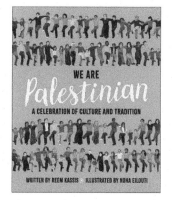

We Are Palestinian is a nonfiction introduction to Palestinian culture. From crafts to agriculture, and geography to food, each page celebrates the depth of Palestinian history and the diversity of its people and traditions. This is an excellent introduction to explorations of culture in general. (Upper elementary and above.) *TP*

A Child's View of Gaza: Palestinian Children's Art and the Fight Against Censorship

By Middle East Children's Alliance
(Pacific View Press, 2012)
79 pp

A Child's View of Gaza: Palestinian Children's Art and the Fight Against Censorship is equally compelling for children, older students, and adults. The captioned illustrations were created by Palestinian children who lived through the Israeli bombardment of Gaza in 2008–09. The pictures were drawn as part of an effort to help children deal with the horrors they had experienced. The nonprofit Middle East Children's Alliance (MECA), arranged to display a collection of these pictures at the Museum of Children's Art in Oakland, California. However, under pressure from the Jewish Federation of the East Bay and other organizations, the museum backed out of the agreement at the last minute. MECA held an art exhibit as a demonstration in front of the museum and then moved the exhibit to a nearby storefront. *A Child's View of Gaza* includes a foreword by Alice Walker. The children's pictures are detailed, colorful, and provide a matter-of-fact yet powerful window into the reality of being a child under attack by planes, bombs, and soldiers. *KDS*

Oranges in No Man's Land

By Elizabeth Laird
(Haymarket Books, 2008)
99 pp.

In *Oranges in No Man's Land*, Ayesha describes her family's experiences during the civil war in Lebanon. When their neighborhood is bombed and Ayesha's family dashes to escape, her mother is killed. Ayesha and her siblings are left under the care of her grandmother because her father is away. They find shelter in an abandoned building

with other refugees from the fighting. When Ayesha's grandmother runs out of her medicine and becomes desperately ill, Ayesha needs all her courage and ingenuity to cross two armed checkpoints and find her grandmother's doctor. Along the way, we see examples of resilience and compassion. *Oranges in No Man's Land* is an easy-to-read novel with challenging content, so a good choice for students learning English or struggling to read at their level of intellectual maturity. There is a realistic, although not overly graphic, depiction of the impact of war on children and their families. There is no overview of what led to the war. We're left with the perspective that wars are a result of mutual prejudices — that if only people were nicer or wanted peace more, wars would cease to exist. This provides an opportunity for teachers to encourage students to think about why people get into fights, and why nations get into wars. Is it just about feelings? When is it a struggle for justice? Or a drive for more power? In the abandoned building, Ayesha makes friends with Samar, a young girl who is deaf, and who teaches Ayesha sign. Ayesha pretends she is deaf to avoid capture at one of the checkpoints. This use of Samar as a plot device felt disrespectful to some reviewers. This would be an important point of discussion with students. (Upper elementary and up.) *TP*

Ida in the Middle

Written by Nora Lester Murad
Illustrated by Kate Cosgrove
(Interlink Publishing, 2022)
223 pp.

Middle school student Ida tries to sit where she is "unnoticeable, like the dust on last year's history books." She seeks to avoid stereotypical insults hurled at her for being from a Palestinian immigrant family. The school's silence aggravates the problem. Ida notes, "Nobody even says the word 'Palestine' in my school. The teachers are afraid to teach anything about the Middle East, even if the topic has nothing to do with politics." As the mother of three girls raised in the West Bank and now living in the United States, author Nora Lester Murad is deeply grounded in the book's characters and themes. And she knows how to captivate middle school readers. Ida eats an olive that sends her time-traveling from her home in Massachusetts to her family's home in the West Bank, introducing readers to both the beauty of their village and the violence of the Israeli occupation that eventually forced her family to leave for their safety. This experience gives Ida the courage and conviction to speak in a school assembly about the realities of the occupation, comparing it to what happened to "Indigenous peoples here. How they were pushed off their land and survived so much violence, as if they weren't human." Stepping out of the shadows, she insists that students and teachers see her and her family's humanity. *DM*

Determined to Stay:
Palestinian Youth Fight for Their Village

By Jody Sokolower
Introduction by Nick Estes
(Olive Branch Press, 2021)
230 pp.

As I read Jody Sokolower's *Determined to Stay: Palestinian Youth Fight for Their Village*, my childhood memories of visits to Palestine flooded my heart with emotion. This book is the perfect blend of well-documented experiences of Palestinians living under brutal military occupation and proof that Palestinians remain steadfast in their dignified fight for liberation. This is exactly the type of book I want my daughter reading in her 9th-grade classroom. *Determined to Stay* includes a series of stories mainly shared from Silwan, a Palestinian village outside the walls of Jerusalem's Old City, historically a densely populated village where generations of Palestinians have resided. Israel illegally annexed Silwan to expand East Jerusalem and Israeli domination over the area. In the process, Israel demolished homes and allowed Israeli settlers to move onto Palestinian land, arresting children and terrorizing residents. *Determined to Stay*: That phrase describes precisely the willpower of the Palestinians in Silwan. Sokolower illuminates this willpower through the stories of those she met during her multiple trips to Palestine. I appreciate Sokolower's commitment to share the voices of the leaders of the Madaa Creative Center and the children of Silwan. The Madaa Creative Center represents the hopes of a multigenerational community of Palestinians who pass on their traditions, create music, and join in dabke as a form of resistance. It is through their eyes and experiences that we gain a better understanding of their struggle. (Middle school and above.) *NSD*

They Called Me a Lioness:
A Palestinian Girl's Fight for Freedom
By Ahed Tamimi and Dena Takruri
(One World, 2023)
288 pp.

In 2017, Ahed Tamimi's story went viral after a leaked video showed her confronting Israeli soldiers who forced their way into her family's home and shot her cousin with a rubber-coated bullet, severely injuring him. Tamimi then slapped one of the soldiers, which led to her arrest and detention. In this memoir, Ahed tells us about her childhood in Nabi Salih, a village near Ramallah in the West Bank. From childhood games playing Israeli Army vs. Palestinians, to family trips to Acre, she relates day-to-day experiences and pivotal moments that reflect life amidst oppression and violence. Tamimi describes her reluctance to become an activist, her increasing militance, and the events that led to her arrest, interrogation, and detention. Through her eyes, we see the

racist power dynamics within the Israeli judicial system. Her account of her time in prison is stark. She is constantly bullied by guards, both physically and psychologically. But Ahed and the other detainees hold classes in their shared cell to continue their education, empowering and inspiring one another. Overall, this book does an excellent job of exposing the oppression of Palestinians in the grip of Israeli apartheid and the resilience of youth and their families. The early chapters, in particular, contain substantial contextual information that may be challenging for some students without scaffolding. (High school and up.) *TP*

Baddawi
By Leila Abdelrazaq
(Just World Books, 2015)
125 pp.

Baddawi, which means bedouin or nomad in Arabic, is the name of Ahmad's refugee camp in Lebanon. Ahmad, who is the author/illustrator's father, grew up in the Palestinian refugee camp in northern Lebanon because his parents were forced out of Palestine in 1948. This accessible graphic novel does a good job describing one long-term impact of the Nakba on Palestinians forced into diaspora. With humor and empathy, the story focuses on Ahmad and the trials he faces as a child and youth, how he copes with the harsh reality  of his situation, and what he makes of it. Eventually he decides to put all his energy and time into his education in order to escape the death and violence that surround him. The story ends as Ahmad heads to the United States to continue his education. Most Palestinian refugees in Lebanon, even generations later, are barred from citizenship and are prevented by Lebanese law from working and from public education. This creates opportunity for discussions of the extent to which refugees in the United States are or are not integrated into U.S. society. (High school and above.) *TP*

Outside the Ark:
An Artist's Journey in Occupied Palestine
By Ellen O'Grady
(2005)
47 pp.

A nonfiction book that relies on firsthand experience of the occupation is the picture book *Outside the Ark: An Artist's Journey in Occupied Palestine* by Ellen O'Grady, an artist-activist who worked for six years in the occupied West Bank and Gaza. O'Grady tells the stories of Palestinians she knew, including 8-year-old Mahmoud, who was killed by Israeli bullets, and 69-year-old Salwa, unable to see her daughter who lives in Jordan and is prohibited by Israel from returning to her village. Although this is a picture book, teachers may find that it is most appropriate for older elementary students. I sometimes found the handwritten cursive text distracting, but the content and illustrations are powerful — each double page merits its own intensive discussion. *KDS*

A Little Piece of Ground
By Elizabeth Laird
(Haymarket Books, 2016)
240 pp.

Elizabeth Laird's *A Little Piece of Ground* is particularly good. It is set in Ramallah, just north of Jerusalem in the occupied West Bank. After a bombing in Israel, Ramallah is under a strict Israeli curfew that prevents people from leaving their homes for days at a time. The main character, Karim, is a 12-year-old boy from a Muslim family who lives in town and is crazy about soccer. His best friend, Joni, from a Christian family, is also crazy about soccer. While kicking a soccer ball against his apartment building during one of the few breaks in the curfew, Karim meets Hopper, who lives close to a refugee camp across town. Hopper takes Karim to a vacant piece of ground near the refugee camp. It is filled with the rubble of demolished buildings, but they think they can convert it into a soccer field. The three boys do exactly that by hauling rocks and rusty machinery to one side of the plot of land. They discover a car buried under the rubble and convert it into a den. One day, while the three boys are playing soccer with boys from the refugee camp, Israeli tanks roll into their soccer field and the boys take off for safety. However, Karim sprains his ankle and is unable to escape; he ends up hiding inside the abandoned car, trapped for several days. The author, a well-known British writer of books for young adults who lived in Ramallah while doing research for this book, does a good job of conveying the friendship and shared interests of the boys and the tension created for Palestinians by life under Israeli occupation. *KDS*

The Shepherd's Granddaughter
By Anne Laurel Carter
(Groundwood Books, 2008)
224 pp.

Canadian author Anne Laurel Carter wrote *The Shepherd's Granddaughter* after living in both Israel and Palestine. Amani is a young girl who lives with her extended family in a West Bank village and wants to follow in the footsteps of her grandfather and become a shepherd. She and her family experience terrifying situations when a group of illegal Jewish settlers occupy a hill overlooking the village. Under the protective eyes of Israeli soldiers, the settlers poison Amani's sheep; destroy her family's ancient olive, fig, and lemon trees; appropriate their land and water sources; and threaten villagers with death if they do not leave their land. Amani observes the demolition of her house by an armored Caterpillar bulldozer and the arrests of two close family members: her father, when he returns home to find his house being demolished, and her uncle, when he and other villagers demonstrate peacefully against the building of a Jewish-only settler road on their land. When Amani's mother returns to Palestine from visiting her dying mother in Canada, she is repeatedly denied re-entry at the Jordanian border. It is only after several days of this intimidation that she is allowed back to her home and family. A subplot focuses on Jonathan, a 16-year-old Jewish American who lives with his father on the illegal settlement, hates what his people are doing to Palestinians, and returns to New York City to become an anti-occupation activist. *The*

Shepherd's Granddaughter does a good job of portraying life under occupation from the perspective of a plucky young Palestinian girl. Amani witnesses disagreements within her extended family around whether to trust Israelis who oppose the occupation and whether to engage in peaceful or armed struggle, which creates an additional context for critical thinking and discussion among students. *KDS*

Where the Streets Had a Name

By Randa Abdel-Fattah

(Scholastic, 2010)

320 pp.

Where the Streets Had a Name, by Randa Abdel-Fattah, an Australian of Palestinian and Egyptian heritage, tells the story of 13-year-old Hayaat, who lives with her family in a cramped apartment in Bethlehem in the occupied West Bank. Hayaat's elderly grandmother is from Jerusalem, but was forced out in 1948 when the state of Israel was declared, and has not been allowed to return. When she becomes sick, Hayaat is convinced that bringing a handful of earth from their ancestral home will help her grandmother get well. This sets in place a dramatic journey for Hayaat and her best friend, Samy, a free-spirited young Palestinian boy. Although their journey is short in distance, it is interminable because of checkpoints and a curfew. The story, told through Hayaat's eyes, provides readers with a clear window into a young teen's life under the Israeli occupation. *KDS*

Jerusalem: Chronicles from the Holy City

By Guy Delisle

(Drawn & Quarterly, 2012)

336 pp.

Jerusalem: Chronicles from the Holy City is a travelogue in the form of a graphic novel. The author/illustrator spends a year living in Beit Hanina near Jerusalem with his family. While his wife works for Doctors Without Borders, Delisle explores the area and takes care of his young children. Delisle is the curious but uninvolved outsider, creating vignettes of his experiences with Palestinians and Israelis as he tries to understand life in the West Bank. Through his eyes, we share his initial encounters with checkpoints, curfews, and other human rights abuses.

We see how different Hebron looks when the guide is an Israeli settler or when it is a Palestinian resident. Although Delisle never takes an explicit position on Israel's impact on Palestinian life, we gradually see that Palestinians are living under a system of apartheid rule. Delisle's wife, whose experiences as a medical worker in Gaza could have provided sharp insights into life there under the siege, has essentially no voice in the book. This prompts the reader to realize that women's voices are largely missing throughout the book. What information and insights are we missing because we only hear from men? *Jerusalem: Chronicles from the Holy City* provides an opportunity for students to decide what they think about Palestine-Israel as Delisle describes incident after incident of life in cities and villages throughout the West Bank. In this way, it's a nonthreatening introduction to the subject. However, in addition to the dearth of women's voices, there is nothing in the book about Palestinian resistance and few explicit descriptions of Palestinian resilience. For serious study, *Jerusalem* needs ancillary videos, articles, and activities to provide context, history, and analysis. (High school and above.) *TP*

Tasting the Sky: A Palestinian Childhood

By Ibtisam Barakat

(Square Fish, 2008)

208 pp.

Ibtisam Barakat's memoir *Tasting the Sky: A Palestinian Childhood* evocatively conveys what it is like to be forced by war out of one's home and familiar life into life as a refugee. Barakat was 3 when her family became refugees during the 1967 war. They joined about 200,000 other Palestinians who fled Israeli forces that invaded East Jerusalem, the West Bank, and Gaza. Barakat and her family lived for several months in Jordan before being able to return to their home in the West Bank, which was then occupied by Israel. The first part of the book is set in 1981. The author is 17, traveling on a bus in the West Bank from Birzeit, where she has gone to check on mail from international pen pals, to her home in Ramallah. Her bus is stopped at a checkpoint and all the passengers are taken to a military detention center, kept

in custody for no reason, and harassed for hours by Israeli police before being allowed to continue on their journey. The second section of *Tasting the Sky* focuses on Barakat's memories of life as a refugee and then under occupation from the age of 3 to 7. Presumably she drew on family members' recollections to augment her own early childhood memories because the descriptions are so detailed. She describes how frightening the war is and what it was like to flee her home and be separated from her family. She describes her family's life in a refugee camp in Jordan and their return to their home on a hill near Ramallah in the West Bank. Because it is in the center of an Israeli training ground, they are not allowed to leave the house during the day. Afraid for her children's safety, Barakat's mother takes her children to live in an orphanage, where she finds work. *KDS*

Background Books

The Question of Palestine
By Edward Said
(Vintage, 1979)
320 pp.

The Question of Palestine by Edward Said is a critical examination of the history, politics, and human dimensions of the Palestinian struggle for self-determination. Said, widely known as one of the most influential Palestinian intellectuals, offers a compelling narrative that challenges Western perceptions of the Israeli-Palestinian conflict. He explores the roots of Palestinian dispossession, the impact of colonialism, and the complexities of identity and representation. It's an essential read for educators seeking to engage with the historical and contemporary realities of Palestine. *SS*

The Ethnic Cleansing of Palestine
By Ilan Pappé
(Oneworld, 2007)
336 pp.

The 1948 Palestine-Israel War is known to Israelis as "The War of Independence," but for Palestinians it will forever be the Nakba, the "catastrophe." Alongside the creation of the state of Israel, the end of the war led to one of the largest forced migrations in modern history. Around a million people were expelled from their homes at gunpoint, civilians were massacred, and hundreds of Palestinian villages deliberately destroyed. Though the truth about the mass expulsion has been systematically distorted and suppressed, had it taken place in the 21st century it would have been called "ethnic cleansing." Prominent Israeli academic Ilan Pappé argues for the international recognition of this tragedy. He asks questions that the world has so far failed to ask to reveal the real story behind the events of 1948. Based on meticulous research, including declassified Israeli archival material, Dr. Pappé's vivid and timely account demonstrates conclusively that "transfer" — a euphemism for ethnic cleansing — was from the start an integral part of a carefully planned strategy, and lies at the root of today's ongoing conflict in the Middle East. *IPS*

The Way to the Spring — Life and Death in Palestine
By Ben Ehrenreich
(Penguin, 2017)
464 pp.

Some commentary about Ehrenreich's book: Molly Crabapple: "In *The Way to the Spring*, Ben

Ehrenreich accomplishes an extraordinary feat of journalism. His portraits of Palestinian resistance are luminous; his writing subtle, meticulously documented, and deeply human, showing the nuanced empathy that slashes through the best funded government propaganda. This is a necessary book." Adam Hochschild: "Ben Ehrenreich's rendition of the Palestinian experience is powerful, deep, and heartbreaking, so much closer to the ground than the Middle East reporting we usually see. I wish there were more writers as brave." Raja Shehadeh: "Of the voluminous amount of writing about the occupation this is one to treasure. He retains an intimacy with his subject without losing his critical distance. So much has been written about the occupation of the Palestinian territories by Israel but rarely with such vividness, eloquence, and success in illuminating complex historical and political realities. This is a superbly intelligent, informative, and critical book about one of the fundamental issues of our time."

The Hundred Years' War on Palestine: A History of Settler Colonialism and Resistance, 1917–2017
By Rashid Khalidi
(Picador, 2020)
320 pp.

Every teacher hoping to teach about the Israeli-Palestinian conflict should first read Rashid Khalidi's essential *The Hundred Years' War on Palestine*. Khalidi, the Edward Said Professor of Modern Arab Studies at Columbia University, outlines what he sees as the six separate-but-connected wars waged on Palestine between World War I up until shortly before the catastrophe unfolding today. It is scholarly, yet personal, as Khalidi was an eyewitness to a number of these wars. The book begins with Khalidi's great-great-great-uncle, the Palestinian scholar and Ottoman official Yusuf Diya al-Din Pasha al-Khalidi, who wrote to Theodor Herzl, Zionism's founding father, in 1899, stressing that Palestine was not an empty land awaiting Zionist settlement: "It is inhabited by others." He concluded, "In the name of God, let Palestine be left alone." As Khalidi demonstrates,

the heart of today's conflicts can be traced back to the original Zionist aspiration of "transforming most of an overwhelmingly Arab country into a predominantly Jewish state." The book's thesis is that "the modern history of Palestine can best be understood in these terms: as a colonial war waged against the indigenous population, by a variety of parties, to force them to relinquish their homeland to another people against their will." Khalidi clearly and compellingly brings this story to life. *BB*

Black Power and Palestine: Transnational Countries of Color
By Michael R. Fischbach
(Stanford University Press, 2019)
296 pp.

"SNCC support for Palestinians clearly was an exercise in the forging of a revolutionary identity: African Americans would support Third World liberation regardless of what whites wanted." This recollection by the Student Nonviolent Coordinating Committee's program director Cleveland Sellers underscores the premise of Michael R. Fischback's book *Black Power and Palestine*. Fischbach scours primary sources to uncover the complex and often changing positions Black leaders in the 1960s and 1970s took on Palestine. The book begins with the political environment that gave rise to the expansion of transnationalism within the African American community and establishes the Black power movement as the epicenter of what became "pro-Palestinian, anti-Israel" viewpoints in the United States. Fischbach writes, "Yet, in issuing strident statements of solidarity with the Palestinians as a people fighting to be free just as they were doing, these activists also were intertwining their own identity and vision of place in America with the Palestinians' struggle." Throughout the book, he also documents the backlash that this burgeoning solidarity caused amongst more conservative Black leaders. *Black Power and Palestine* celebrates the metamorphosis of an African American identity that made them powerful allies on the international stage and champions against colonialism in Palestine. *KR*

19 Varieties of Gazelle:
Poems of the Middle East
Edited by Naomi Shihab Nye
(Greenwillow, 2005)
142 pp.

Naomi Shihab Nye has written or edited several anthologies of poetry focused on the Middle East. In her collection *19 Varieties of Gazelle: Poems of the Middle East*, she writes about being Arab American, about being Palestinian American, about her family, and about living in the West Bank. The poems are beautifully crafted and evocative. For example, toward the end of the poem "Going to the Spring," about women collecting water in a traditional way, she writes:

> These feet write history on the dirt road
> and no one reads it, unless you are here
> to read it, unless you are thirsty
> and cup your hands where the women
> tell you to hold them,
> throwing your head back
> for the long sweet draft.
> *KDS*

The Flag of Childhood:
Poems from the Middle East
Edited by Naomi Shihab Nye
(Aladdin, 1998)
100 pp.

The poems in this volume, written by poets from 14 countries, including Palestinians and Jewish Israelis, explore and honor daily life in the Middle East, and life for Middle Eastern immigrants and their children in North America. The collection offers readers a beautifully worked window into what Nye refers to in the introduction as a complicated center of dramatic cultural and religious history. The revered Palestinian writer and poet Mahmoud Darwish wrote primarily for adults. However, his compelling poetry captures life for Palestinians, from their forced dislocation when the state of Israel was formed, through exile and occupation, and many of his poems can be shared with intermediate grade readers. One example is "Identity Card"; the penultimate stanza captures the losses that Palestinians have experienced:

> Write down!
> I am an Arab
> You have stolen the orchards of my ancestors
> And the land which I cultivated
> Along with my children
> And you left nothing for us
> Except for these rocks.
> So will the State take them
> As it has been said?!
> *KDS*

Websites

Teach Palestine
teachpalestine.org
(2024, updated regularly)

Teach Palestine is an indispensable resource by and for K–12 teachers and teacher educators focused on bringing Palestine into classrooms and schools. It is a project of the Middle East Children's Alliance (MECA), based in Berkeley, California. MECA is a nonprofit organization working for the rights of children in the Middle East by sending humanitarian aid, supporting projects for children, and educating North American and international communities about the effects of U.S. foreign policy on children in the region. Several of the lessons in this book began as articles at Teach Palestine; and the project's co-coordinators are major contributors to the book, Samia Shoman as an author and book editor, and Jody Sokolower as an author of multiple pieces. *ZEP*

Visualizing Palestine
visualizingpalestine.org
(2024, updated regularly)

Visualizing Palestine is a nonprofit "dedicated to using data and research to visually communicate Palestinian experiences to provoke narrative change." The graphic storytelling at Visualizing Palestine can help students "see" Palestinian reality in new ways, but also prompt students' own imaginative visual projects to story Palestine. For example, one January 2024 illustration depicts school buses lined up into the distance: "It would take 177 buses* to carry the Palestinian children killed by Israeli forces in Gaza. (*72 children per bus.)" Another illustration depicts the disparity in water usage for cooking, hydration, and hygiene: Israel — 230 liters per person/per day; World Health Organization minimum per person/per day — 100 liters; Gaza, before the war per person/per day — 88; Gaza today — 3 liters per person/per day. Share these and others at the site with students and have them develop their own. And see Visualizing Palestine images throughout this book, pp. 48–49, 69, 120, 139. *BB*

Zinn Education Project
Teaching About Palestine-Israel and the
Unfolding Genocide in Gaza
zinnedproject.org
2024

The Zinn Education Project — coordinated by Teaching for Change and Rethinking Schools, the publisher of this book — launched the site on "Teaching About Palestine-Israel and the Unfolding Genocide in Gaza" shortly after Oct. 7, 2023. A description at the site explains, "One cannot understand this tragedy without acknowledging its history. While many education groups provide resources for teaching about the crisis as a "conflict" rooted in antisemitism and Islamophobia, that sole emphasis is misleading. Students need to examine how the current crisis is shaped in large part by settler colonial history, and the role played by world powers. As educators, we must help our students make historical explanations for today's violence. . . Lessons at the Zinn Education Project are filled with examples of how ideas of social inequality justified horrific injustice — the theft of land from Native Americans, the enslavement of Africans, the genocide of Jews, the incarceration of Japanese Americans, and so much more. Our curriculum

must put empathy at the center, inviting our students to critique policies and practices that begin from the premise that some people's lives are worth more than others'." The site seeks to offer educators "resources to help students probe the long history of colonialism and resistance in Palestine-Israel, the role that our own government has played — and to imagine what justice looks like." *ZEP*

Pali Answers
PaliAnswers.com
2024

Teachers are called upon to be instant experts about the latest world crisis. And usually, we are not. Some of us have studied Palestine-Israel for years, yet some of us have only recently had our hearts touched by what we see in the media, and have committed ourselves to learn more as we teach our students. Needless to say, widespread misinformation — even lies — infect the discourse about the conflict in Gaza and the Occupied Territories, and Israel, so knowing what is true can be a challenge. Pali Answers is a new crowdsourced still-in-process database of short responses designed explicitly to help people contend with anti-Palestine myths. For example: "It all started on Oct. 7." Response: "This kind of historical amnesia and dishonest selective historiography enables Israel to keep breaking international law with impunity. As the U.N. secretary-general said, 'It is important to recognize the attack by Hamas did not happen in a vacuum.' Palestinians have been subjected to over 100 years of war, displacement, occupation, and discrimination by Israel and her imperial backers." Myth: "There was no Nakba, it was the Arab armies that attacked Israel in 1948." Response: "More than 250,000 Palestinians had already been ethnically cleansed out of Palestine before any Arab army had set foot in Palestine. Israel's ethnic cleansing plan was laid out from the 1930s and carried out starting in 1947. Arab armies at no point aimed to destroy Israel, they tried to maintain as much of the territory as possible and prevent an even larger genocide." Tough question from a student? Check out PaliAnswers.com. *BB*

Democracy Now! The War and Peace Report
Hosted by Amy Goodman and Juan González
democracynow.org
Monday – Friday, 60 min.

This is the indispensable newscast. For years, the daily, hour-long *Democracy Now!* has featured stories about struggles for racial justice, the impact of climate chaos, student activism around the world — and the ongoing crisis in Palestine-Israel. As horrific and hard to watch as the daily news can be, *Democracy Now!* offers a "people's history" focus on the activists who know how tough things are but keep working to make a difference. Recent segments have featured the poignant, eloquent case brought by South Africa accusing Israel of committing genocide in Gaza; a Chicago ER doctor testifying to the viciousness of Israeli attacks on Gaza hospitals, but also to the heroism of those working to keep people alive in impossible conditions; the Palestinian journalist Akram al-Satarri, on what it means to report the news in the Occupied Territories in "The Struggle to Survive, Stay Sane"; Tal Mitnick, the first Israeli jailed for refusing military service in what he calls the "revenge war" on Gaza; and so much more. Bring to life the insights from the film *The Occupation of the American Mind* on the manufacture of propaganda by asking students to compare, say, *ABC World News Tonight* with *Democracy Now!* — whose voices matter, whose stories get told, what history is explored? *BB*

Films

Israelism
Directed by Erin Axelman and Sam Eilertsen
(Tikkun Olam Productions, 2023)
84 min.

"Something is deeply wrong here, and it is breaking my heart. What we've been told is that the only way that Jews can be safe is if Palestinians are not safe. And I guess the more I learned about that, the more I came to see that as a lie." Those are the words of Simone Zimmerman, who grew up in Los Angeles, attended Jewish day school, colored Israeli flags, went to Jewish camps, lived in Israel on a high school exchange program, and even spent time acting the role of an Israeli soldier — and then decided to get answers to her questions about the lives of Palestinians. The heart of the wonderful film *Israelism* is transformation: young Jews fundamentally changing not just their attitudes about Israel, Palestine, and Palestinians, but about their own role in the world — coming to see themselves as solidarity activists. The filmmakers begin by introducing us to a host of pro-Israel proponents and their arguments: Israel is the place you can go to be safe; Israel is the insurance policy; I cannot separate Judaism and Israel — that is my identity; it's cool to be an Israeli soldier. The film unravels these conclusions and attitudes through the stories of U.S. Jews whose experiences contradict conventional pro-Israeli positions. At almost an hour and a half, *Israelism* is long, but because it is poignant and filled with point-counterpoint storytelling, it makes for a student-friendly film. *BB*

The Occupation of the American Mind: Israel's Public Relations War in the United States
Directed by Loretta Alper and Jeremy Earp
(Media Education Foundation, 2016)
(Three versions: 21 min./45 min./84 min.)

Here is Israeli Prime Minister Benjamin Netanyahu, depicted in *The Occupation of the American Mind*: "I think Americans largely get it. They know who the good guys are and who the bad guys are." The film's premise is that U.S. attitudes about Palestine and Israel have been shaped by a decades-long propaganda campaign that has framed Israel as the victim, the aggrieved — the good guys — and the Palestinians as terrorists, "irrational Muslim fanatics" — the bad guys. As the film points out, pro-Israeli propaganda in the United States requires widespread amnesia — blotting out the history of early Zionist settlement in a land that at the start of the 20th century was 94 percent Palestinian Arab; the 1948 ethnic cleansing of more than 700,000 Palestinians; the 1967 occupation of East Jerusalem, the West Bank, and Gaza; Israel's 1982 invasion of Lebanon; and more. Israeli propaganda erases history, and it erases land — as the conflict in Palestine-Israel has always been centered on who will control the land. *The Occupation of the American Mind* helps students recognize how, in the words of Sut Jhally, executive director of the Media Education Foundation, the media and politicians consistently frame "Palestinian resistance as terrorism and Israeli aggression as self-defense." (Helpfully, the filmmakers make available a transcript of the full film: mediaed.org/transcripts/The-Occupation-Of-The-American-Mind-Transcript.pdf.) *BB*

The Night Won't End
Directed by Kavitha Chekuru
(Al Jazeera English, 2024)
78 min.

The Night Won't End is heartbreaking and one of the most compelling tools for educators to expose the devastation caused by Israel's war on Gaza and the role the United States has played in facilitating it. Because journalists have been barred from entering Gaza, Al Jazeera worked with a team of Palestinian journalists to follow three families as they recount their horrific experiences. With stunning cinematography and first-person interviews with relatives of victims, the documentary powerfully exposes the nightmare of Israel's assault. This includes one of the most comprehensive accounts of the murder of 6-year-old Hind Rajab, shot along with six of her relatives and two paramedics coming to her rescue. In addition to telling the gut-wrenching stories of Palestinians navigating months of war, the film carefully presents the Biden administration's continued support for Israel's atrocities despite clear violations of international humanitarian law. *AS*

Remembering the Gaza War: Ibrahim's Tree
By Jen Marlowe
(Donkeysaddle Projects, 2019)
10 min.

In 2009, Israeli forces demolished the Awajah family's home. An Israeli soldier shot and killed their 9-year-old son, Ibrahim. Despite this trag-edy, the family rebuilt what they envisioned as their "dream house." However, during the 2014 assault on Gaza, Israel destroyed their new home as well, severing the olive tree that Ibrahim had lovingly planted as a young child. This video documents the Awajah

family's journey from one devastated home to the next, with Ibrahim's tree standing as a powerful symbol of resilience, regeneration, and the unwavering sumoud — steadfastness — for which Palestinians are renowned. *Ibrahim's Tree* is the fourth installment in a five-part series, produced in collaboration with Donkeysaddle Projects, the Institute for Middle East Understanding (IMEU), and Just Vision, highlighting the profound human impact of Israel's 2014 assault on Gaza. Through this poignant narrative, the series sheds light on the enduring strength and spirit of those who continue to resist and rebuild in the face of unimaginable adversity. *JH*

Vows to My Homeland
(Shoruq and Middle East Children's Alliance, 2023)
Arabic with English subtitles
10 min.

Shoruq, a cultural and community center in Dheisheh Refugee Camp near Bethlehem, took Palestinian youth to visit their ancestral villages. Sarah Faraj was one young participant, and the livestream of her visit is seen by Aya, a teenager living in Gaza. Aya asks Sarah to visit her ancestral village, al-Jura, located a few miles north of the Gaza Strip. Aya surprises her grandmother Um Nabeel with a video call with Sarah, who takes them on a live virtual tour of al-Jura, the village Um Nabeel calls home and refuses to forget. This short, heartfelt video captures the intergenerational Palestinian refusal to forget about their homelands, and would make an excellent introduction to studying forced migrations, the Nakba, Gaza, and/or the right of return. (6th grade and above.) *TP*

I Am from Palestine

Written by Rifk Ebeid
Directed by Iman Zawahry
Animated by Lamaa Jawhari
(Rifk Books, 2023)
6 min.

It is young Saamidah's first day at school. The teacher's opening assignment — "to celebrate diversity" — asks students to go up to the classroom's world map and put "a mark where your family came from." No doubt, it is a problematic assignment for a bunch of reasons, but for Saamidah, it is an impossible assignment. Saamidah's family is from Palestine, and as on so many world maps, Palestine is missing. Jennifer has no problem putting a pin in the United Kingdom. Lily's pin goes in Germany. Saamidah searches for Palestine on the classroom map. There is Israel. There is Jordan. But as the teacher says with a frown, "There is no Palestine on the map. I'll mark Israel for you." At home Saamidah asks her father, "Baba, where am I from?" Through story and song, Saamidah joyfully travels to Palestine in her imagination, and then returns to school, map in hand, to educate her class — and her teacher. The short, delightful *I Am from Palestine* could be used at different grade levels, in different ways. *BB*

Flying Paper

Directed by Nitin Sawhney and Roger Hill
(Flying Paper Productions, 2014)
Arabic with easy-to-read English subtitles
51 min.

This gentle film focuses on 14-year-old Musa, his 12-year-old sister Widad, and their younger siblings and neighbors. The children are building kites as part of a school-sponsored effort to break the Guinness World Record for number of kites flown from the same place. We watch the children build and test their kites and later join thousands of kite-flying students on a Gaza beach. Children talk about the impact of the siege on themselves and their families, but it's in the background. This rare video opportunity to see Palestinian children just being children would make a good introduction to a deeper look at the lives of Palestinian children under occupation or to a discussion of how children participate in carrying culture from one generation to the next. *Flying Paper* might be a little long for elementary school students; some sections in the middle could easily be skipped. (Upper elementary, secondary.) *TP*

Frontiers of Dreams and Fears

Directed by Mai Masri
(Nour Productions Film, 2001)
Arabic with English subtitles
55 min.

This documentary follows the experiences of two young girls — Mona, who lives in the Shatila refugee camp in Beirut, Lebanon, and Manar, who lives in Dheisheh refugee camp near Bethlehem in Palestine's West Bank. Through written correspondence, the girls form a friendship and compare their experiences. After the Israelis are forced out of southern Lebanon in 2000, the friends are able to meet at the border fence between Lebanon and the West Bank, solidifying their relationship despite their physical separation. They are joined by hundreds of Palestinian refugees, reaching across the border wire to touch family members and friends they haven't seen in decades. Manar tells Mona about her trips to Palestinian villages that Israelis destroyed. At a friend's request, Manar visits Mona's family's village as well, relaying how beautiful but depleted the area is now. These sequences contribute to the ongoing theme of right of return, which the children repeatedly reference as a source of hope. The documentary overall does an excellent job demonstrating the shared experiences of oppression for young Palestinians, embedded in the everyday highs and lows that are universal for adolescents, and highlighting their resilience and commitment to their heritage and rights. (Upper elementary, middle, secondary.) *TP*

Inside Israeli Apartheid

By Yumna Patel
(Palestine Productions, 2022)
22 min.

This short video introduces the concept of apartheid and its relevance to Israeli policies toward

Palestinians. It discusses the factors that constitute a definition of apartheid and how they are experienced by Palestinians every day. Through exposing different facets of Israeli rule over Palestinians — from segregated housing to control of movement from one place to another, to hierarchies of citizenship, etc. — the video reveals the policies and legal mechanisms that marginalize and discriminate against Palestinians. Although there are limitations to an anti-apartheid framework (equality under the law is not the same as liberation), this video is a good resource as an introduction — the brief historical information and up-to-date conditions demonstrate in an easily accessible format the severity of the human rights violations taking place. (Middle, secondary.) *TP*

My Neighbourhood
Directed by Julia Bacha and Rebekah Wingert-Jabi
(Just Vision, 2012)
Arabic and English with English subtitles
26 min.

This short film chronicles the story of Mohammed El Jurd, a Palestinian 11-year-old whose family is forced out of their home in the East Jerusalem neighborhood of Sheikh Jarrah by Israeli settlers. In fact, the settlers are trying to take over all the homes in Sheikh Jarrah. Mohammed comes of age in the midst of unrelenting tension with the Israeli settlers and growing resistance among both Palestinians and progressive Israelis. In addition to Mohammed, there are interviews with members of his family, other evicted residents, Israeli settlers, and Israelis who come to see the injustice and join the demonstrations, including one Israeli mother who is influenced by her teenage children to join the movement to save Sheikh Jarrah. (Upper elementary, middle and high school, post-secondary.) *TP*

The Present
Directed by Farah Nabulsi
(Philistine Films, 2020)
Arabic and English with English subtitles
25 min.

This great introduction to Palestine for younger students focuses on Yasmine and Yusef, a young girl and her father traveling from one West Bank town to another to buy Yasmine's mother a new refrigerator as an anniversary gift. The film centers on their experiences at the Israeli checkpoint that lies between their house and the appliance store. Yasmine watches as her father is interrogated, ridiculed, and briefly caged by the Israeli soldiers, while Israeli cars breeze through the checkpoint without question. Finally, Yasmine and Yusef make it through. On the trip back, pushing the refrigerator on a wobbly dolly, the father endures more abuse, only to discover that the refrigerator won't fit through the narrow Palestinian gate; the soldiers refuse to let him use the wide Israeli passage. Tempers mount between Yusef and the soldiers. It seems that the day will end in tragedy, but Yasmine takes the lead. Taking advantage of the soldiers' distraction, she calmly pushes the refrigerator through the Israeli gate and toward her home. Because the relationship between Yasmine and her father is so transparent and tender, students from elementary school on will have a strong connection to the story and many questions. This makes *The Present* an excellent cultural energizer to start learning about Palestine. (Upper elementary, secondary.) *TP*

Secret Hebron: The School Run
Directed by Donna Baillie
(Journeyman Pictures, 2003)
In Arabic, Hebrew, and English with English subtitles
28 min.

This video shows young Palestinian children in the West Bank city of Hebron who risk being attacked by Israeli soldiers as they try to go to school each morning. Israel keeps the children under curfew for months at a time, making it impossible for them to travel on the "Israeli only" streets to get to school. The youngsters scrabble across the roofs of buildings in an effort to avoid the soldiers below. The film shows the efforts of groups like the Christian Peacemaker Teams to help the children get safely to school. Although the presence of international observers sometimes helps, Israeli soldiers regularly use percussion grenades, tear gas, and rubber bullets against the children. The first section of this video provides an excellent example for elementary and older students of the impact of the occupation on Palestinian children. However, as the video continues, it focuses on the efforts of international peacekeepers to get "clarity" about the regulations, which takes the focus off the children and the efforts of Palestinian parents, teachers, and the community to get them to school despite the occupation. (Elementary, middle, high school.) *TP*

Farha
Directed by Darin J. Sallam
(TaleBox, Laika Film & Television, Chimney, 2021)
Arabic with English subtitles
92 min.

Farha is a story about the 1948 Nakba told through the perspective of a teenage Palestinian girl. The film is set in the 1948 Palestinian countryside on the eve of the Zionist military campaign of ethnic cleansing. The viewer sees the world through the eyes of Farha, the daughter of the village's leader, and learns of her dreams of going to school in the city. Her hopes and excitement for a big life change are quickly diminished when Farha becomes aware of the looming threat against her father and their village. When her village is suddenly attacked by Zionist militias, the viewer watches Farha's life fall apart. In the chaos of the invasion, Farha is locked in a cellar by her father to keep her safe. She escapes and is left to tell her story and bear the burden of what she has witnessed. *Farha* is interesting for high school students as the story is told from a youth perspective. Farha's youthful hope while on the cusp of an exciting life change resonates with high schoolers. This film is also a valuable conversation starter and addition to any lesson on Palestine, human rights, ethnic cleansing, and forced migration as it adds a personal and emotional tone, so necessary when discussing the Nakba. *Farha* also accurately portrays the events of the 1948 Nakba. (Secondary and above.) *TP*

5 Broken Cameras
Directed by Emad Burnat and Guy Davidi
(Kino Lorber, 2021)
In Arabic with English subtitles
90 min.

Emad Burnat, a Palestinian farmer, chronicles the struggle of Bil'in — a West Bank village threatened by illegal Israeli settlements on their land and the construction of Israel's "separation wall." Burnet receives his first camera in 2005 to film the protests in his village as his youngest son Gibreel was born. Structured around the destruction of each of Burnat's five cameras, the film chronicles five years of Bil'in's creative resistance, the price the community pays for their extraordinary determination, and the Israeli forces' increasingly brutal repression — contrasted with Gibreel's growth from infancy to childhood. This film is a strong vehicle for talking about why Palestinians are so committed to staying on their land and for looking at the impact of Israeli settlements on Palestinian land and communities. Note: One could get the impression from this video that Palestinian women are only marginally involved in fighting for Palestinian land and independence. As an additional resource, *Budrus*, also about Palestinian struggle against the "separation wall," focuses on the leadership of young women. (High school, post-secondary.) *TP*

3,000 Nights
By Mai Masri
(Nour Productions Film, 2015)
Arabic with English subtitles
99 min.

After false accusations of conspiring to help a Palestinian child accused of being a terrorist, Layal is arrested and taken to an Israeli women's prison. From the moment she arrives, we see the discrimination and oppression that Palestinians face. Incarcerated Israeli women are allowed personal goods in their cells and their own clothing; the treatment by the guards is noticeably better and less volatile. The Palestinian women, on the other hand, are easily identified (and thus targeted) by their uniforms and barren cells; they are forced to work the worst jobs, and are often terrorized by the Israeli prisoners. Soon after she is imprisoned, Layal discovers she is pregnant. The warden coerces her, in exchange for a visit with her husband, into informing on the other Palestinian prisoners. After she gives birth in chains, Layla is repeatedly forced to decide between the Palestinian women who have supported her and the future well-being of her child. The film's climax occurs when the women prisoners organize a hunger strike, and Layal must decide what to do. *3,000 Nights* does an excellent job portraying the situation of Palestinian political prisoners, and the proximity of Palestinian and Israeli women within the prison spotlights the differences in their experiences. We see the targeting they face, and their insistence on defending themselves and asserting their dignity. Finally, with the birth of Layal's son, the film showcases how committed Palestinians are to fostering hope and cultural identity with new generations: Despite their bleak circumstances and surroundings, the Palestinian women inside create a community that loves and provides for the child in the best ways they can. (Secondary and above.) *TP*

Budrus

Directed by Julia Bacha
(Just Vision, 2009)
Arabic and English with English subtitles
80 min.

Budrus is about the struggle against the Israeli "separation barrier" in one village in the West Bank. Palestinian community organizer Ayed

Morrar works to unite Palestinian political factions and Israeli supporters to save Budrus, his village near Ramallah, from destruction by Israel's construction of the apartheid wall. An exciting aspect of the video is the focus on Morrar's 15-year-old daughter Iltezam, who launches a women's contingent that quickly moves to the front lines. The video raises important issues around the role of youth in building community struggles and counters stereotypes of Palestinian women and girls as passive or victims. (Secondary and above.) *TP*

The Crossing

Ameen Nayef
(Odeh Films, 2017)
Arabic with English subtitles
10 min.

This short film is about three Palestinian siblings, all young adults, who must cross an Israeli checkpoint to visit their sick grandfather. The opening scenes imply the difficulty of obtaining the travel permits (which were granted only after their grandfather became terminally ill) and highlight the tension with which the siblings approach the crossing — despite their permits, it is likely they will be turned away. Once they arrive at the checkpoint, they watch the border guard turn away other individuals who have permits in a vindictive and seemingly random fashion, denying entry and refusing to provide any justification (and speaking to Palestinians in Hebrew or English only). At first, this is the case for the siblings as well. In a final attempt to convince the guard, the eldest sibling reveals that their grandfather is not sick but already dead. This deeply personal revelation, made in desperation to convince the indifferent guard, shocks the younger siblings and underlines the heartbreaking nature of the moment. High school students find the family dynamics among the siblings compelling, so *The Crossing* is helpful to begin discussions on checkpoints and their impact on Palestinians' ability to travel for work, family, education, and health care. The checkpoint guard appears alone; students need to be aware that his behavior and treatment of the individuals at the checkpoint is, of course, not singular in nature, but rather reflects the systemic denial of Palestinian rights. (Secondary and above.) *TP*

Farming Without Water: Palestinian Agriculture in the Jordan Valley

(EWASH Palestine, 2014)
7 min.

This short film introduces the strain under which Palestinian farmers continue to live in the Jordan Valley. Water shortages prevent farmers from growing productive crops, while right next door the Israeli water company Mekorot pumps millions of gallons from the ground to supply water to illegal settlements. Israel has systematically denied Palestinians their right to dig wells or build water infrastructure since 1967, when the Israeli army completed its occupation of all of historic Palestine. No Palestinian has received a permit to build a water structure since 1967, and Israeli authorities routinely demolish "illegal" water infrastructure. (Middle school, high school, post-secondary.) *TP*

The Great Book Robbery:
Chronicles of a Cultural Destruction
Directed by Benny Brunner
2911 Foundation and Al Jazeera English, 2012
In Arabic, English, and Hebrew with English subtitles
57 min.

In 1948, the newly created state of Israel looted 70,000 Palestinian books. *The Great Book Robbery* tells the story. Israeli historians, Palestinian writers, and Palestinian refugees describe how Zionist forces worked with Hebrew University to seize the private libraries of Palestinian intellectuals as they were expelled from their houses, including volumes of great historical value. Palestinian prisoners were commandeered to do much of the looting. These books are still held, labeled Absentee Property, in the National Library in Israel and are inaccessible to Palestinian scholars. The film raises issues about the relationship between universities and military strategies that are relevant to the United States as well; another connection is to recent controversies as countries and Indigenous peoples demand the return of artwork stolen during colonial conquest. Note: The terms "abandoned homes" and "absentee property," both used in the film, are political ones. Palestinian families left their homes by military order, by news of massacres in other villages, and by force. Palestinians did not "abandon" their homes by choice. (High school, post-secondary.) *TP*

The Lobby — USA
(Al Jazeera, 2017; released by Electronic Intifada 2018)

The Lobby — USA is a four-part undercover investigation by Al Jazeera into Israel's covert influence campaign in the United States. It documents efforts to silence discussion about Israel and Palestinian human rights, particularly on college campuses. The film was made by Al Jazeera. Shortly before its scheduled release, it was censored when Qatar, the gas-rich Gulf emirate that funds Al Jazeera, came under intense Israel lobby pressure not to air the film. In March 2018, The Electronic Intifada and other independent news sources began releasing leaked excerpts of the video. Although it is too long to show in class in its entirety, the exposé of Israeli intelligence attacking U.S. college students make excerpts compelling to high school and college students. *TP*

Occupation 101: Voices of the Silenced Majority
Directed by Abdallah Omeish and Sufyan Omeish (Triple Eye Films, 2006)
90 min.
Occupation 101 is a well-documented exploration of Palestinian life under Israeli occupation. The first few minutes of the video place Palestinian resistance within the historical context of Ireland, Algeria, the U.S. Civil Rights Movement, and South Africa. It describes the first waves of Jewish immigration, rising tensions between Palestinians, Zionists, and the British during the 1920s and 1930s, and the 1948 Nakba — expulsion of 750,000 Palestinians from their homes and villages. Also covered are the 1967 war, the First Intifada (which began in 1987), the Oslo Peace Process, illegal settlement expansion, the Second Intifada (which began in 2000), the separation wall, and the Israeli withdrawal from Gaza. More recent military assaults on Gaza are not included. The film includes substantial voice-over narration that may be difficult for English language learners. Note: Within the movie a statement is made about the United Nations upholding and defending Palestinian human rights. The history of the U.N. in Palestine is complex; for example, the U.N. Relief and Works Agency for Palestinian Refugees in the Near East (UNRWA) provides critical food, health care, and education for Palestinians in refugee camps in the West Bank, Gaza, Lebanon, Syria, and Jordan. At the same time, all other refugees internationally come under the mandate of the UNHCR, the U.N. Agency

for Refugees, which works to repatriate refugees whenever possible. The UNRWA does not work for repatriation; this categorization weakens international support for the Palestinian right of return. (High school, post-secondary.) *TP*

Palestinian Girls Make Videos About Their Lives

These five short videos — *Frightening Day, Prisoner, Dream Become True, The Last Smile*, and *Dancer for Freedom* — were created by Palestinian teenage girls at Shoruq, a cultural and community center in Dheisheh Refugee Camp near Bethlehem. Each portrays an aspect of their lives under Israeli occupation. *TP*

Roadmap to Apartheid

Directed by Ana Nogueira and Eron Davidson
(Journeyman Pictures, 2012)
English with some subtitles
95 min.

Roadmap is a clear and accessible exposition of the many parallels between apartheid in South Africa before 1994 and in Israel. Students will learn lots about the history of both countries. The film focuses on the differences between petty apartheid (e.g., segregated drinking fountains) and grand apartheid (structures like ID cards, access to land, jobs, natural resources). This can spark classroom conversations to compare and contrast apartheid in South Africa and Israel with structural racism in the United States. The video may be too long for some classes; the first 30 or 35 minutes make a clear case for why Israel is an apartheid regime. At approximately 1:11, the focus shifts to resistance with a discussion of the First Intifada, moving on to the role of international solidarity. (Secondary and post-secondary.) *TP*

Slingshot Hip Hop

Directed by Jacqueline Reem Salloum
(2008)
Arabic, English, and Hebrew with English subtitles
80 min.

This video by a Palestinian American woman filmmaker braids together the stories of young Palestinians living in Gaza, the West Bank, and inside Israel as they discover hip-hop and begin to use it as a tool to protest Israeli colonial control. The central focus is on the Lyd hip-hop group RAM. As RAM leader Tamer Nafar explains, "Our music is one-third hip-hop, one-third literature, and one-third . . ." — here he points out the window at the struggles of Palestinian youth inside 1948 Israel. Hip-hop artists in Gaza and Dheisheh Refugee Camp near Bethlehem are also featured. The video includes young women hip-hop artists and the additional challenges they face from traditional attitudes about women. *Slingshot Hip Hop* is an excellent introduction to Palestine for middle and high school students and lends itself to broader discussions of the use of the arts in changing political consciousness, speaking truth to power, and building collective resistance. (Middle school, high school.) *TP*

"Why Are Muslims So . . ."

By Sakila Islam and Hawa Rahman
(18th Annual Brave New Voices International Youth Poetry Slam Festival Finals, 2015)
5 min.

This award-winning spoken word piece by two Muslim young women is an excellent introduction to Islamophobia. For teaching materials connected to the poem, see Alison Kysia's lesson "What Is Islamophobia? Interpersonal vs. Structural Discrimination," posted at Teaching for Change's "Challenge Islamophobia" site. *TP*

The Wanted 18

Directed by Amer Shomali and Paul Cowan
(Kino Lorber/National Film Board of Canada, 2014)
In Arabic, English, and Hebrew with English subtitles
75 min.

This excellent movie, a combination of interviews and animation, documents how the town of Beit Sahour, on the outskirts of Bethlehem, participated in the First Intifada (1987–1993). In a community effort to resist the economic impact of the Israeli occupation, they begin growing their own food and refusing to pay Israeli taxes. They buy 18 cows to supply the community with milk rather than buying it from Israelis. The movie documents their growing resistance and Israeli efforts to repress them. *The Wanted 18* shows how the occupation affected Palestinian lives in a day-to-day way during this period and offers an in-depth look at a local community's participation in the

First Intifada. Toward the end of the film, Beit Sahour activists describe the negative effect on their organizing of the Oslo Accords, providing an opportunity to explore the content, controversy among Palestinians, and impact of the Accords. Other issues raised include youth throwing stones at Israeli military vehicles and milk trucks, taxation without representation, organizing strategies, and the efficacy of boycotts. The narration centers on interviews with Palestinians who led the effort; unfortunately, few women's voices are included. Israeli soldiers who led and participated in the repression of Beit Sahour are also interviewed. **Note:** Scattered throughout are animated sequences in which the cows talk. The cows were originally purchased from an Israeli settlement, and in the beginning of the film they use anti-Palestinian slurs, including "raghead," and call anti-settlement Jews "Israeli peaceniks"; these are issues to discuss with your students. (High school and post-secondary.) *TP*

Al Nakba
Directed by Rawan Damen
(Al Jazeera English, 2013)
Four-part series, each just over 45 min.

Most useful as background material for educators and post-secondary students, this documentary by Rawan Damen, a Palestinian woman filmmaker, is an in-depth exploration of the roots, events and continuing impact of the expulsion of Palestinians from their homes and land in 1948. Episode I starts with Napoleon Bonaparte's 1799 effort to promise Palestine to the Jewish people in exchange for loyalty to France against England and covers the early Zionist movement. Episode II starts with the Palestinian revolt of 1936–39, aimed at securing national independence from the British Empire and an end to Zionist immigration to Palestine. Episode III focuses on the U.N. Partition Plan and the events leading up to 1948. Episode IV focuses on 1948 and the aftermath. Arab, Israeli, and Western historians and eyewitnesses provide the central narrative, accompanied by archival material and documents, many only recently released. (Advanced high school, post-secondary, and teacher background.) *TP*

Editors of *Teaching Palestine*

Bill Bigelow taught high school social studies for many years. He is curriculum editor of *Rethinking Schools* magazine and author or co-editor of several Rethinking Schools books: *A People's History for the Classroom, The Line Between Us: Teaching About the Border and Mexican Immigration, Rethinking Columbus, Rethinking Globalization: Teaching for Justice in an Unjust World, Rethinking Our Classrooms – Volumes 1 and 2*, and *A People's Curriculum for the Earth: Teaching Climate Change and the Environmental Crisis*. Bigelow co-directs the Zinn Education Project, a collaboration between Rethinking Schools and Teaching for Change. He lives in Portland, Oregon, with his wife, Linda Christensen.

Jesse Hagopian is a Seattle-based educator and author of *Teach Truth: The Struggle for Antiracist Education*. His African ancestors were enslaved on plantations in Mississippi and Louisiana, and his Armenian great-grandfather survived the Armenian genocide and immigrated to the United States. Hagopian is a Rethinking Schools editor, a founding member of Black Lives Matter at School, a member of Black for Palestine, and the director of the Zinn Education Project's Teaching for Black Lives campaign. In 2011, he participated in Eyewitness Palestine's first African Heritage delegation to Palestine-Israel. Hagopian is also the co-editor of B*lack Lives Matter at School: An Uprising for Educational Justice, Teaching for Black Lives, Teacher Unions and Social Justic*e, and the editor of *More Than a Score: The New Uprising Against High-Stakes Testing*.

Suzanna Kassouf is an Arab American educator and activist in Portland, Oregon. She is a contributor to *Rethinking Schools* and the Zinn Education Project, is a co-editor of the forthcoming Rethinking Schools book *Teaching Environmental Justice* and is a 2024–2026 Zinn Education Project Prentiss Charney Fellow. She was a co-founder of the youth-led climate justice organization Sunrise Movement PDX. Kassouf teaches social studies in Portland Public Schools.

Adam Sanchez is the managing editor of *Rethinking Schools* magazine. He is Jewish and has family in Israel. He taught high school social studies for more than a decade in Portland, Oregon, New York City, and Philadelphia. He is the editor of *Teaching a People's History of Abolition and the Civil War* and a forthcoming book about teaching Reconstruction. He was the Zinn Education Project (ZEP) 2017–2018 Teacher Organizer and Curriculum Writer and continues to be a ZEP Teacher Leader.

Samia Shoman is a first-generation Californian with Palestinian heritage. She has dedicated more than 25 years to advancing racial and social justice in education. After 16 years as a social science teacher, Shoman transitioned into administration, where she leads an alternative high school focused on supporting multilingual learners. She has collaborated with California educators to design and implement authentic Ethnic Studies frameworks. Shoman also lectures in the Arab and Muslim Ethnicities and Diaspora Program at San Francisco State's College of Ethnic Studies and has worked with educators nationwide to develop curriculum and articles focused on teaching about Palestine. As the co-coordinator of the Middle East Children's Alliance's Teach Palestine project, Shoman advocates for transformative, culturally relevant education in the classroom and beyond.

Index

Rethinking Multicultural Education
Teaching for Racial and Cultural Justice
Edited by Wayne Au

This new and expanded third edition demonstrates a powerful vision of anti-racist, social justice education. Practical, rich in story, and analytically sharp, **Rethinking Multicultural Education** reclaims multicultural education as part of a larger struggle for justice and against racism, colonization, and cultural oppression — in schools and society.

Paperback • 418 pages • ISBN: 978-0-942961-53-9
$24.95*

Teaching for Black Lives
Edited by Dyan Watson, Jesse Hagopian, Wayne Au

Teaching for Black Lives grows directly out of the movement for Black lives. We recognize that anti-Black racism constructs Black people, and Blackness generally, as not counting as human life. Throughout this book, we provide resources and demonstrate how teachers can connect curriculum to young people's lives and root their concerns and daily experiences in what is taught and how classrooms are set up. We also highlight the hope and beauty of student activism and collective action.

Paperback • 368 pages • ISBN: 978-0-942961-04-1
$29.95*

The New Teacher Book THIRD EDITION
Finding purpose, balance, and hope during your first years in the classroom
Edited by Linda Christensen, Stan Karp, Bob Peterson, and Moé Yonamine

Teaching is a lifelong challenge, but the first few years are the hardest. This expanded third edition of **The New Teacher Book** offers practical guidance on how to flourish in schools and classrooms and connect with students and families.

Paperback • 352 pages • ISBN: 978-0-942961-03-4
$32.95*

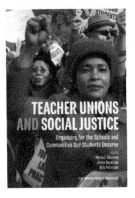

Teacher Unions and Social Justice
Organizing for the schools and communities our students deserve
Edited by Michael Charney, Jesse Hagopian, and Bob Peterson

An anthology of over 60 articles documenting the history and the how-tos of social justice unionism. Together, they describe the growing movement to forge multiracial alliances with communities to defend and transform public education.

Paperback • 448 pages • ISBN: 978-0-942961-09-6
$29.95*

RESOURCES FROM Rethinking Schools

ORDER ONLINE: www.rethinkingschools.org

CALL TOLL-FREE: 800-669-4192